SOFTWARE ARCHITECT
BOOTCAMP

ISBN 0-13-027407-0

90000

9 780130 274076

WWW.WWISA.ORG

The Worldwide Institute of Software Architects (WWISA) is a non-profit professional organization dedicated to establishing a formal profession of software architecture and providing information and services to software architects and their clients—analogous to the formation of the American Institute of Architects roughly 140 years ago. The essential tenet of WWISA is that there is a perfect analogy between building and software architecture, and that the classical role of the architect needs to be introduced into the software construction industry.

The architect, whether designing structures of brick or computer code, forms the bridge between the world of the client and that of the technical builders. This critical bridge has been missing from the software industry, resulting in a decades-long software crisis. Entire software structures are dysfunctional or have been scrapped entirely—before seeing a single "inhabitant." We have simply been building huge, complex structures without architects, and without blueprints.

WWISA was established in 1998 and now has over 1,000 members in 37 countries. Membership is open to practicing and aspiring software architects, professors, students, CIOs, and CEOs. Members participate to promote training and degree programs, develop architectural standards and guiding principles, and work toward creating a standard body of shared knowledge. We are our client advocates; clients are our driving force. We hope to become the clients' bridge to successful software construction by helping them leverage the full range of technology.

SERIES VISION

Software technology is critically important to the world's businesses and human society. However, software engineering remains a chaotic, immature discipline, unable to systematically deliver successful systems. What's missing is software architecture. But, many questions about software architecture, going much deeper than academic discussions, remain unresolved. In particular, how do we apply software architecture on real-world projects and across business enterprises?

At the same time, many successful practitioners of software architecture know how to answer these questions from experience. From among these practitioners our series authors are carefully selected. Often they work in companies that rely upon software system success as their core business model (e.g., business systems, telecommunications, and financial services). These innovative software architects have developed systematic disciplines for doing work that consistently surpasses the industry averages for on-time, on-budget deliveries that meet users' needs and expectations. Some of these experts utilize published standards and patterns for software architecture. Others can share unique lessons learned through professional experience. We have discovered significant commonalities in practical software architecture knowledge which can be useful across most software applications. Together, the joint knowledge of innovative software architects represents the next generation of practice for leading technologists in the software discipline.

The mission of the Software Architecture Series is to publish a common body of knowledge for the software architecture discipline. Software architecture is a specialty distinct from software engineering, programming, and project management. A software architect balances and resolves design forces from many perspectives, including system stakeholders and system developers. Software architects are responsible for a much wider and more interesting range of issues (technical, intuitive, and human factors) than we typically associate with project management. Software architects create technical plans that coordinate the work of groups of programmers, resolving significant systemwide risks and project/technical inefficiencies. The software architect role is an important career path for lead programmers and other IT professionals, as an alternative to project management.

In this series, our goal is to establish the knowledge base for the software architect career path. We hope to share the comprehensive knowledge of successful software architects in a way that fundamentally changes how people develop software, to show better ways of working, and to develop individuals (such as yourselves) into world-class professionals drawing from the acquired knowledge of a wide range of peers in the software architecture profession. We share these goals with a nonprofit organization, the Worldwide Institute of Software Architecture (WWISA), a co-sponsor of this book series.

In conclusion, knowledge is power, particularly for software architects. We are giving to you—the next generation of software architects—the best of our knowledge in the hope that you will fundamentally change the software profession, through your individual practices, toward a mature discipline, which achieves systematic success in the development of software systems. We hope that you as software architects derive all of the benefits and professional recognition that is due to you. In this transition, we do not expect your personal career to be trouble-free and easy. But we do know that software architecture is one of the most exciting fields of endeavor, and we welcome you into our worldwide community!

THOMAS J. MOWBRAY, PH.D.
SERIES EDITOR

SOFTWARE ARCHITECTURE SERIES

Thomas J. Mowbray, Ph.D., Series Editor

▶ *Confessions of a Software Architect*
Bowman

▶ *Software Architecture: Organization Principles and Patterns*
Dikel, Kane, Wilson

▶ *Software Architect Bootcamp*
Malveau, Mowbray

▶ *Architecting with RM-ODP*
Putman

▶ *Design of Software Architecture*
Scheer

▶ *Software Architecture: An Introduction to the Profession*
Sewell, Sewell

SOFTWARE ARCHITECT BOOTCAMP

RAPHAEL MALVEAU

THOMAS J. MOWBRAY, PH.D.

PH PTR

PRENTICE HALL PTR
UPPER SADDLE RIVER, NJ 07458
WWW.PHPTR.COM

Library of Congress Cataloging-in-Publication Data

Malveau, Raphael C.
   Software architect bootcamp/Raphael Malveau, Thomas J. Mowbray.
     p.cm.
   Includes bibliographical references and index.
   ISBN 0-13-027407-0
   1. Software engineering. 2. Computer architecture. I. Mowbray, Thomas J. II. Title.

QA76.758 .M27 2001
005.1--dc21

                                                       2001021243

Editorial/Production Supervision: *Faye Gemmellaro*
Acquisitions Editor: *Paul Petralia*
Marketing Manager: *Bryan Gambrel*
Editorial Assistant: *Justin Somma*
Cover Design: *Alamini Design*
Cover Design Director: *Jerry Votta*
Buyer: *Maura Zaldivar*

Prentice Hall books are widely used by corporations and government agencies for training, marketing, and resale.

The publisher offers discounts on this book when ordered in bulk quantities.
For more information, contact Corporate Sales Department, phone: 800-382-3419;
fax: 201-236-7141; e-mail: corpsales@prenhall.com
Or write: Prentice Hall PTR,
        Corporate Sales Department,
        One Lake Street,
        Upper Saddle River, NJ 07458

Printed in the United States of America
10 9 8 7 6 5 4 3

ISBN 0-13-027407-0

Prentice-Hall International (UK) Limited, **London**
Prentice-Hall of Australia Pty. Limited, **Sydney**
Prentice-Hall Canada Inc., **Toronto**
Prentice-Hall Hispanoamericana, S.A., **Mexico**
Prentice-Hall of India Private Limited, **New Delhi**
Prentice-Hall of Japan, Inc., **Tokyo**
Pearson Education Asia Pte. Ltd.
Editora Prentice-Hall do Brasil, Ltda., **Rio de Janeiro**

INSPIRATION
"All we know is only a handful of what we don't know."
—*Hindu Proverb*

This book is dedicated to our families:
Carrie Malveau
and
Kate Mowbray, CPA

CONTENTS

Two   SOFTWARE ARCHITECTURE:
             BASIC TRAINING   41

NINE   SOFTWARE ARCHITECTURE:
          PSYCHOLOGICAL WARFARE   233

Preface

Software architecture is an emerging discipline and an exciting career path for software professionals. We encourage both new and experienced practitioners to read this book as an aid to becoming better software architects. You may have noticed that most software books today do not say much about software architecture. Here, in this volume, we've concentrated the knowledge that you need to be the most effective architect possible.

As co-authors, we have lived through the experience of graduating from "member of technical staff" developers to becoming practicing software architects at the most senior levels of our respective companies. We are technical people, not managers, and we enjoy the technical nature of our work. We enjoy parity of salary and benefits with the senior managers at our respective firms. In other words, we are none-the-worse-for-wear as a consequence of choosing a software architecture career. We think that many of our readers would like to gain from our experience. Hence this book.

This is more than a book about software architecture. It is a field manual that can train you. We choose the pseudomilitary style, because it embodies an essential attitude. As a software architect, you need many survival skills— some technical, some political, some personal. While neither author has military experience, we have seen software architecture become a battleground in many ways. It is a battleground of ideas, as developers compete to forward their own concepts. It is a battleground for control of key design decisions that may be overruled by managers or developers, perhaps covertly. It is a battle-ground with many risks, since architects are responsible for a much wider range of technical and process risks than most managers or individual developers.

If you are a practicing software architect, we know that you are a busy professional. After buying this book, we would suggest that you peruse the table of contents and the index for topics that are new to you. Focus on those sections first. When you have time, we suggest that you attempt a cover-to-cover read-through, to familiarize yourself with all of the covered topics and terminology.

If you are new to architecture and want to become a software architect, we suggest that you do a cover-to-cover read-through beginning with the first chapter. Work the exercises provided, which will add an experiential learning element to your experience base.

RAPHAEL MALVEAU
THOMAS J. MOWBRAY, PH.D.
McLean, Virginia, U.S.A.

Acknowledgments

We would like to express our thanks for all of the generous support of our friends and the technical contributions of our fellow software architects. In particular, we wish to recognize: Jan Putman, Kirstie Bellman, Liz Zeisler, Thad Scheer, Marc Sewell, Laura Sewell, Hernan Astudillo, Theresa Smith, Roger Hebden, Chip Schwartz, Jack and Gillian Hassall, John Eaton, Dr. Amjad Farooq, John Holmes, John Weiler, Kevin Tyson, Kendall White, Chibuike Nwaeze, Dave Dikel, David Kane, John Williams, Bhavani Thuraisingham, Jim Baldo, Eric Stein, John Hetrick, Dave Gregory, John Bentley, Nigel Pates, Richard Taylor-Carr, Dan Lam, Garrett Fuller, David Broudy, Mike Baba, Burt Ellis, Matthew Presley, Robert Davis, Peter Lee, Linda Kemby, Georgene Murray, Alfredo Aunon, Jim Gray, and Woody Lewis.

INTRODUCTION

So you want to become a software architect? Or perhaps you are already a software architect, and you want to expand your knowledge of the discipline? This is a book about achieving and maintaining success in your software career. It is also about an important new software discipline and technology, software architecture. It is not a book about getting rich in the software business; our advice helps you to achieve professional fulfillment. Although the monetary rewards are substantial, often what motivates many people in software architecture is being a continuous technical contributor throughout their career. In other words, most software architects want to do technically interesting work, no matter how successful and experienced they become. So the goal of this book is to help you achieve career success as a software architect and then maintain your success.

In this book we cover both heavyweight and lightweight approaches to software architecture. The role of software architect has many aspects: part politician, part technologist, part author, part evangelist, part mentor, part psychologist, and more. At the apex of the software profession, the software architect must understand the viewpoints and techniques of many players in the IT business. We describe the discipline and process of writing specifications, what most people would consider the bulk of software architecture, but we also cover those human aspects of the practice which are most challenging to architects, both new and experienced.

So what does a software architect do? A software architect both designs software and guides others in the creation of software. The architect serves both as a mentor and as the person who documents and codifies how tradeoffs are to be made by other software designers and developers. It is common to see the architect serve as a trainer, disciplinarian, and even counselor to other members of the development team. Of course, leadership by example will always remain the most effective technique in getting software designers and developers on the same page.

1.1   ADVICE FOR SOFTWARE ARCHITECTS

"Success is easy; maintaining success is difficult."—J.B.

If you have a focus for your career, gaining the knowledge you need in order to advance can be relatively easy. For software professionals, simply building your expertise is all that is needed in most corporate environments. For example, we often ask software people what books they have read. In the West, most professionals are familiar with design patterns (see Section 1.3). And many have purchased the book by Erich Gamma and co-authors that established the field of design patterns [Gamma 94]. Some have even read it. However, it always surprises us how few people have read anything further on this important topic.

For software architect books, the situation is even worse. Possibly the reason is that there are fewer popular books, but more likely it is that people are not really focused on software architecture as a career goal. In this book series, by publishing a common body of knowledge about software architecture theory and practice, we are eliminating the first obstacle to establishing a software architecture profession. However, making this information available does not automatically change people's reading habits.

So, if the average software professional only reads about one book per year, just think what you could do in comparison. If you were to read three books on design patterns, you would have access to more knowledge than the vast majority of developers on that important topic. In our own professional development, we try even harder—at least a book each month, and if possible, a book every week. Some books take longer than a week—for example, the 1000-page book on the Catalysis Method [D'Souza 98]. In our opinion, it contains breakthroughs on component-oriented thinking, but so few people are likely to read it thoroughly (except software architects), that it becomes a valuable intellectual tool for making you (the reader) a thought leader, as the entire industry moves through the difficult transition to component-based development.

> *"Particularly for social systems, it's the perceptions, not the facts, that count"* [Rechtin 97].

Getting ahead on book reading is a clearcut way to differentiate yourself from the software masses. Converting your book learning to real-world success is also straightforward. You can apply your knowledge on your current projects. You can convert your knowledge into briefings and tutorials that put you in visible leadership and teaching roles. You can share you knowledge at conferences and professional groups. And you can write. The key transition that leads to success starts with sharing your knowledge one-to-one (i.e., inefficiently) and proceeding to share with many at a time. In our own careers, when we began to share knowledge in one-to-many situations, the appearance of success came with it. Since, for most people, appearance is reality, success is easy to attain. The much more difficult challenge is maintaining success, once you've achieved it.

Word of Caution

The software architecture career path is a difficult one for many reasons. While becoming a competent software architect can be difficult, maintaining your skills is usually even harder. Here are some key reasons why the architecture career is difficult:

► Nascent Body of Knowledge
► Confusion and Gurus
► Professional Jealousy
► The Management Trap
► The Software Crisis

We discuss each of these in the subsections that follow.

Nascent Body of Knowledge

First of all, the body of software architecture knowledge is not well established. Software architecture is a relatively new field of computer science. Not much software architecture is taught in schools. Academics have not yet sorted out the fundamentals; there is still much discussion and disagreement on the basics.

However, many practicing software architects believe that sufficient knowledge does exist. The practice of software architecture is much more mature than many will admit. Hopefully, you will gain this understanding, too, after reading further.

In the absence of widespread agreement about software architecture theory, you have to be your own expert. You have to acquire your own set of knowledge and a strong set of beliefs about how to do software right. No one book or software method will give you everything that you need to be an effective software architect.

"Technical problems become political problems" [Rechtin 97].

Confusion and Gurus

Many published software approaches claim to provide the benefits of software architecture, but most of them can't deliver on their promises. In fact, the software industry has created many technology fads and trends, on the basis of incomplete principles. When these approaches are applied in practice, software projects fail. And guess what? The overwhelming majority of corporate development projects do fail—by being cancelled, from overspending, or for under-delivery.

These failures are characteristic of a vast corporate software market, populated with companies that are struggling to deliver their internal software. New products and software development ideas are constantly being produced, in a never-ending attempt to meet the needs of the struggling software masses. Consequently, despite all the failures, the software products industry has thrived.

As a software architect, you have to be an evangelist and leader for your software team. From the myriad conflicting software approaches and products you need to sort out what works and what does not. This is not easy, because a tremendous onslaught of marketing information generated by vendors and industry experts tends to contradict your architectural messages. It is your fate to have your architectural decisions frequently contradicted and obsolesced by the commercial software industry. One of your key skills as an architect is to make sound decisions that can survive the ravages of time and commercial innovation.

Professional Jealousy

The more successful you become, the more some people will resent your success. Many software professionals are genuinely nice people. But many people in our profession have large egos. We all have egos that can be abrasive, but whether you intend to compete on the basis of ego or not, professional competition can create serious problems in software organizations and in your career, unless you are careful.

"Challenge the process and solution, for surely someone else will"
[Rechtin 97].

Professional jealousy is a factor that you will have to watch for vigilantly. You must learn to conduct yourself with a certain degree of humility and be prepared to defend yourself when necessary. Never take any comment personally; it's always a mistake. Consider a situation where you are meeting someone for the first time and they appear to be acting quite rudely. In the eyes of people who have known them for an extended period of time, they may very well be acting in their usual manner.

The Management Trap

As you become more successful in your software career, you may be joining the ranks of management, since most companies organize around a single management ladder. If you are good at what you do, it is natural for management to want you to mentor and supervise other people doing it, too. The company can try to get the productivity of several good performers based upon your experience.

As your administrative responsibilities increase, your time to perform technical work can decrease dramatically. Because you spend less time on technical tasks and on maintaining your technical skills, you can lose your technical edge. If you chose a software career because you enjoyed technical work, you can lose one of your most important motivations for your work.

Being a software architect is quite different from being a manager. A software architect is a direct technical contributor, whereas a manager contributes indirectly by coordinating the actions of other people. Together, managers and architects make highly effective leadership teams. In our experience, combining the two roles can work only temporarily.

As you advance as a manager, eventually a superior will tell you to
stop touching the keyboard (i.e., programming).

You as a software architect can avoid becoming a manager if you establish a personal professional policy. If you don't want management duties, you must learn how to say so. For many of us, one of the most difficult transitions is learning how to say "No." For example, you have to avoid lateral promotions that lead to management and administrative roles.

In some organizations you will become trapped in a management role, because the company does not have a technical ladder. At a certain level of seniority (typical of software architects), you may be surprised, one day, to find yourself assigned responsibilities on the management organization chart. Once this is decided, it is very hard to reverse. The best approach is to declare your expectations (e.g., for technical assignments) when you first take the job. And repeat your policy often.

Defining Software Architecture

An increasing number of software professionals are claiming the title: software architect. In our opinion, very few of these people understand what software architecture is.

Have you ever been involved in a discussion of the question: "What is architecture?" The term "architecture" is one of those most often misused. Below we describe one of the common misuses; then we answer the question "What is architecture?" with a conceptual standard that is in widespread use today (see Section 1.2).

Misuse of the Term "Architecture"

Too often, architectures are used as sales tools rather than technical blueprints. In a typical scenario, a fast-talking technical manager (the "architect") presents a few high-level viewgraphs to convince you of the greatness of his product or system. This is a presentation of a marketing architecture. Most marketing architectures are directed externally at customers and not at software developers. Marketing architectures are fine for advertising the features of commercial products, but they provide only limited technical information for developers.

The problem with marketing architectures is that they are decoupled from the development process. The so-called architect is a manager who delegates most technical details to individual developers. Unless the architect manages the computational model (including subsystem interfaces), the architecture is unlikely to deliver any real technical benefits. Architectural benefits that are easily compromised include system adaptability (for new business needs) and system extensibility (for exploitation of new technologies).

Despite the many competing definitions, experts emphasize the importance of architecture, especially for component-based applications. As component reuse and software complexity increase, architecture is growing dramatically in importance. In subsequent sections we discuss several architecture-centered approaches, which support business change, technology innovation, and design reuse. Reuse of architectural designs benefits component reuse, because design reuse is often much more effective than software reuse alone.

Before Architecture

High-quality, flexible software is one goal of architecture-centered development. In recent years, popular development approaches assumed that *bad software is better*. In other words, getting software delivered quickly is better than delivering quality software which supports change and reuse. Well-known process models and vendor regimes are founded on the *bad-is-better* principle.

Architecture-centered approaches accommodate reuse and change more effectively, because there is a planned system organization, specifically designed for these purposes, i.e., the system architecture. In our opinion, the practice of software architecture is essential for component-based development. *Bad is better* was the thesis; software architecture is the antithesis.

Of course, we do not want to lose the inherent benefit of *bad is better*, i.e., rapid delivery. Architecture-centered approaches utilize several techniques, including pragmatism, architecture planning, and architecture reuse, which jointly support increased productivity, reduced risk, and minimum time-to-market.

The Software Crisis

Many of us have serious misconceptions about the capabilities of current software approaches. Based upon surveys of corporate software projects in the United States, the realities of software development are as follows [Brown 98]. About one-third of all software projects are cancelled. Average projects expend twice as much budget and schedule as initially planned. After delivery, the majority of systems are considered unsuccessful because they have far fewer capabilities than expected. Modification and extension of systems are the most expensive cost drivers and very likely to create new defects. Overall, virtually all application software projects produce *stovepipe systems,* brittle software architectures that underperform on requirements.

The software crisis in corporate development became apparent decades ago, when procedural software technologies were popular. Subsequent, object-oriented approaches (such as the Object Modeling Technique) have been equally unsuccessful for corporate developers. These outcomes have been repeatedly confirmed by research [Brown 98].

Three key factors are exacerbating the software crisis:

► requirements change
► commercial innovation
► distributed computing

A significant part of the problem is rising user expectations. User requirements for systems have increased much faster than corporate developers' capability to deliver. Requirements changes are more frequent, as businesses maneuver for competitive advantage with strategic corporate software.

Another confounding factor is the destabilizing force of accelerating technology innovation, in both commercial software and hardware platforms. Corporate developers have difficulty finding compatible configurations of software products and are forced to upgrade configurations frequently as new products are released. Software maintenance due to technology upgrades is a significant corporate cost driver.

Owing to predominance of the Internet and geographically diverse enterprises, distributed computing is an essential feature of many new applications. Traditionally, software designers assumed homogeneous configurations, centralized systems, local communications, and infrequent failures. Today's highly distributed enterprises require heterogeneous hardware/software, decentralized legacy configurations, and complex communications infrastructure. The resulting computing environments have frequent partial system failures. Distributed computing reverses many key assumptions that are the basis for procedural and object-oriented software development.

The software industry has established object orientation (OO) as the mainstream technology. OO is the technology adopted by new corporate development projects because it is universally supported by software tool vendors. Masses of legacy programmers are training for object-oriented development (e.g., C++ and the Java programming language) as corporations create new strategic systems. Unfortunately, these developers and corporations are likely to become the next generation of disillusioned participants in the software crisis. However, the organizations that survive and thrive with this technology, must use it in sophisticated new ways, represented by componentware.

1.2   SOFTWARE ARCHITECTURE AS A DISCIPLINE

As a professional discipline, software architecture has at least a dozen schools of thought. Some of the major schools of thought include:

► Zachman Framework [Zachman 97]
► Open Distributed Processing (ODP) [ISO 96]

▶ Domain Analysis [Rogers 97]
▶ Rational's 4+1 View Model [Booch 98]
▶ Academic Software Architecture [Bass 98]

Alternative architecture approaches share concepts and principles, but their terminologies differ greatly. Each architecture school is relatively isolated from the others. In the literature of any given school, perhaps one or two other schools are acknowledged, however briefly. None of the schools appear to make any significant use of the results of the others. Since the terminology between these groups varies significantly, communication is difficult, especially between practitioners using different architecture approaches. Upon further study, we find that the goals of each school are quite similar, and each school has some unique value to offer.

In addition to these schools, there are many vendor-driven approaches that are tied to specific product lines, such as Netscape ONE, Sun Enterprise JavaBeans, and Microsoft BackOffice. In fact, every vendor appears to have a unique architectural vision for the future founded upon its own product lines.

Many vendors actually have minimal understanding of application architecture. Thus, I focus here on those approaches which consider key application drivers with appropriate product support for underlying capabilities.

Architecture Approaches

Here is a brief tour of the major schools of software architecture thought.

Zachman Framework

Derived from IBM research and practice, the Zachman Framework is a traditional architecture approach; i.e., it is decidedly non-OO. The Zachman Framework is a reference model comprising 30 architecture viewpoints. The reference model is a matrix, which intersects two paradigms: journalism (who, what, when, why, where, and how) and construction (planner, owner, builder, designer, subcontractor). Architects choose from among these viewpoints to specify a system architecture.

Open Distributed Processing

A formal standard from ISO and ITU (telecommunications), Open Distributed Processing (ODP) defines a five-viewpoint reference model (enterprise, information, computational, engineering, and technology). ODP defines a comprehensive set of terminology, a conformance approach, and viewpoint correspondence rules for traceability. The product of seven years of standards work, ODP is a recent adoption that fully supports OO and component-based architecture. In fairness, I should note that ODP is my primary approach to software architecture.

Domain Analysis

A process for the systematic management of software reuse, domain analysis transforms project-specific requirements into more general domain requirements for families of systems. The requirements then enable the identification of common capabilities, which are used as the basis for horizontal frameworks and reusable software architectures. An important capability of this approach is the definition of robust software designs, which are relatively resistant to requirements and context changes.

4+1 View Model

A four-viewpoint approach is under development by Rational Software. The viewpoints include: logical, implementation (formerly "component"), process (i.e., runtime), and deployment. The "+1" denotes *use case* specifications supporting requirements capture. This approach is closely aligned with the Unified Modeling Language and the Unified Process.

Academic Software Architecture

Academic software architecture comprises a community of computer science researchers and educators constituting an academic field. Their educational efforts are focused on basics and fundamentals. In their research contributions, this community avoids proven architectural standards and practices in order to achieve originality, theoretical formality, and other academic goals.

Common Principles

It is often said that the principles of software are simple. For example, let's consider (1) simplicity and (2) consistency. Architects agree that managing complexity (i.e., achieving simplicity) is a key goal, because it leads to many architectural benefits, such as system adaptability and reduced system cost. For example, a simpler system is easier to test, document, integrate, extend, and so forth.

> *"Explore the situation from more than one point of view. A seemingly impossible situation might become transparently simple"* [Rechtin 97].

Simplicity is most necessary in the specification of the architecture itself. Most architectural approaches utilize *multiple viewpoints* to specify architecture. Viewpoints separate concerns into a limited set of design forces, which can be resolved in a straightforward and locally optimal manner.

Consistency enhances system understanding and transfer of design knowledge between parts of the system and between developers. An emphasis on consistency contributes to the discovery of commonality and opportunities for reuse. Architects agree that unnecessary diversity in design and implementation leads to decidedly negative consequences, such as brittle system structure.

Architecture Controversies

The principal disagreements among architecture schools include: (1) terminology, (2) completeness, and (3) a priori viewpoints.

Architects disagree on terminology due to their backgrounds or schools of thought. For example, when discussing software interfaces, the consistency principle is variously called: standard interfaces, common interfaces, horizontal interfaces, plug-and-play interfaces, and interface generalization. We can also argue that *variation-centered design* (from design patterns) and *component substitution* are largely based upon consistent interface structure.

Unnecessary diversity of terminology leads to confusion, and sometimes to proprietary advantage. Some vendors and gurus change terminology so frequently that keeping up with their latest expressions becomes a time-consuming career.

Differences in terminology lead to miscommunication. In contrast, some distinct areas of disagreement among architecture schools can't be resolved through improved communications alone.

The notion of *complete models* is promoted by legacy OO approaches (e.g., OMT), the Zachman Framework school, and various others. These groups have promoted a vision that complete models (describing multiple phases of development) are a worthwhile goal of software development projects. Other schools would argue that multiple models are not maintainable, that unnecessarily detailed models are counterproductive, and that architectural significance should be considered when selecting system features for modeling.

These contrary notions can be summarized in terms of the principle of *pragmatism*. We side with the pragmatists for the above reasons and because most software systems are too complex to model completely (e.g., multithreaded distributed computing systems). Pragmatism is a key principle to apply in the transition from document-driven to architecture-centered software process.

The selection of architecture viewpoints is a key point of contention among architecture schools. Some schools have preselected a priori viewpoints. Some schools leave that decision to individual projects. The Zachman Framework is an interesting case, because it proposes 30 viewpoints, from among which most projects select groups of viewpoints to specify.

Variable viewpoints have the advantage that they can be tailored to address the concerns of particular system stakeholders. Predefined viewpoints have the advantage that they can accompany a stable conceptual framework and a well-defined terminology, as well as predefined approaches for resolving viewpoint consistency and architecture conformance.

Innovative Software Architecture

There are many active and successful schools of software architecture thought. Software architecture is a discipline unified by principles, but divided by terminology. The various architecture schools can be viewed as different branches of an evolutionary progression.

The Zachman Framework has evolved from the traditional non-OO approaches. ODP is an outgrowth from object-oriented and distributed-computing paradigms that has achieved stability, multiindustry acceptance, and formal standardization. Both Zachman and ODP approaches have enjoyed significant success in production-quality software development. Domain analysis has demonstrated its worth in defining robust, domain-specific software architectures for reuse. The 4+1 View Model is an approach undergoing development, in parallel with the Unified Process.

All of the above can be described as innovative software architecture approaches. They are being applied in practice, based upon various levels of proven experience. Academic research in software architecture is defining a baseline for architecture knowledge that resembles a lowest common denominator of the above approaches. Fortunately, the academic community has legitimized the role of the software architect, regardless of whether their guidance is useful to innovative architects.

In our opinion, software architects should have a working knowledge of the innovative approaches described above. In addition, they should utilize one of the product-quality architecture frameworks in daily practice. Component architecture development is a challenging area, requiring the best of stable conceptual frameworks supporting sound architectural judgment.

The Architecture Paradigm Shift

The nature of information systems is changing from localized departmental application to large-scale global and dynamic systems. This trend is following the change in business environments toward globalization. The migration from relatively static and local environments to highly dynamic information technology environments presents substantial challenges to the software architect (Figure 1.1).

A majority of information technology approaches are based upon a set of traditional assumptions (Figure 1.2). In these assumptions the system comprises a homogeneous set of hardware and software which is known at design time. A configuration is relatively stable and is managed from a centralized system management configuration. Communications in traditional systems are relatively predictable, synchronous, and local. If the state of the system is well known at all times and the concept of time is unified across all the activities, another key assumption is that failures in the system are relatively infrequent and, when they do occur, are monolithic. In other words, either the system is up or the system is down.

In the building of distributed application systems, most of the assumptions are reversed. In a distributed multiorganizational system it is fair to assume that the hardware and software configuration is heterogeneous. The reason is that different elements of the system are purchased during different time frames by

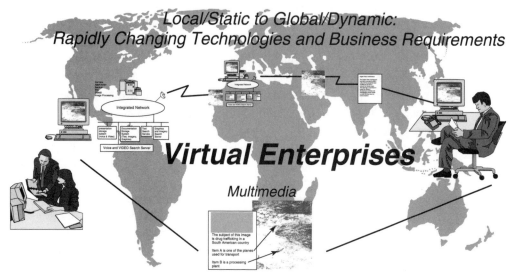

FIGURE 1.1 Virtual Enterprise Paradigm Shift

TRADITIONAL SYSTEM ASSUMPTIONS
- Homogeneous hardware/software
- Stable, centrally managed configuration
- Synchronous and local: processing, state, time, and communications
- Infrequent, monolithic failures

DISTRIBUTED SYSTEM ASSUMPTIONS
- Homogeneous hardware/software – evolving configurations
- Remote, autonomous processing
- Distributed, replicated, non-uniform: state and time
- Asynchronous, insecure, variable: communications
- Frequent partial system failures

FIGURE 1.2   Traditional and Distributed-Systems Assumptions

different organizations and many of the decisions are made independently. Therefore in a typical configuration you have a variety of information technology. It is also the case that hardware and software configurations are evolving. Occurring within any organization are turnover in employees and evolution of business processes. The architecture of the organization impacts the architecture of the information technology. As time progresses, new systems are installed, systems are moved, new software is acquired, and so on. When multiple organizations are involved, these processes proceed relatively independently, and the architect must accommodate the diverse evolving set of configurations.

In distributed systems, the assumption is that there is remote processing at multiple locations. Some of this remote processing is on systems that were developed independently and therefore have their own autonomous concept of control flow. This reverses the assumption of localized and unified processing resources. There are some interesting implications for the concepts of state and time. The state of a distributed system is often distributed itself. The state information may need to be replicated in order to provide efficient reliable access at multiple locations. It is possible for the distributed state to become nonuniform in order to get into error conditions where the replicated state does not have the desired integrity and must be repaired. The concept of time-distributed systems is affected by the physics of relativity and chaos theory. Electrons are traveling near the speed of light in distributed communication systems. In any large system there is a disparity between the local concepts of time, in that this system can only have an accurate representation of partial ordering of operations in the distributed environment. The total ordering of operations is not possible because of the distances between information process. In addition, distributed communications can get quite variable and complex. In a distributed system there are various qualities of service which communications systems can provide. The communications can vary by timeliness of delivery, the throughput, the levels of security and vulnerability to attack, the reliability of communications, and other factors. The communications architecture must be explicitly designed and planned in order to account for the variabilities in services.

Finally, the distributed system has a unique model of failure modes. In any large distributed system components are failing all the time. Messages are corrupted and lost, processes crash, and systems fail. These kinds of failures happen frequently and the system must be architected to accommodate for them.

In summary, distributed processing changes virtually all of the traditional system assumptions that are the basis for most software engineering method-ologies, programming languages, and notations. To accommodate this new level of system complexity, architects have three new needs.

First, architects need the ability to separate complex concerns, in particu-lar to separate concerns about business-application functionality from concerns about distributed-system complexity. Distributed computing is a challenging and complex architectural environment unto itself. If systems are built with tra-ditional assumptions, architects and developers are likely to spend most of their time combating the distributed nature of real-world applications. Problems and challenges of distributed computing have nothing to do fundamentally with business-application functionality.

The purpose of information technology is to establish new business processes. By separating concerns, we can focus on the business functionality that is the true purpose of the information system. Ideally, architects would like to separate distributed-system issues into categories of design, where the majority of components are purchasable as commodity communication infra-structure.

Object-oriented architects also need the ability to future-proof the infor-mation systems that they are planning. It is important to accommodate com-mercial technology evolution, which we know is accelerating and beginning to provide substantial challenges for architects and developers. Future-proofing also requires the ability to adapt to new user requirements, since requirements do change frequently and account for a majority of system software cost over the life cycle. It is important to plan information systems to support the likely and inevitable changes that users will require in order to conduct business.

A third need for object-oriented architects is the ability to increase the likelihood of system success. Corporate developers to date have had a very poor track record of creating successful systems. The object-oriented architect is responsible for planning systems with the maximum probability of delivering success and key benefits for the business. Through proper information technology planning, we believe that it is possible to increase the likelihood of system delivery on time and on budget.

In confronting these three needs, authorities in software engineering and computer science tend to agree that architecture is the key to system success. Authorities in areas ranging from academia to commercial industry are declaring that software architecture is essential to the success and management of information systems. There is a long and growing list of software authorities who have come to this conclusion. Unfortunately, it is not always clear to everyone what software architecture truly is. In order to provide clarification, we need to take a look at some of the reference models which provide definitions of software and systems architecture (Figure 1.3).

The needs that we are discussing have been thoroughly considered by many authorities. There are two leading meta-architecture frameworks that guide the development of software system architecture. One of the popular frameworks originated at IBM and is called the Zachman Framework. The Zachman Framework predated the popularity of object orientation and took the perspective of separating data from process. In the Zachman Framework there are six information system viewpoints as well as five levels of design abstraction. The original Zachman Framework published in 1987 contained

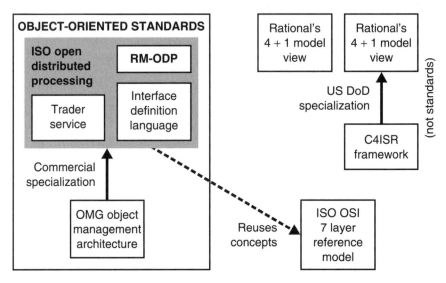

FIGURE 1.3   Software-Intensive Systems Architecture Reference Models

viewpoints for the network, the data, and the process of the information system [Zachman 97]. A subsequent revision introduced three additional viewpoints. The current framework resembles the set of traditional journalistic questions, which include who, what, when, why, where, and how. Each viewpoint in the Zachman Framework answers a chief set of questions to ensure that a complete system engineering architecture is created.

The Zachman Framework formed a matrix of architecture descriptions which are also organized in terms of levels. There are five levels of description above the information system implementation. They range from architectural planning done by individual programmers at the finest grain to the overall enterprise requirements from the investors' perspective of the information system. In total, the Zachman Framework identifies 30 architectural specifications, which provide a complete description of the information system. In practice no real-world project is capable of creating these 30 or more detailed plans and keeping them all in synchronization. When the Zachman Framework is applied, systems architects partition the viewpoint into various categories and create architectural specifications that cover all of the different Zachman descriptions without having to create the large number of specification documents that the Zachman Framework implies. One example is a very successful architecture initiative by the United States Department of Defense called the C4ISR architecture framework, where C4ISR stands for Command and Control, Computers, Communication, Intelligence Surveillance, and Reconnaissance. The C4ISR architecture framework is used to describe DOD information technology at the highest echelons of the organization. The primary benefit in this case is that different service organizations and agencies can communicate their architectural plan through common-viewpoint description.

Beyond the Zachman Framework, object-oriented architects have discovered additional needs for defining computational architecture and other viewpoints which are not obvious applications of the Zachman principles. The international standards organization (ISO) has also considered these architectural issues. Recently completed is the ISO reference model for open distributed processing called RM-ODP. This model belongs to a category of ISO standards called open distributed processing (ODP). ODP is an outgrowth of earlier work by ISO in open systems interoperability. The Open Systems Interconnection (OSI) seven-layer reference model identified an application layer which provided minimal structure and guidance for the development of application systems. In fact, the seventh layer for applications groups remote procedure calls, directory services and all other forms of application level services within the same architectural category, not defining any particular structure or guidance for this significant category of functionality.

A Standard for Architecture

Among the various architecture approaches, there is a useful international standard that defines what information systems architecture means, the Reference Model for Open Distributed Processing (RM-ODP) [ISO 96]. We will cover it as one way to think about software architecture. This model is representative of mature software architecture practice today.

RM-ODP defines five essential viewpoints for modeling systems architecture:

► Enterprise Viewpoint
► Information Viewpoint
► Computational Viewpoint
► Engineering Viewpoint
► Technology Viewpoint

The five viewpoints provide a comprehensive model of a single information system.

An *enterprise* viewpoint contains models of business objects and policies. Enterprise policies include permissions, prohibitions, and obligations. An *information* viewpoint includes the definition of information schemas as objects. Three kinds of RM-ODP schemas include static, invariant, and dynamic. A *computational* viewpoint includes definitions of large-grained object encapsulations, including subsystem interfaces and their behaviors. These three viewpoints define architecture in a manner that makes distributed computing transparent. An *engineering* viewpoint exposes the distributed nature of the system. The distribution transparencies supported by infrastructure are declared explicitly. The allocation of objects onto processing nodes is also specified. RM-ODP defines a reference model of distributed infrastructure called a *channel* which is used to model all forms of middleware connections.

RM-ODP defines eight distribution transparency properties. It is interesting to note that only a handful of these properties are supported by major commercial infrastructures (without resorting to niche-market products). For example, CORBA products provide full support for access, location, and transaction transparency, with some support for failure and persistence transparency. Microsoft's Distributed Component Object Model (DCOM) provides support for persistence and transaction transparency, with limited support for the other properties.

Open distributed processing and its reference model are the result of ten years of formal standardization work at ISO. The reference model for open distributed processing is object oriented. It provides a referenced model that was intended to address three fundamental goals: (1) to provide a standard framework for further work and additional detailed standards under the open distributed processing initiative, (2) to provide a set of common terminology and concepts that could be applied for the development of product and application systems for open distributed processing, (3) to provide a guideline for object-oriented architects to specify software systems. This third purpose is directly relevant to the day-to-day practices of systems architects.

Open distributed processing includes several other standards which are significant (Figure 1.3). In particular, it has adopted the interface definition language from CORBA as a notation for a specified computational architecture. It also has a standard for the trader service, which is the key directory service supporting the discovery of application functions in distributed systems. The trader service has subsequently been adopted as a commercial standard through the object management group. The group's object management architecture is a commercial specialization of open distributed processing.

All together, the OMG's consensus standards and the ISO open distributed processing form a set of software architecture standards that are useful intellectual tools for most software architects and developers.

RM-ODP has three completed standards documents. Part one of the standards is a non-normative overview and summary of the overall concepts and terminology. All three parts of the adopted standard are cosponsored by the International Telecommunications Union ITU-T through their X.900 series. The cosponsorship of both ISO and ITU-T represents a broad international consensus on this guideline for object-oriented architecture.

Part two of the standard is the foundations document, comprising a glossary of standard terminology for object oriented distributed systems.

Part three of the standards is the architecture document. It defines the various viewpoints for object-oriented architecture along with their structuring rules and various open distributed processing functions which enable distributed computing.

Altogether, these three standards documents comprise less than 200 pages of documentation with the normative parts, part two and part three comprising about 100 pages. Even though this is a relatively short standard, it provides a great deal of valuable information. Many ISO standards are relatively inscrutable to the practicing software engineer; this standard is no exception. However, we believe that the effort to understand it is very worthwhile, given the challenges of distributed computing in business process change that need to be resolved.

Who supports RM-ODP? RM-ODP is the product of formal standards bodies including ISO and IEEE. The IEEE is an accredited standards organization reporting to ISO; therefore, the IEEE is a voting participant and joint supporter of RM-ODP as well. RM-ODP is the formal standards basis for the object management group's object management architecture and all of the resulting technologies that the group has adopted which form the basis for distributed object computing and technologies that are available commercially. RM-ODP is also accurately used in several mission-critical industries which depend upon information technology for their income. In particular, RM-ODP is applied across the telecommunications industry through the telecommunications information network architecture consortium, and RM-ODP is actively used by telecommunication companies such AT&T, Lucent, and Nortel. In the telecommunications industry, information technology is their business, and distributed information systems success is essential to maintaining their competitive advantage.

Also applying ODP actively is the financial services industry. Companies such as Merrill Lynch, Morgan Stanley, and various mortgage lending organizations are applying RM-ODP to define new information systems concepts. The deployment of new information technologies is becoming one of the key competitive advantages that these companies have for creating new market channels to distribute and transact new financial instruments and securities, and perform other financial services. For these industries failure of information systems directly affects bottom-line profitability and is usually not an option. If these influential companies accept this architectural approach and apply it actively, can your organization afford not to consider its benefits?

The RM-ODP comprises five standard viewpoints. Each viewpoint is a perspective on a single information system (Figure 1.4). The set of viewpoints is not closed, so that additional viewpoints can be added as the needs arise. Another of their purposes is to provide information descriptions that address the questions and needs of particular stakeholders in the system. By standardizing five viewpoints, RM-ODP is claiming that these five stakeholder perspectives are sufficient for resolving both business functionality and distributed systems issues in the architecture and design of information systems. RM-ODP is an elegant model in the sense that it identifies the top priorities for architectural descriptions and provides a minimal set of traceability requirements which are adequate to ensure system integrity.

The enterprise viewpoint of our RM-ODP takes the perspective of a business model. The enterprise models should be directly understandable by managers and end users in the business environment. The enterprise viewpoint ensures that business needs are satisfied through the architecture and provides a description which enables validation of these assertions with the end users.

The information viewpoint defines the universe of discourse in the information system. The perspective is similar to the design information generated

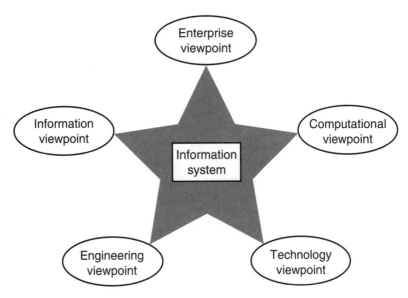

FIGURE 1.4 Architecture Viewpoint Perspectives

by a database modeler. The information viewpoint is a logical representation of the data and processes on data in the information system.

Each of the five RM-ODP viewpoints is object oriented, and they provide a complete model of the system from the given perspective. The information viewpoint is an object-oriented logical model of the information assets in the business and how these assets are processed and manipulated.

The computational viewpoint partitions the system into software components which are capable of supporting distribution. It takes the perspective of a designer of application program interfaces for componentware. The computational viewpoint defines the boundaries between the software elements in the information system. Generally, these boundaries are the architectural controls that ensure that the system structure will embody the qualities of adaptability in management of complexity that are appropriate to meet changing business needs and incorporate the evolving commercial technology.

The engineering viewpoint of RM-ODP exposes the distributed nature of the system. Its perspective is similar to that of an operating system engineer who is familiar with the protocol stacks and allocation issues that are necessary to define the distributed processing solutions for the information system.

The fifth viewpoint is the *technology* viewpoint. It defines the mappings between the engineering objects and other architected objects to specific standards and technologies including product selections. The viewpoint is similar to that of a network engineer who is familiar with the protocol standards and products available commercially which are appropriate selections to configure the information system.

All five RM-ODP viewpoints are co-equal in the sense that they do not form levels of description; rather each viewpoint provides a complete model of the information system that is object oriented and corresponds to the other viewpoints. Each defines various constraints on the design of the information system that provide various architectural benefits for each of the system's stakeholders. The RM-ODP viewpoints enable the separation of concerns which divide the business and logical functionality of the system from the distributed computing and commercial technology decisions of the architecture.

The first three viewpoints identify informational and computational characteristics. The enterprise and information viewpoints are purely logical views of the business, represented as object-oriented models (Figure 1.5). The computational viewpoint is independent of the distribution of software modules, but it must define computational boundaries which are enabled for distribution. The CORBA IDL notation for specifying computational interfaces is appropriate for this purpose. IDL provides a way to define computational interfaces which are independent of the distribution and deployment issues in enterprise development. The first four viewpoints—enterprise, information, computational, and engineering—are independent of specific implementations. In other words, the majority of the architectural design is independent of the specific product selections which configure the system. This property of RM-ODP enables the evolution of technology components without impacting the overall architectural constraints defined in the first four viewpoints. The engineering viewpoint defines qualities of service and distribution transparencies which

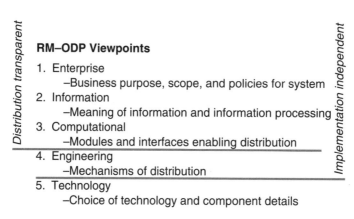

FIGURE 1.5   Characteristics of Architecture Viewpoints

evolving technology selections must support. The terminology of RM-ODP assists in providing concise descriptions of these technology requirements.

RM-ODP contains many terminology definitions which are useful concepts for object-oriented architects. Some of the key definitions in RM-ODP are the distribution transparencies. RM-ODP defines in distribution transparencies which specify the qualities provided by distributed computing infrastructure (Figure 1.6). Currently available commercial infrastructures provide some subset of these, such as location, and access transparencies provided by CORBA along with partial support for persistence in transaction transparency. Additional transparencies are available through niche-market products and through custom implementations which are enabled by proper architectural separation of infrastructure requirements from technology selections. Technologies which do not provide access transparency, such as Microsoft COM+ and the distributed computing environment, do not adapt well to the future evolution of distributed systems (Figure 1.7).

RM-ODP provides standard definitions for distributed infrastructure objects that enable abstract descriptions of engineering constraints. Figure 1.7 is an example of the engineering objects which RM-ODP defines. These engineering objects are capable of defining the characteristics of all forms of distributed infrastructure, including remote procedure calls, screening data interfaces, and asynchronous interfaces for signaling. Among the most important features of RM-ODP are its definitions supporting conformance assessment. After all, what is the purpose of architectural documentation unless we

Distributed Transparency	Architectural Guarantee
Access	Masks platform-protocol difference in data representation and invocation mechanisms
Failure	Masks failures and recoveries of other objects
Location	Masks the use of location information to find & bind to objects
Migration	Masks awareness of changes in location of the object from itself
Relocation	Masks changes in the location of an interface/service from clients
Replication	Masks the existence of replicated objects that support common states and services
Persistence	Masks activation and deactivation of objects (including the object itself)
Transaction	Masks coordination of activities to achieve consistency

FIGURE 1.6 Distribution Transparencies

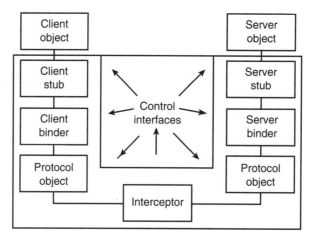

FIGURE 1.7   Distribution Channel Model

can assess conformance—that is, make sure that the implementation of the system corresponds to the written and intended architectural plans.

RM-ODP defines four categories of conformance and proceeds to specify how conformance is represented in an architectural plan. The first category is called *programmatic conformance*. This is the usual notion of behavioral testing of software interfaces. Many of the programmatic conformance points will occur in the computational viewpoint specification of RM-ODP based architectures.

Perceptual conformance includes testing at user interfaces in communications ports that represent external boundaries to the system. Usability and user interface testing can be defined through perceptual conformance assessment. *Interworking conformance* involves testing between systems implementations. It is not sufficient for individual systems to have programmatic conformance in order to guarantee interoperability. Interworking conformance includes interoperability testing between working implementations, which is an additional requirement beyond programmatic conformance.

Interchange conformance involves testing of the exchange of external media, such as disks and tapes. It ensures that information that is stored on external media can be interpreted and assimilated in other systems that conform to the same standards. RM-ODP also defines correspondence requirements between the various viewpoints of application architecture. In general, the objects defined in each of the viewpoints do not have to be explicitly correspondent, because they represent independent description of the system representing various levels of granularity of descriptions and constraints.

Several key points of correspondence must be ensured. The computational viewpoint must support any dynamic behaviors that are specified in the information viewpoints. The information viewpoint represents the information in the information system and its processing. Whenever a process occurs, it must be explicitly allocated to the internal operation of one of the computational modules or it must be explicitly allocated to a particular computational interaction—in other words, invoking a software interface to cause the processing of information. In addition, there is an explicit correspondence requirement between the computational and engineering viewpoints. In general, engineering objects outnumber computational objects, because the engineering viewpoint exposes the objects in the distributed infrastructure, which may be numerous. For every computational interface defined in the computational viewpoint, there must be an explicit correspondence to engineering interfaces in the engineering viewpoint objects. The computational boundaries must map onto distributed engineering objects so that the distribution strategy is clarified by the architecture.

Applications and Profiles

Open systems standards (such as RM-ODP) are purposely generic so that they apply to all domains. To make standards deliver their benefits, a *profile* is required. A profile is an implementation plan for how the standard is applied within a context. Several profiles of RM-ODP are in use today.

The 4+1 View Model is a viewpoint-based architecture approach supported by OO tools such as Rational Rose. The viewpoints include:

► Use Case View
► Logical View
► Process View
► Implementation View
► Deployment View

The *use case* view models enterprise objects through a set of scenarios. The *logical* view includes object models of packages, classes, and relationships. The *process* view represents control flows and their intercommunications. The *implementation* view defines the modular structure of the software. The *deployment* view identifies the allocation of software onto hardware. An architecture defined as a 4+1 View Model covers aspects of all 5 RM-ODP viewpoints.

RM-ODP is being applied in several industries, including financial services and defense. For example, the United States Department of Defense (DoD) has a profile of RM-ODP, called the Command, Control, Communications, Computers, Intelligence, Surveillance, and Reconnaissance Architecture Framework (C4ISR-AF). C4ISR-AF defines three viewpoints: operational architecture, system architecture, and technical architecture. An information viewpoint is also specified.

Before applying the framework, DoD services defined their architectures using disparate conventions. C4ISR-AF is currently used by all DoD services to describe their architectures. The framework is enabling technology exchanges across diverse system development programs. Reuse opportunities and common interoperability solutions are being identified and defined as a result.

Viewpoint Notations

Within each viewpoint, the RM-ODP approach uses formal notations (or specification languages) that support architecture description.

One of the most useful notations for specifying computational viewpoints is the ODP interface definition language (ODP IDL). ODP IDL is a related international standard that is identical to CORBA IDL. It enables the specification of object encapsulations that can be implemented on multiple infrastructures, such as CORBA, Microsoft COM, and the Adaptive Communication Environment (ACE). Since ODP IDL is programming-language independent, a single interface specification suffices to define interoperable interfaces for C, C++, Ada95, COBOL, Smalltalk, the Java programming language, and Microsoft IDL. These mappings are defined by open systems standards and supported by commercial products.

Another useful notation for describing architecture viewpoints is the Unified Modeling Language (UML). UML is an object-oriented notation recently adopted by the Object Management Group. UML is also supported by Microsoft in its respository and development environment technologies.

Although it is not widely publicized, RM-ODP is providing architectural benefits in multiple industries. RM-ODP is a formal standard that defines how to describe distributed OO architectures. In practice, RM-ODP's viewpoints, models, and transparency properties are useful conceptual tools for object-oriented architects.

1.3   DESIGN PATTERNS AND SOFTWARE ARCHITECTURE

We view software architecture as an eclectic practice, combining ideas from many areas of computer science and software engineering. Reuse of these ideas and existing knowledge is paramount to the effective practice of the architectural discipline. Luckily, the popular movement of design patterns has codified and documented a great deal of software knowledge for this purpose. We believe that software architects should also be pattern literate.

What the design patterns community has done is to make the reuse of lessons learned into a popular, trendy approach. Patterns represent a rejection of originality as a technical goal, including an active avoidance of the Not-Invented-Here (NIH) syndrome.

Design Patterns

Design patterns are a significant extension to object-oriented paradigm. Design patterns are documented representations of software engineering knowledge. They are intended to capture expert-level knowledge and important lessons learned. Design patterns are a departure from previous object-oriented guidance in several respects. Patterns document essential design knowledge, transcending original object-oriented notions. Originally, object orientation was based upon modeling of the natural world as objects. To design effective software systems, more sophisticated structures are needed that are unique to software.

Design patterns have more stringent requirements for documenting knowledge. Design patterns should represent *proven solutions*, not merely wishful thinking about how software should be done. This concept is embodied in the so-called *rule of three*. Informally, the rule of three states that: "A single design occurrence is an event, two occurrences are a coincidence, and three occurrences are a pattern." To the design patterns authors, there is a more literal meaning, that patterns are proven solutions applied by one or more communities of experts on a recurring basis.

Design patterns also introduce the notion of *design force,* also called *issues* or *concerns*. Design patterns document these forces explicitly and elaborate the solution in terms of resolving the design forces.

In order to facilitate problem solving, it is useful to find ways to separate design concerns—design elements which are implicitly responsible for resolving all potential concerns, those that are potentially unstable (when subject to scrutiny), and those that may require voluminous documentation to justify the design. Explicit reference models for separation of concerns have been proposed for software engineering and other fields of engineering endeavor.

Figure 1.8 also contains a software design-level model proposed by Shaw and Garlan showing three levels [Shaw 96]. In comparison, the software community does not have a sophisticated view of how to separate design concerns,

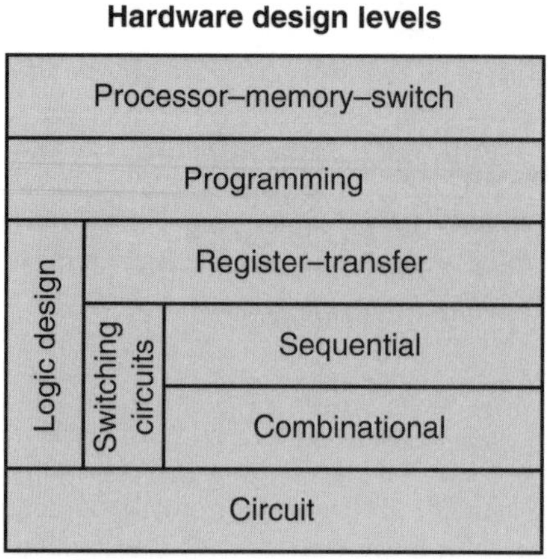

Hardware design levels

Processor–memory–switch		
Programming		
Logic design	Switching circuits	Register–transfer
		Sequential
		Combinational
Circuit		

FIGURE 1.8   The Concept of Design-Level Models

and it is also not known what the components are that comprise each of these levels. In the software design model, the *machine* level represents the binary software that is part of the operating system and commercial products that cannot be modified by the application developer. The *code* represents the program that is the domain of application development, and the third level is the *architecture,* which provides a model of how the system is partitioned and how the connections between the partitions communicate. The shortcomings of this simple model are that it does not represent any significant separation of concerns and that important properties such as interoperability between systems are not considered.

Software Design-Level Model

Figure 1.9 shows the software design-level model that we propose in our book called *CORBA Design Patterns* [Mowbray 97a]. This model was originated by one of the founders of the design pattern movement, Richard Helms, and describes in a recursive fractal fashion what the various levels of software design are in terms of objects. At the micro levels we have individual objects, and the design principles that apply to those individual objects are usually object specific. There is a class of patterns called idioms which represent design guidance for language-specific issues. These issues are fairly fine grained.

The next level up is called *micro architecture* patterns. In micro architectures we have small configurations of objects, generally a handful of objects that give us sophisticated ways of organizing our software structure to support variability in other qualities of design. The framework level then takes a number of micro architecture patterns and combines them into a partially completed

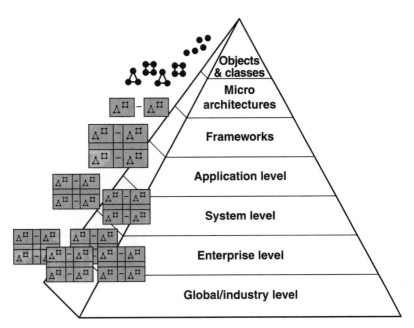

FIGURE 1.9   Software Design-Level Model

application with reusable software. Above the micro level, we have completed applications and systems. The *application* level represents the application of zero or more frameworks to provide an independent program. We encounter issues such as user interface programming which are significant in software development. At the *system* level, we take a number of applications which play the role of subsystems and integrate those applications to create a working system environment. The system level is where many of the design forces applicable to programming are changed in terms of their priorities. Management of complexity and change becomes critical at the system level and above.

At the *enterprise* level, we have a number of different systems which are integrated across an organization or virtual enterprise of organizations working in conjunction. The enterprise level is the longest scale of internally controlled operating environments.

The global industry level is represented by the Internet, the commercial market, and the standards organizations, which comprise the largest scale of software systems. Figure 1.10 represents the separation of design forces which occurs as we move throughout these various levels. Overall, the management of risk is a force which applies at all levels when we make software decisions. At the finer-grained levels, management of performance and functionality issues is very important and perhaps dominates any of the other design forces

▶ **The universal force**
  • Management of risk

▶ **Primal forces**
  • Management of performance
  • Management of functionality
  • Management of complexity
  • Management of change
  • Management of IT resources
  • Management of technology transfer

FIGURE 1.10   Prevalent Forces in Software Decisions

that apply horizontally across all the levels. Looking at the system level, the key design forces here include the management of change and the management of complexity. We come to this conclusion due to the writings of other authors. In particular Horowitz writes that the adaptability of systems is the primary quality which is missing where the majority of system cost is due to changes in requirements reference [Horowitz 93]. Shaw and Garlan identify the management of complexity as the key design force at the system architecture level [Shaw 96].

Above the system level the environment changes on a more frequent basis. Each system must be modified to support individual business processes; at an enterprise level with multiple systems the change accumulates as people move and the organization evolves on a daily basis. Management of the resources at the enterprise level and of technology transfer to support capabilities such as design and software reuse becomes more significant and important. At the *global* and *industry* levels, the management of technology transfer become predominant. When something is published on the Internet, it is instantly accessible on a global basis to virtually any organization or individual. Using the management of technology transfer design force, it is important to manage the information that the enterprise discloses in terms of software intellectual capital as well as the information that the organization exploits.

Figure 1.11 shows the overall priorities for these horizontal design forces as they apply to the coarser-grained levels. Here we show that at the system architecture level the management of change is the predominant force, because it is linked directly to the cost of the system in published work. We also identify as a second priority the management of complexity, because it is a design force that is emphasized by academic authorities in software architecture. Priorities at the other levels are indicated to show how the perspective of each of the architectural designers at these levels varies by the scale of software design. We see these as guidelines for making sure that the appropriate priorities are

Horizontal Force	Component Programming	Component Integrator	Software Architect	Enterprise CIO	Global CEO
Performance	1				
Functionality	2	1			
Complexity		2	2		
Change			1	2	
IT Resources				1	2
Tech. Transfer					1

FIGURE 1.11 Priorities for Key Design Forces

allocated to decisions that are made at each of these levels. The reference model helps us to organize patterns knowledge and identify priorities for design forces that are horizontal across all the levels. Design patterns are a modern approach to providing technical guidance. The breakthrough that design patterns provide is the capability of applying lessons learned and reusing design information across organizations.

Design patterns represent a high-quality academic research movement that has its own conference series and visibility at most other technology events. The origin of design patterns comes from actual bricks-and-mortar building architecture. The original vision for design patterns included a design level model which we did not discover in other authors' work. We believe that design patterns represent the right approach for documenting guidance and solving technical problems in software architecture and system development. Figure 1.12 shows an example of a popular design pattern called the model view controller. This is a pattern that applies at the framework level and provides an approach for reusing software objects that contain data and processing which must be viewed and controlled in many different ways.

The model view controller pattern includes model objects, view objects, and controller objects. The model object is the reusable component. It represents the data in the system and the encapsulating processes which need to be represented and controlled in several ways. The view objects represent various visualizations of that information, and there can be many simultaneous views that may be presented to groups of users. The controller objects represent various business processes or mechanisms for controlling the processing of the data. The model view controller pattern has been around at least since the invention of Smalltalk and has been reapplied at several different scales of

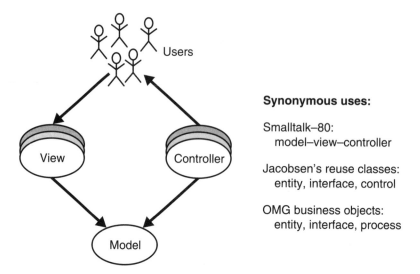

FIGURE 1.12   Model View Controller Pattern

software by various groups, including UML's business classes and the OMG business object task force which defines business objects in an analogous set of categories [Mowbray 97b]. Figure 11.6 shows the overall structure of design patterns. The essence of any design pattern is a problem–solution pair. The problem is explained and expanded in terms of the applicable design forces and any contextual forces which may be present. The solution resolves the design forces in a particular manner. The selection of any solution is a commitment, and a commitment provides some benefits as well as consequences. In addition, selection of a solution may lead to additional problems where other patterns are appropriate.

Design patterns are distinguished from other forms of software literature in that design patterns are presented in terms of a standard outline or template. Several templates have been published that meet the needs of various software design models. Figure 1.13 is a listing of the template developed for the CORBA design patterns [Mowbray 97a]. In this template there is a separation between the solution description and the variations of the solution, which may vary by structure and by scale of application. Making this separation allowed the authors to clarify the base solution at a particular scale and then to describe the variations and nuances of applying the pattern in separate sections of the template. The design pattern template is a rhetorical structure that ensures consistent coverage of the key questions that people may need to answer in order to apply the design information. In particular, when justifying the application

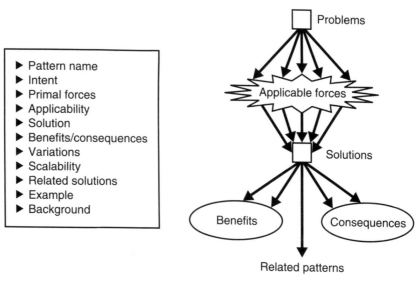

FIGURE 1.13   An Example Pattern Template

of a pattern, it is important to understand the benefits and potential consequences of the pattern to understand the real tradeoffs in design. If the design pattern authors have properly documented the pattern, they have identified those points of debate explicitly so that the users of the pattern do not have to reinvent that information.

Figure 1.14 is an example of a CORBA design pattern that applies in general to technologies beyond CORBA for system building. The problem is that most systems have vertical solutions, where each software module has a unique interface corresponding to each software implementation. The vertical solutions lead inevitably to stovepipe interdependencies between the modules in the system. By adding the common interface pattern to a system, we can capture the common interoperability information so that the software modules can interoperate without explicit dependencies upon particular implementations. The common interface pattern is a fundamental principle that is applied in standardization work and in software architectures in general.

Figure 1.15 shows a related pattern which applies the common interface in a more general and sophisticated context. In this pattern, called the horizontal vertical metadata pattern, we have a static architecture for a system defined in terms of a common interface with vertical interface extensions; also we are adding some dynamic architecture elements represented metadata. A key tradeoff described in the pattern talks about how dynamic architecture and static architecture can be varied to represent different portions of the design. Dynamic

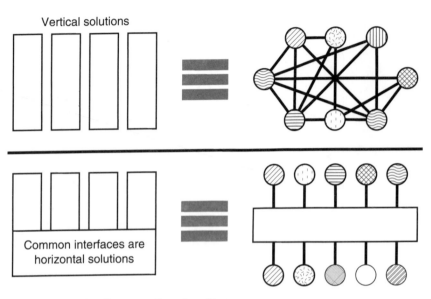

FIGURE 1.14   Common Interface Pattern

architecture is one of the key solutions for implementing variability and adapt-ability in software architectures.

Figure 1.16 shows how the horizontal-vertical-metadata pattern is actu-ally an instance of a more general concept that is applied across standards organizations and profiling entities all the way down to a system level of

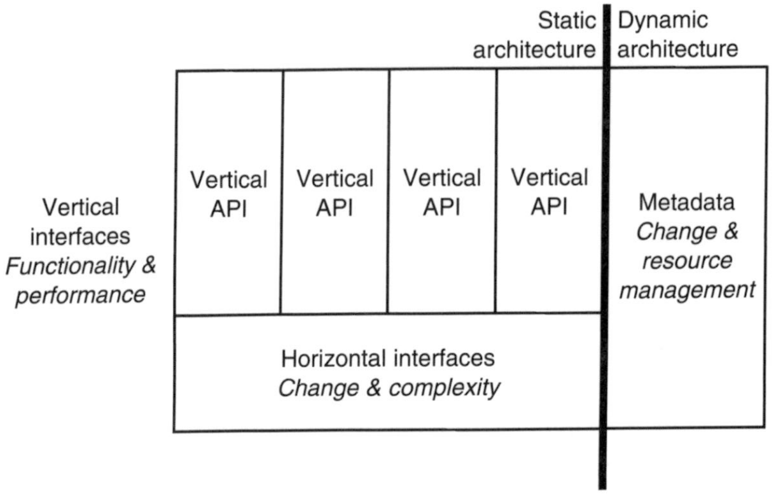

	Static architecture	Dynamic architecture			
Vertical interfaces *Functionality & performance*	Vertical API	Vertical API	Vertical API	Vertical API	Metadata *Change & resource management*
	Horizontal interfaces *Change & complexity*				

FIGURE 1.15   Horizontal Vertical Metadata Pattern

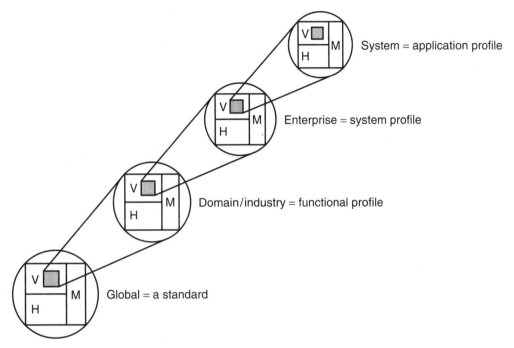

FIGURE 1.16   Pattern Applicability at Multiple Scales

deployment. This application of the horizontal-vertical-metadata pattern is directly analogous to the functional and system profiles that we describe in Chapter 4, where the functional profile is a vertical extension of a global standard. A system profile is a vertical extension of a functional profile, and any particular application system is a vertical instance of a system profile.

Figure 1.17 shows an application-level pattern and how it is applied. We present this example to give you a flavor of what is involved. In this case we are showing a UML sequence diagram. Before the pattern is applied, there is a simple request and return transaction which actually causes the client program to block while it is occurring. It turns out that this is the default behavior of most distributed computing infrastructures such as remote procedure calls and CORBA. We can improve the performance of this configuration by adding a moderate amount of complexity and, after applying the pattern, we can return a reference to the result which will be computed in parallel and then retrieved later (Figure 1.17).

Figure 1.18 shows a table of several examples of design pattern languages. Much of the available pattern documentation addresses a specific software design level. More recent work on CORBA design patterns and

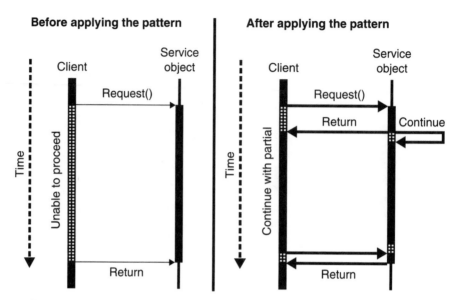

FIGURE 1.17   Partial Processing Sequence Diagram

pattern-oriented software architectures has addressed several levels of abstraction where these level are explicit. At the idiom level of design patterns we are concerned with individual objects. Idiom documentation has been widely available in the form of programming language guidebooks. Idioms represent expert programming techniques. These are techniques that one would rediscover after substantial use of a language. If software engineers are maintaining software written by other people, it is essential to understand idioms in order to understand the intentions of the programmers applying these sophisticated ideas.

	Gamma Design Patterns	Buschmann Architecture Patterns	CORBA Design Patterns	Fowler Analysis Patterns
Software Scale	Micro-Architecture	Micro to System	System	Objects to Micro
Most Useful to	OO Programmer	System Architect	System Architect	OO Analyst
Key Horizontal Forces	Change	Change Complexity Performance	Change Complexity	Functionality Change

FIGURE 1.18   Comparison of Design Pattern Languages

One of the first published design pattern languages described microarchitecture patterns [Gamma 94]. The goal of the gamma pattern language was to invent a new discipline of variation-centered software design. The gamma pattern language is organized in terms of several categories including creational patterns, structural patterns, and behavioral patterns. When applying the gamma patterns, complexity of design is increased with the benefit of potential support for potential modification of the software. Gamma patterns have become very popular and are applied widely in software engineering organizations today.

AntiPatterns

A recent development in the patterns community is called AntiPatterns. An AntiPattern differs from an ordinary pattern in that it is a solution pair rather than a problem–solution pair (Figure 1.19). An AntiPattern starts with a problematic solution. The reason why the solution is there is due to various contextual forces. The AntiPattern solution leads to various kinds of symptoms and consequences, and the consequences can be quite devastating. The AntiPattern proceeds to

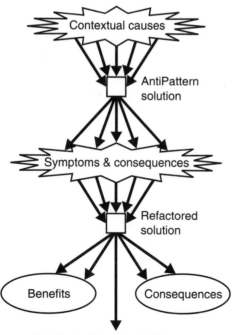

FIGURE 1.19 AntiPatterns

define a potential solution for migrating the problematic solution to a refactored solution providing improved benefits. AntiPatterns are fundamentally about software refactoring. Refactoring is modification to software to improve its structure or quality. Common examples of AntiPatterns include stovepipe systems, spaghetti code, and analysis paralysis. AntiPatterns are further explained in the book *AntiPatterns* published by John Wiley & Sons in 1998 [Brown 98].

1.4   CONCLUSIONS

In order to realize the benefits of software components and object technology, much more effective guidance is needed than the naive application of objects which characterized the first generation of these technologies. Design patterns are a highly effective and academically based guidance approach that is now being practically applied in many software development shops. The technology and skills transfer available through design patterns can lead to some important benefits, including reducing software risks, enhancing the effectiveness and productivity of the software developer, and making successful practices repeatable.

In particular, the reference model for open distributed processing is the formal standard for object-oriented architecture. This reference model is widely used because it is effective for defining distributed systems. The model is used in many industries where mission-critical systems must be successful. RM-ODP separates complex concerns for the specification of distributed systems. RM-ODP enables future proofing because it defines an approach for specifying architectural plans which are independent of distribution and technology choices. We believe that RM-ODP is a key architectural guideline for object-oriented systems and should be applied in your organizational practices.

1.5   EXERCISES

EXERCISE 1.1   Define your career plan for the next two years. As your career progresses to higher levels of seniority, you will be expected to require redirection on a less frequent basis, with the maximum being about once a year. We believe that planning is essential, so making a career plan at this early stage of your reading would be a positive step. Identify your goals, and then identify what you need to know in order to achieve your goals (i.e., knowledge gaps). Be brutally honest.

EXAMPLE SOLUTION: Three years ago, my goal was to continue in technical architecture roles and increase my knowledge in several areas, so that I could be a more complete contributor. In particular, I wanted to gain extensive experience in UML modeling, design patterns, and software process and to reconnect with programming fundamentals. I also wanted to gain some management experiences to add to my resume. I wanted to give the research and development cycle one more go, for both personal and professional reasons. After all, I joined this industry because I loved programming. At the back of my mind was a desire to help some friends in small commercial businesses, but I sorely lacked experience in this area, having worked mostly for large defense contractors and think tanks. Having a list of what I wanted to learn, I next consulted the Internet, the world's most extensive collection of free resources. I located several books, training courses, and other information that helped me identify specific learning targets.

Being a relatively independent middle manager in the technical ladder, I adjusted my workload to align with my goals. I prepared a tutorial on UML and defined an architecture using UML notation, which was within the scope of our research. I downloaded the latest version of the Java programming language from Sun Microsystems and began programming the first phase of the architecture prototype. I was having fun and achieving my goals while performing useful architecture research and evangelism for my firm, which was in the midst of UML adoption. Reviewing my results with co-workers enriched my learning experience and helped my firm to move forward on UML-related initiatives. Also I pursued directed readings and attended a patterns workshop, which greatly enriched my knowledge of the field.

Having achieved a modicum of success on this path, I was ready for the next phase. Time to replan. In the pre-Y2K days, the software industry was very profitable. Opportunities abounded. I lacked much of the essential knowledge to help my friends in small commercial businesses (my ultimate goal). In addition, I wanted to do more technical architecture work, on a faster cycle. Defining a new architecture every month would be ideal, but that kind of opportunity was not available at my current firm. Also, business in my firm was in a cooling-off period.

A career change was in order. I took a job at a very stable, highly reputable small commercial firm; e.g., their paychecks came regularly and they always cleared the bank. This new firm knew everything that I wanted to learn—a perfect match. At the library I discovered the book resources to learn the requisite areas of knowledge that I was lacking, a bit of business training, and so forth. I was able to read about these matters and apply them on the job daily. I was able to complete several interesting architecture projects, including a financial system specification, a middleware architecture specification for a large telecommunications firm, and a high-level architecture for a real-time system. In addition, I was able to do a great deal of UML modeling, learn

Visual Basic and C++, and do some CORBA programming. I was also teaching courses on the topics that I wanted to master—excellent progress, by any standards of performance. At this point, I had achieved the technical goals that I had set two years earlier. Time to re-plan, as this exercise continues in real life.

EXERCISE 1.2   Select an architecture framework for use in your current firm (or customer's organization)—for example, RM-ODP, Zachman Framework, or 4+1 Model View. Write a brief profile description about how the framework should be applied in your organization.

       BACKGROUND FOR SOLUTION: We believe that having a framework is far superior to working without one. Whatever framework you choose, certain conventions and guidelines for applying it in your organization will need to be managed. The need for these profile conventions is most obvious in the selection of the Zachman Framework. Since you have 30 candidate specifications to write, you must address two issues. First, 30 specifications is too much work, and you should compress and simplify the amount of effort required to plan a system. Focus on the useful, practical elements for your domain of application. Combine elements as appropriate to ensure coverage without elevating the document-driven aspects to an unreasonable level. Second, if there is no profile, you can't possibly expect any two architectures to be comparable. You should select essential and optional viewpoints to be specified, and define what they mean in your organization's terminology. You can also propose conventions for how these viewpoints will be documented, such as a template for each viewpoint, and notational conventions. We believe that these steps are required for any responsible application of these powerful frameworks.

EXERCISE 1.3   Create a pattern system for use in your organization. Select patterns from among the available pattern catalogs to cover the areas of greatest concern and need in your organization.

       BACKGROUND FOR SOLUTION: A "pattern system" is documented in a simple tabular form. Use page 380 of [Buschmann 96] as your starting point. The pattern-system table contains a listing of the names of each pattern, along with their book page reference, for quick retrieval. Implicit in this exercise is the selection of the key patterns catalogs (i.e., books) that would be readily available to every developer. Remember: Patterns are lessons learned. The purpose of this exercise is to create a job aid so that your developer can more effectively apply lessons learned. We suggest that you consider including sources such as [Fowler 97], [Gamma 94], and [Mowbray 97a, b] to your list of candidate catalogs.

SOFTWARE ARCHITECTURE: BASIC TRAINING

This chapter on basic training for software architects presents the fundamental tools you require in order to be effective. In the military, basic
training is used to challenge and motivate cadets and to demonstrate
both the demands and rewards of a military career. Similarly, software architects must be motivated individuals who have the desire to confront the challenges of technical leadership in a software development effort. However,
motivation is not enough. A software architect must be equipped with the intellectual tools to concretely realize in software an architectural vision.

This manual takes a hands-on approach that not only presents the best architectural practices in the industry but also provides concrete real-world examples and exercises for applying the presented material to circumstances common
throughout the software industry. Basic training will cover the fundamental concepts of software technology, which provide a foundation for software architecture. Software technology has evolved through many trends and alternatives for
software development. Currently, mainstream software practice has evolved
from procedural software to object orientation (Figure 2.1). With the increasing
adoption of enterprise Java and Microsoft COM, component-orientation is the
next major paradigm. In corporate development, most new-start projects are
adopting object orientation because it is supported by the majority of commercial
development environments. As we will discuss, object orientation has a very
weak notion of software architecture, which leads to serious shortcomings. The
emerging trend of component orientation is replacing old approaches with strong
elements of architectural design.

Software architects must be able to articulate these development paradigms clearly, along with appropriate uses of enabling technologies. In any given project, an eclectic mixture of development paradigms (including relational database management) can be useful to achieve the best results. Each paradigm has something useful to offer, including mature development tools. An interesting discussion of multiparadigm programming is presented in [Coplien 99].

2.1   SOFTWARE PARADIGMS

Today, most organizations will find their technology skill base engaged in one of the three major paradigms: procedural, object oriented, or component oriented. Where you are today is highly specific to your organization and your staff skills. Procedural and object paradigms are closely tied to programming-language choice, but you will find that component orientation is different in that it is more closely associated with the selection of an infrastructure.

Procedural programming languages include FORTRAN, COBOL, Pascal, BASIC, and many others. In procedural technology, the program comprises the process for executing various algorithms. The process is separated from the data in the system, and the process manipulates the data through direct access operations. This is a direct outcome of the stored-procedure programming systems from which computer technology originates. When the program and data are separated, there are many potential interdependencies between parts of the program. If the data representation is modified, there can be substantial impacts on the program in multiple places.

An example of data–process separation is the year 2000 problem, in which simply adding some additional digits to the date representation has catastrophic consequences for procedural software. Unfortunately, because the majority of systems are built with procedural technology, the dependencies upon these data representations can cause systemwide program errors and the necessity for line-by-line program review and modification.

Object-Oriented Paradigm

Object-oriented programming languages include Smalltalk, C++, and the Java programming language ("the Java language"). These languages support the encapsulation of data with accessor code in terms of abstract data types (commonly called classes). In object-oriented programming languages, the encapsulation capabilities are sufficient for reasonably sized programs. As long as software modules are maintained by individual programmers, encapsulation is sufficiently robust to provide some intrinsic benefits. However, we shall see that language-specific encapsulation is insufficient to support software reuse and distributed systems.

In object-oriented technology, the basic paradigm is changed to enable a separation of concerns. Figure 2.1 shows the object-oriented technology paradigm in which the program is broken up into smaller pieces called *objects*. Each object contains some of the data of the system, and the program encapsulates that data. In other words, access to the data is only available through using the program through which it is directly associated. In this way, the system is partitioned into modules which isolate changes. Changes in data representation usually only impact the immediate object which encapsulates that data.

Objects communicate with each other through messages. Messages can have an impact upon state—in other words, changing the data—but only through the encapsulated procedures which have an intimate relationship to the local data. For small-scale programs, the object paradigm is effective in its isolation of change. However, the paradigm is not perfect for all of its potential uses.

Technology and System Scale

When the size of the system is scaled so that many programmers are involved, the encapsulations have been found to be insufficient to isolate change across systems. In this case, additional component-oriented infrastructures are needed to provide industrial-strength encapsulations of the data and associated programs.

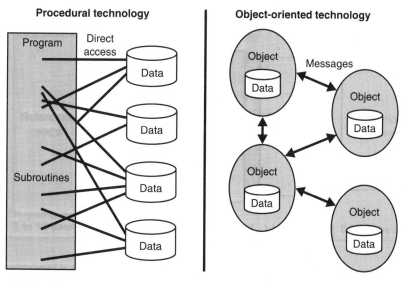

FIGURE 2.1   (a) Procedural Paradigm and (b) Object-Oriented Paradigm

One example is the CORBA interface definition language, which defines object-oriented interfaces that are sufficiently opaque to support the integration of large-scale distributed systems. In fact, the encapsulation mechanism, or IDL, is powerful enough to enable the transparent integration of multiple programming languages such as Smalltalk and the Java language as well as the object-oriented communication across heterogeneous systems which may involve multiple operation systems and protocol stacks.

Objects Are the Commercial Baseline

Object-oriented technology is in widespread use today. It has been said that the procedural technologies originated from academia but the object-oriented technologies originated from commercial organizations. In fact, object-oriented technologies have many interesting origins which go back virtually to the beginning of computer science. Today, object technology is the dominant paradigm for commercial software. Virtually every vendor in the software business is providing object-technology solutions which, together with component infrastructures, can enable interoperability between software vendors in various software environments.

For example, corporate development organizations today are migrating from procedural languages such as C and COBOL to object-oriented languages which have gained substantial popularity in recent years. Languages such as the Java language have made a dramatic impression on society as a whole. An awareness of the Java language is so commonplace that even the man on the street is familiar with the terminology for this tool of software developers.

OBJECT-ORIENTED ARCHITECTURE: AN OXYMORON

For the majority of practitioners, object orientation is devoid of a software architecture approach. This is manifested in multiple ways in object-oriented methods and culture. Starting with what is generally regarded as the original source for OO thinking, Wirfs-Brock's 1990 book, *Designing Object-Oriented Software,* there was a notion of software architecture, including the discovery of subsystems through inspection of collaboration diagrams. It merited an entire chapter of Wirfs-Brock's method in 1990. In the next decade, little was written about architecture in the OO methodology community. Major OO methodology books had at most a few paragraphs concerning architecture, which were a faint reflection of Wirf-Brock's architecture notions.

Since virtually nothing was written about architecture in the literature, most OO practitioners had no architecture guidance. There was no reason to consider architecture important. This has led to great confusion on OO projects, as team members struggle to manage complexity and scalability with OO methods not designed to address them.

In general, OO methods involve successive refinement of object models, where most analysis objects are eventually transformed into programming objects. In our terminology, we called these approaches model-based methods. The assumption that each analysis object will inevitably become a programming object is a major obstacle for OO thinkers to overcome in order to understand architecture. In architectural models, specification objects represent constraints, not programming objects. They may or may not be transformed into programming objects; that is an independent decision of the developer.

OO also opposes architecture in other subtle ways, related to project culture. OO encourages project teams to be egalitarian (e.g., CRC cards), where all decisions are democratic. On such a project, there is no architect role, because there is little separation of decision making between members of the development team.

OO encouraged "bad-is-better" thinking in development, a philosophy which is virtually the opposite of architectural thinking. Using "bad is better," the external appearance of a working implementation greatly outweighs any requirement for maintainable internal structure. In other words, rapid iterative prototyping, with ruthless disregard for architectural principles, is a normal, healthy environment for OO development.

The topic of architecture has resurfaced only recently in OO literature, with the newfound popularity of componentware. Now it is customary to include a token chapter on architecture in most methodology books, whereas in the heyday of OO, architecture was virtually taboo. In one sense, componentware is a response to the shortcomings of OO. Componentware, with its emphasis on larger-variable-grained software modules, is a clear step toward an architectural mindset.

Databases and Objects

Database technologies are also evolving toward objects. The database technologies originated with several different models. In recent years, the relational model of databases has been predominant. More recently, object-oriented databases have become a substantial technology market, and databases which combine object orientation and relational concepts are becoming prevalent.

Database query languages, such as Structured Query Language (SQL), are being extended in standards work to support object-oriented concepts. One reason why this is occurring is that the kinds of applications people are creating require substantially more sophisticated types of data representations and types of query algorithms for searching and manipulating the information.

Object in the Mainstream

Object technology is used today in most application areas and vertical markets. Dozens of projects are being pursued by government organizations in object technology as well as commercial industry. A principal advantage of technology is that it enables the implementation of new business processes which provide competitive advantage to organizations. Society is changing toward increasing dependence upon information technology. The use of object technology enables rapid system implementation and various forms of labor saving through software reuse mechanisms. Even though the largest number of lines of software are still written in procedural languages such as COBOL, it is becoming clear that this paradigm is changing.

Toward Components: Scripting Languages

Proponents of scripting languages claim that there are a larger number of scripting language programmers than there are of any other kind [Ousterhout 98]. Scripting languages such as the JavaScript language, TCL shell programming languages, and Visual Basic enable pre-existing software (e.g., components) to be easily integrated into application configurations.

Since object-oriented software and object technology is the dominant commercial paradigm, it is important to understand the major flavors of commercial technologies which are available for the architecture of software systems. The two major categories include commercial off-the-shelf proprietary software and commercial off-the-shelf open systems software (see Section 2.2).

Componentware: The Component Orientation Paradigm

Moving to the next level of software sophistication requires fundamental changes in systems thinking, software processes, and technology utilization. The next major area of technology, componentware (or component orientation), contains key elements of the solution to today's critical software problems.

The componentware approach introduces a set of closely interrelated techniques and technologies. Componentware introduces a sophisticated mindset for generating business results. These componentware elements include:

► Component Infrastructures
► Software Patterns
► Software Architecture
► Component-Based Development

Componentware technologies provide sophisticated approaches to software development that challenge outdated assumptions. Together these elements create a major new technology trend. Componentware represents as fundamental a change in technology as object orientation did in previous generations. We will discuss these componentware technologies after a brief introduction to componentware's unique principles.

Components versus Objects

Componentware can be understood as a reincarnation of object orientation and other software technologies. Distinguishing componentware from previous generations of technology are four principles: encapsulation, polymorphism, late binding, and safety. This list overlaps with object orientation, except that it eliminates the emphasis on inheritance. In component thinking, inheritance is a tightly coupled, white-box relationship that is unsuitable for most forms of packaging and reuse. Instead, components reuse functionality by invoking other objects and components instead of inheriting from them. In component terminology, these invocations are called *delegations.*

> *"One person's architecture is another person's detail. One person's system is another person's component" [Rechtin 97].*

By convention, all components have specifications corresponding to their implementations. The specification defines the component *encapsulation* (i.e., its public interfaces to other components). Reuse of component specifications is a form of *polymorphism* which is strongly encouraged. Ideally, component specifications are local or global standards that are widely reused throughout a system, an enterprise, or an industry.

Componentware utilizes composition for building systems. In composition, we integrate two or more components to create a larger entity, which could be a new component, a component framework, or an entire system. Composition is the integration of components. The combined component acquires joint specifications from the constituent component.

If the components have matching specifications for client calls and services, then they can interoperate with no extra coding. This is often called plug and play integration. When executed at runtime, this is a form of *late binding*. For example, a client component can discover a component server through an on-line directory, such as the CORBA Trader Service. With matching client and service interface specifications, the components can establish a run-time binding to each other and interact seamlessly through the component infrastructure.

In a perfect world, all components would be fully conformant with their specifications and free from all defects. Successful operation and interoperation of components depend on many internal and external factors. *Safety* properties can help because they can minimize entire classes of defects in a component environment. As society becomes increasingly dependent upon software technology, safety has become a serious legal concern and one of the most important areas of computer science research.

For example, Java's garbage collection feature guarantees memory safety, or freedom from memory deallocation defects (which are problematic in C++ programs). Other kinds of safety include type safety (guaranteed data type compatibility) and module safety, which controls the effects of software extension and component composition.

Component Infrastructures

The componentware revolution has already arrived in the form of component infrastructures. Major platform vendors have bet their futures on componentware product lines. In particular, Microsoft, Sun Microsystems, IBM, and the CORBA consortia have established significant componentware infrastructures through massive technology and marketing investments.

These component infrastructures (Microsoft COM, Sun Enterprise Java-Beans, and CORBA request brokers) are dominant infrastructures for overlapping industry segments—Microsoft COM+ on the desktop; the Java language for cross platform applications; and CORBA for corporate networks and the Internet. Interestingly, these technologies are also mutually interoperable, with Microsoft, Sun, IBM, and others supporting the CORBA Internet Inter-ORB Protocol (IIOP) for Microsoft COM and Java Remote Method Invocation (although the Java language works equally well with CORBA). In the following paragraphs, we'll compare these infrastructures briefly.

Microsoft has been promoting the Component Object Model (COM) and follow-on products for several years. COM is a single-computer component infrastructure. OLE and ActiveX define componentware interfaces based upon

COM. In theory, the Distributed Component Object Model (DCOM), now called COM+, extends the capabilities of COM over networks and the Internet. With these technologies, Microsoft has funded a major corporate strategy promoting a worldwide migration to componentware over the past five years. Future Microsoft plans indicate that it will continue its componentware initiative for the forseeable future.

Sun Microsystems' invention of the Java language is a continuing evolution of programming-language features, infrastructures, and related class libraries. The Java language technology has created tremendous industry excitement and support from independent developers. The extensions for JavaBeans and Enterprise JavaBeans establish an evolving component model that rivals COM and ActiveX in the cross-platform application space. Enterprise JavaBeans and the IBM San Francisco project are using Java Remote Method Invocation (RMI) for distributed computing, one of several proprietary infrastructures available to Java language programmers. While proprietary Java language infrastructures do provide convenience for programmers, they lack one key capability: ease of interoperability with other programming languages. This may be a serious limitation for corporate projects because it hampers legacy integration and cross-language development which is commonplace for server applications. Another, more subtle, issue is that Java application programming interfaces (APIs) are not standard. For popular technologies like JDBC, vendors often customize the APIs as they create their value-added versions of the Sun reference technologies.

The Common Object Request Broker Architecture (CORBA) is an open systems standard for distributed infrastructure supported by multiple vendors, industry consortia, and formal standards bodies. Recently there has been a surge in CORBA licensing in corporate development organizations, with a surprising array of Fortune 500 companies adopting CORBA for enterprise projects, including banks and manufacturers. From its inception CORBA has supported both object and componentware models. With today's CORBA products supporting multiple component interfaces in a single encapsulated servlet, CORBA is an ideal infrastructure for componentware development involving heterogeneous hardware/software, multiple programming languages, or distributed computing. Recently, CORBA has been extended to support the capabilities of message-oriented middleware and domain-specific API standards (health care, manufacturing, financial services, and so forth). Just like any other technology, CORBA products do have limitations (e.g., memory leaks, conformance, performance). However, for a standard established in 1991, it is amazing how well the CORBA architecture has weathered cataclysmic innovations in other technologies and emerged ever stronger (e.g., the Java language and the Internet).

Java application servers have overtaken CORBA's role in many Internet-savvy organizations. What CORBA lacks is direct support for scalability, reliability, and maintainability. These capabilities are standard features supported by most Java application servers today.

Componentware infrastructures are having a significant impact on software development. In many respects, these infrastructures are well on their way to becoming mainstream development platforms. Because all of them are becoming interoperable (through CORBA IIOP), there is a well-understood relationship between infrastructure models. Their similarities are much greater than their proprietary differences might imply.

Infrastructure selection is one of the most discussed, but least important, aspects of implementing componentware. For corporate developers, the most critical issues are confronted well after infrastructure selection. These issues include: how to master designing with the technology, how to architect systems, and how to coordinate one's development efforts. These areas are covered in the next three sections.

Component Software Patterns

Software patterns comprise a common body of software knowledge which can be applied across all component infrastructures (see Section 1.3). The most famous category of software patterns, called *design patterns*, comprises proven software design ideas which are reused by developers. Other important categories of patterns include analysis patterns and antipatterns. Analysis patterns define proven ways of modeling business information that can be directly applied to the modeling of new software systems and databases.

Software patterns are a necessary element of componentware. The development of new, reusable components requires expert-level quality of design, specification, and implementation. Proven design solutions are necessary to establish successful component architectures and frameworks for families of applications. Often, there are too many variables to take chances on unproven design concepts.

The popularity of software patterns can be explained as a response to the practical shortcomings of object orientation. Antipatterns explain the common mistakes that people make when developing object oriented software systems (as well as other types of systems). Much more is needed than basic object-oriented principles to build successful systems. Design patterns explain the additional, sophisticated ideas that are required for effective software designs. Analysis patterns present the sophisticated ideas necessary for the effective modeling of concepts and data.

It is still commonplace in software development to reinvent design ideas, incurring the risks and delays of trial-and-error experimentation. If fact, most software methods encourage reinvention as the normal mode of development. Considering the challenging forces of requirements change, technology innovation, and distributed computing, we consider reinvention to be an unnecessary risk in many circumstances. This comment is especially applicable to the development of components, where the costs of defects and redesigns can affect multiple systems.

Altogether, software patterns can be described as *knowledge reuse*. It is interesting to note that most patterns are considered as simple as common sense by expert-level developers. However, for the majority of developers, patterns are a necessary part of technical training that can help them to achieve world-class results.

Component Software Architecture

Software architecture concerns the planning and maintenance of system structure from earliest system concept through development and operations. Good architectures are stable system structures which can accommodate changes in requirements and technologies. Good architectures ensure the continuous satisfaction of human needs (i.e., quality) throughout system life cycles. Reusable components are examples of good architecture. They support stable interface specifications, which can accommodate changes due to reuse in many system contexts.

Software architecture plays an important role in component design, specification, and use. Software architecture provides the design context within which components are designed and reused. Components have a role in predetermining aspects of software architecture. For example, a component framework may predefine the architecture of a significant portion of a system.

One of the most exciting aspects of software architecture for componentware is supporting distributed project teams. A software architecture comprises a system specification that enables parallel, independent development of the system or its parts. A proper software architecture defines computational boundaries (i.e., API) that divide the system into separate testable subsystems. These subsystems can be outsourced to one or more distributed project teams.

Component-Based Development

Component-based development is software development with a difference. Many process aspects are reused, such as iterative, incremental development. The primary componentware difference is the specialization of technical roles.

Three key componentware roles are software architect, component developer, and application developer. These differ from object-oriented approaches, which promoted notions of all-purpose programmers, committee-based design, and architecture after-the-fact.

A typical leadership team for a project comprises a software architect and a project manager. The architect works in conjunction with management to make key technical decisions, those with systemwide impact. The architect is responsible for technical planning of the system and for communicating these plans with developers. Since the architect coordinates systemwide design decisions, many other technical decisions are the responsibility of developers. To be effective, the architect must have the highest levels of experience and technical training, with outstanding skills in design, specification writing, and spoken communication.

The best component developers are also the most talented programmers. They design and program the building blocks from which the application will be constructed. The architect defines the major boundaries behind which component-based services will be provided. Reuse of preexisting components is evaluated with respect to an organizational software repository. For new component requirements, the component developers design and construct new software, updating the organizational repository. Typically, components will implement the horizontal functions and lower-level aspects of the system, reducing the need for application developers to reinvent these capabilities. Component developers make intensive use of software patterns, applying several overlapping patterns to each component design and implementation.

Application developers are responsible for integrating components and implementing the vertical requirements of the system, including user interfaces. They apply preexisting components to the solution of application-specific problems. Application developers must communicate with end users having some domain expertise.

Generally, component developers use systems programming languages, such as the C++ and Java languages, while application developers use scripting languages, such as the JavaScript language, TCL, Python, and Visual Basic. Systems programming languages allow more control of low-level issues but are more difficult to use for application building. Scripting languages provide a higher level of abstraction, with a corresponding reduction of up to 8:1 in lines of code needed to implement a given requirement, compared to systems programming languages.

Componentware is the next major software technology trend. In many ways, it has already arrived and is readily available for commercial exploitation. This revolution is actively supported by major vendors, including Microsoft, Sun, IBM, and the CORBA vendor consortia. The most important aspects of componentware are not the choice of technologies, but how these are applied. Successful adoption of componentware must include the reuse of software patterns, the planning of software architecture, and the establishment of component-based development teams.

The componentware revolution is an exciting opportunity to avoid the inadequacies of outdated software approaches. Componentware enables you to survive and thrive when facing the challenges of requirements change and rapid commercial innovation. Componentware delivers the benefits of software reuse and enables outsourcing to distributed project teams.

2.2   OPEN SYSTEMS TECHNOLOGY

Proprietary software is a non-standards-compliant product of a single vendor. That single vendor controls the form and function of the software through many iterations of product releases. When today's systems are built, they are dependent upon commercial software to varying degrees. Commercial software is the primary form of software reuse and in practice is a much more effective form of reuse within individual enterprises.

One reason why commercial software is a more powerful form of reuse is due to an economy of scale. Large numbers of copies of the software are distributed to customers, and the software can be debugged and quality controlled to a degree which exceeds the in-house development capabilities of even the largest end-user enterprises. When end-user enterprises depend upon proprietary software, they are dependent upon the vendors' continued support for existing capabilities, and architecturally many end users depend upon future features which the vendors claim will be added to the software. When proprietary software is packaged in the form of a public specification or standard, the specification is usually a direct representation of that single software implementation.

Often, when proprietary specifications are put forward in the public domain, it is unlikely that the proprietary implementation will be modified. This leaves the impression that proprietary software can also be an open system standard, when in fact there is no possibility of modification of the underlying technologies. This phenomenon is especially true when millions of software licenses have been distributed and are running on existing software systems. When proprietary technology is put forward, vendors use unique interpretations of software concepts to describe their products. These interpretations can include fundamental modifications to object-oriented principles.

"Successful architectures are proprietary, but open" [Rechtin 97].

The most significant aspect of proprietary technology is the provision of application program interfaces (APIs). The APIs to proprietary software define the boundary between a proprietary implementation and any value-added application software which either an independent software vendor or the end user provides to build application systems. As proprietary software technologies evolve through multiple releases, the application program interfaces can change.

New capabilities are continuously added to proprietary software, and this exacerbates the complexity of application program interfaces. In many cases the complexity of the program interfaces available with proprietary software greatly exceeds the functionality needs of end-user organizations. It then becomes appropriate for the end-user organizations to attempt to manage this complexity in various ways. We will cover complexity-management concepts in several chapters.

In addition to adding new capabilities to proprietary program interfaces, vendors also on occasion may obsolesce interfaces in software. When program interfaces are obsolesced, there can be a significant maintenance impact upon application software. As proprietary software evolves through multiple releases, it is important for users to continue to upgrade the software to remain in synchronization with the mainstream support activities from the proprietary vendor. When the end users' systems fall behind more than two cycles, it is often necessary to completely repurchase and reintegrate the commercial software in order to synchronize with the currently released version. Many end users have found an almost complete obsolescence of application program interfaces within a few cycles of product release.

In summary, proprietary software releases and the evolution of the program interfaces become a treadmill for application programmers and independent software vendors to maintain synchronization with available and supported software. There is a conflict of interests between the application users and the proprietary software vendors, because the vendors' majority of profits can be driven by the sale of software upgrades.

The other major category of commercial software is open systems technologies (Figure 2.2). An open system technology is fundamentally different than a proprietary technology. In an open system technology, there is multivendor consensus to develop a specification that is independent of proprietary implementations. This is the case of most formal standards activities and many consortium standards activities which are becoming increasingly prevalent. In an open systems technology, the specification governs the behavior of the implementations.

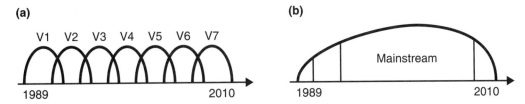

FIGURE 2.2   (a) Proprietary Technology and (b) Open Systems Technology

One of the key benefits is a consistency of implementation interfaces across multiple vendors. Additional benefits include uniformity of terminology and software interfaces, because the open systems technology requires multiple vendors to reach consensus. Another benefit is an increased level of technology specification and an extended life cycle. Since product developments are in parallel across multiple vendor organizations, the corresponding marketing activities which create the demand for the technology are also synchronized and coordinated. A key benefit of open systems technology is the interoperability that it provides between commercial software vendors. The distinction between open systems and proprietary technologies is particularly appropriate for object-oriented systems, which are becoming the mainstream of application development, as object technology is already the mainstream of commercial technology.

Commercial information technology is evolving. Additional capabilities are being added and becoming available through commercial technology that increasingly satisfy application needs. However, there is also a significant amount of reinvention in commercial technology of fundamental capabilities such as operating systems and programming languages.

In some commercial technologies, such as office automation, word processors, and spreadsheets, a continual reorganization of functionality is presented to the end user without significant extension of capabilities. In many people's view the rate of technology evolution on the commercial side is relatively slow in comparison to the growth in needs for competitive application developers. Commercial technology is put forth to satisfy the needs of large numbers of users. The generality of this software exceeds the need of any individual application user. In order to adapt commercial technologies to application needs, there is a requirement for software development and installation which customizes the commercial software to the needs of specific applications (Figure 2.3).

The requirement to customize commercial technology is often called *profiling,* a concept that we will cover in more detail in Chapter 4. In addition to the profiling software, substantial application-specific software is required to create application systems. Because of the relatively primitive capabilities

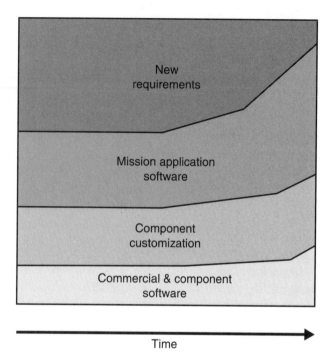

New
requirements

Mission application
software

Component
customization

Commercial & component
software

Time

FIGURE 2.3   Commercial Software Customization

available commercially for many application needs, this drives an increasing demand to build more and more application-specific software to complete the architecture for application systems. As systems evolve from single-user and departmental-level applications, to the enterprise with greater interoperability capabilities, the functional gap between available commercial software and individual user software will continue to increase.

The architecture of applications software systems is increasingly important in how systems support user needs. The majority of systems that have been created outside of the telecommunications industry are integrated using procedural and other paradigms which often lead to ineffective solutions. In fact, for systems created by corporate development organizations, a majority of the software projects are considered unsuccessful at completion. From an architectural perspective, many of these systems resemble the configuration in Figure 2.4 for stovepipe systems. In a stovepipe system there are a number of integrated software modules. Each software module has a unique software interface. This unique software interface corresponds to a single program implementation.

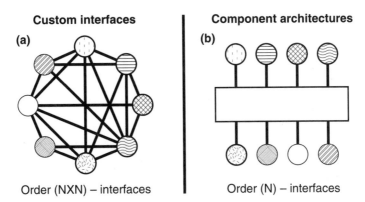

FIGURE 2.4 (a) Stovepipe Systems and (b) Component Architectures

When the system is integrated, there are many one-to-one dependencies between various part of the system. These dependencies are unique integration solutions. As the scale of the system increases with the number of modules, the number of dependencies increases by the square of the number of modules. This increase in complexity has many negative consequences. In particular, as a system evolves it becomes less and less amiable to modification and extension. System extension happens to be one of the major cost drivers in application development; it can account for as much as half of all software cost [Horowitz 93].

An alternative way of architecting systems includes a planned definition of software interfaces which provide a greater level of uniformity across the integrated solution. Component architectures are application systems which are defined using consistent application program interfaces across multiple instances of software subsystems (Figure 2.4). Component architectures reduce the dependency between software modules. The reduced dependency enables the system to be extended and support larger scales of integration. A properly architected component system has complexity which scales with the number of software modules in terms of the complexity of the software integration.

2.3 CLIENT SERVER TECHNOLOGY

Client server technologies are the result of the evolution of software technology supporting application systems. In particular, the evolution of client server technologies has been an important factor in the expansion of information technology across an increasing range of application business processes. Originally client server technologies focused on file sharing. File sharing is still the dominant paradigm of the Internet today with protocols such as HTTP supporting access to global file systems available across the Internet. File server technologies evolve into a second generation of capabilities dominated by a database server technology. It is important to note that the file server technologies were closely linked with the evolution of distributed computing technologies.

Increasingly, client-server technologies are being replaced by N-Tier component-oriented solutions. Based upon Java application servers, the N-Tier solutions include support for thin-client user interfaces with increased scalability and reliability.

One of the most successful networking technologies came from Sun Microsystems and is called network file server. Sun Microsystems was successful in encouraging the de facto standardization of that technology by providing free reference technology access in terms of source code for implementation on arbitrary platforms. Network file server technology is based upon open network computing, another Sun Microsystems technology which was one of the first successful generations of distributed computer technology. Network file server was a procedurally based technology closely tied to the C programming language, as was the other important remote-procedure-call technology called the distributed computing environment. Both of these technologies resulted in file-sharing capabilities which were widely implemented. The database server technologies utilized these underlying distributed computing capabilities to provide remote access to database systems from a variety of client platforms.

Another important technology that arose during the database generation was that of transaction-processing monitors. Transaction-processing monitors enable the consistent and reliable maintenance of data integrity across distributed systems. Transaction processing technology continues to be an important add-on capability to distributed computing technologies to ensure robustness and integrity of implementations.

Groupware technologies also arose in the late 80s and early 90s starting with e-mail and evolving to higher forms of interactivity, some of which we can see on the Internet today, such as chat rooms and videoconferencing. Recently, the technologies of object orientation, distributed computing, and the Internet are beginning to merge to support adaptable computing environments which can scale to global proportions. This generation of technologies is called *distributed objects* and is characterized by technologies such as CORBA and the Java language (Figure 2.5).

The client server technologies initially arose as an evolution of mainframe-based technologies. Mainframe-based technologies were a natural outgrowth of single-processor systems which date back to the origins of

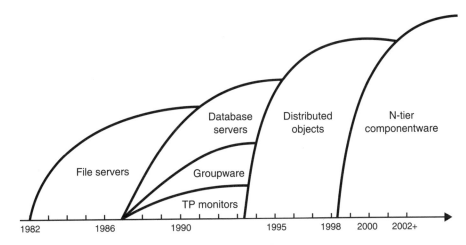

FIGURE 2.5 Origins of Client Server Technologies

computing. In a mainframe technology, the processing and management of data in the system is completely centralized. The mainframe is surrounded by a number of peripheral client terminals which simply support presentation of information. In the client server generation of technologies, the client computer has become a significant processing resource in its own right. Client systems which arose during the personal computer revolution are now capable of processing speeds which rival and greatly exceed that of former minicomputer and mainframe computer generations. Initially, in order to support access to data in departments and enterprises, client server technology supported the connection through local area networking to the back-end mainframe minicomputer and workstation server systems. The technology at the software level supporting this communication is called *middleware.*

> *An element "good enough" in a small system is unlikely to be good enough in a more complex one [Rechtin 97].*

Initially, middleware was installed as a custom capability to support client server networking between PCs and server platforms. As technology evolves, middleware is becoming embedded in the operating system so that it is a natural capability of client platforms as well as server platforms. Client systems with embedded middleware can now support on-board services to applications running locally and across the network. This evolution of client server technology to an embedded capability has added many new challenges to the implementation of application systems. In fact, there are various antitheses to the client server evolution, including a resurgence of the mainframe platform as a significant business of IBM and the capability called the *network computer* which begins to resemble the dumb terminal of mainframe days (Figure 2.6).

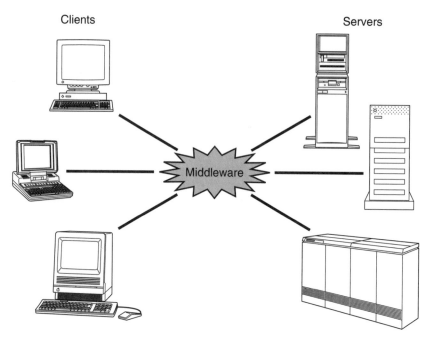

FIGURE 2.6   Role of Middleware

Object technologies are organized around client server capabilities. Object technologies come in two primary categories. Some are organized to serve the process of software development (Figure 2.7). Examples of these technologies include object-oriented analysis and object-oriented design. Object-oriented analysis comprises the definition of information technology capabilities that are models of current and future business processes. Object-oriented modeling provides rich capabilities for representing business entities and business processes. This is in contrast to procedural and relational database technologies, which require the application designer to compromise the representation of the business environment to the constraints of the technology in terms of control flow and data representation. Object-oriented analysis, because of the natural correspondence of state information in process, provides a mechanism for modeling reality which is relatively easy to communicate with end users. Because the end-user communication is facilitated, the design and validation of object-oriented systems is greatly enabled.

Object-oriented design is another major software phase which has been successful commercially in the software process market. Object-oriented design comprises the planning of software structure and capabilities that support the reduction in software defects and rapid prototyping of software capabilities.

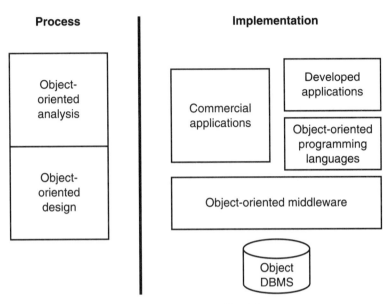

FIGURE 2.7   Middleware Reference Model

The other major category of object technology focuses on the implementation. At the center is object-oriented middleware technology. Object-oriented middleware supports distributed computing and the integration of various heterogeneous software technologies including operating systems, programming languages, and databases. Object-oriented programming languages are the direct expression of the object paradigm. Object-oriented programming languages support the encapsulation of data with process in the form of abstract data types in component objects. There are numerous object-oriented programming languages as there are procedural languages. The predominant languages for object-oriented programming include C++ Smalltalk and the Java language but there are significant communities supporting Eiffel, and other languages. Object-oriented middleware allows these languages to interoperate to form applications. Object-oriented programming languages are one possible choice for implementation of application software. It is also possible to utilize object-oriented analysis and design to support programming in procedural languages. This occurs frequently, as many corporate development environments use procedural languages for their mainstream languages, such as the C programming language and COBOL.

Another important technology is that of object-oriented database management systems and their closely related cousin, extended relational database systems. Object-oriented middleware supports the integration and distribution of all of these database capabilities. In the case of object-oriented database systems, middleware can support the publishing and access of data objects across distributed heterogeneous systems. Object-oriented analysis and design are also used in the definition of database capabilities which are then implemented in ordinary relational technologies. Object-oriented programming languages can then be used with relational databases to build systems. This practice is commonplace.

Relational database technologies continue to be a practical implementation technology for many forms of applications. The occurrence of pure object-oriented systems will continue to be relatively rare as legacy application technologies are carried forward into future target systems. Distributed object technologies (i.e., component infrastructures) are appropriate for the integration of legacy applications. The encapsulation capabilities of distributed object technologies provide some distinct advantages to the integration of legacy systems and the extension of those systems with new object-oriented capabilities.

One of the important qualities of object orientation is that the developer should not have to be concerned about the underlying implementation. If the underlying implementation is procedural or is object-oriented, it should not and does not matter if the applications are properly encapsulated. Distributed object middleware supports the opaque encapsulation property which makes this possible. The integration of commercial software with legacy and object-oriented applications is also enabled due to these encapsulation properties (Figure 2.7).

Object-oriented middleware technologies can be viewed as an outgrowth of their procedural producers. Beginning with operating systems, procedural technologies supporting interprocess communication were added to enable file sharing and the evolution of client server capabilities (Figure 2.8). Some of these technologies include the remote-procedure-call technologies such as ONC and DCE. The remote-procedure-call technologies were preceded by socket-level technologies, which are a more primitive form of messaging. Today, all of these technologies are still used actively in application systems and on the Internet. The object-oriented middleware technologies provided a next generation of capabilities which bundled more of the application functionality into the infrastructure.

It is interesting to note that previous generations of interprocess communication technology were marketed with the promise of universal application interoperability. Component-oriented technology is marketed the same way today. Distributed object-oriented middleware has the advantage of retrospection on the shortcomings of these previous technology generations. It was found that even though remote-procedure-call technologies enabled the integration of distributed software, the primitive level of these technologies required substantial application programming in order to realize systems. Once the systems were implemented, the systems tended to be fairly brittle and difficult to maintain. We can see many of the same shortcomings in the current generation of the component object model from Microsoft.

Microsoft, in 1996, released the distributed component object model (DCOM) as a multimedia middleware technology for the Internet. DCOM still exposed many of the lower-level primitive details which were the downfall of remote procedure calls. DCOM added some object-oriented capabilities and a natural integration support for C++ programming. Simply adding the capability to support C++ doesn't necessarily overcome the procedural route that exposed excessive complexity to distributed system developers in the DCOM predecessor called the distributed computing environment.

The common object request broker architecture for CORBA was the first technology to be designed from the ground up to support distributed object-oriented computing. Figure 2.8 shows that there is a partitioning of a technology market between the Microsoft technology base and virtually all other information technology vendors. The other vendors support various open system technologies that are the result of consensus standards processes. CORBA is universally accepted as the vendor-independent standard for distributed object middleware. CORBA simplifies distributed computing in several ways. The most significant advance is the language independence that CORBA

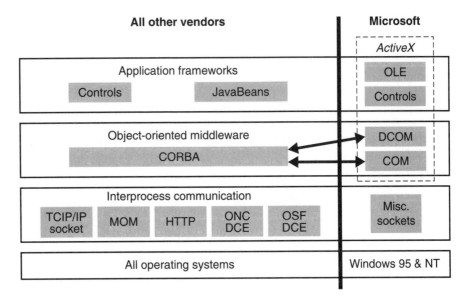

FIGURE 2.8   Distributed Technologies in Context

provides, allowing multiple programming languages in heterogeneous environments to interoperate using object messaging.

Above the middleware layer are other technologies which support further integration of application functionality. In the Microsoft technology base, they have grouped these technologies into a brand name called ActiveX. The ActiveX technologies are being obsolesced and replaced with Windows 2000+ technologies called COM+. The COM+ technologies include a substantial reinvention of middleware capabilities that eliminate interface definition languages, and it is likely that the language independence of the middleware will be compromised. The COM+ technologies are not yet available in a robust development configuration. The CORBA capabilities are widely available today and support multiple programming-language integration from multiple vendor platforms. Layered on top of the CORBA capabilities are various other technologies, some of which are still in development. These include JavaBeans and the CORBA component model, which is the distributed heterogeneous extension of JavaBeans technology.

CORBA technologies are the product of an open systems consortium process called the object management group, or OMG. The OMG has over 700 member organizations including all major vendors in the information technology, such as Sun Microsystems, Hewlett Packard, IBM, Netscape, and Microsoft. The OMG has addressed the problem of application software interoperability by focusing on the standardization of programming interfaces. With previous generations of remote-procedure-call technologies, the only widely adopted standard interface was the network file server, which is really the most primitive form of software interoperability beyond exchange of removable media. It is important for end users to provide their requirements and interact with open systems processes because they shape the form of technologies which will be used for end-user system development. In particular, sophisticated users of technologies can encourage open systems consortia and software vendors to provide more complete capabilities to enable the development of complex systems. This reduces technology risk and creates more leverage for application developers.

The CORBA technologies are centered around the object request broker which the component standardizes (Figure 2.9). In the object management architecture which is the route node of OMG diagrams, there are several categories of objects. The object request broker is distinguished because it is the object through which all the other categories of object communicate. The object management architecture is conceptually a layered architecture which includes increasing levels of specificity for domain application implementation.

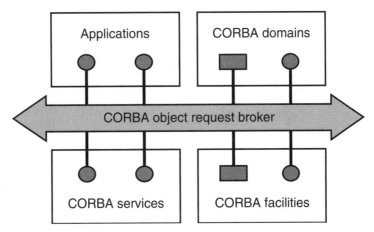

FIGURE 2.9 Object Management Architecture

The most common capabilities embodied by object technologies are standardized through the object request broker. The next level of capabilities are called the CORBA services, which provide enabling functions for systems implementation. The CORBA services are comparable in functionality to current operating-system services which are commonly bundled with platforms. The CORBA services provide the first step toward a distributed operating system capability which supports the integration of application software and commercial software across all types of platforms and environments.

The next level of capabilities is called the CORBA facility. CORBA facilities are common horizontal functions which may not be appropriate in every application domain. These functions include system management and compound document as well as printing and other capabilities. The CORBA domains are standard interfaces for the direct support of application domain interoperation. The application domains include health care, manufacturing, finance, and many other categories. The final category of distributed objects is the application objects. These include all of the other interfaces which will not be explicitly standardized. Application object interfaces include commercial proprietary interfaces, as well as custom interfaces that are built for a particular application system.

CORBA technology is widely available today and is a mainstream technology available on virtually every operating-system platform. Some of the more innovative platforms, including the Netscape Communicator which could be considered an operating-system platform in its own right, are bundling

CORBA with all of their deliverable licenses. Microsoft also supports the CORBA technology market by delivering specifications that enable interworking with the Microsoft infrastructure workings. The OMG has standardized interworking specifications for both COM and COM+ generations of Microsoft technologies. These standards are available on products on major CORBA implementation systems today.

In addition, third-party vendors are providing direct support for CORBA. These include vendors like Black and White software who provide graphical user interface development tool kits, database vendors, system management vendors, and specialty market vendors such as realtime and computer-aided software engineering tools. The key capability that CORBA provides, which is fundamental to object orientation, is the interface definition language. The interface definition language is a notation for defining software boundaries. IDL is a specification language which enables the description of computational software architectures for application systems as well as international standards for interoperability.

The interface definition language from CORBA has also been adopted by the international standards organization and the formal standards counterparts for telecommunication systems. IDL is the international standard DIS14750. As such, IDL is a universal notation for defining application program interfaces in software architectures. Because IDL is programming-language independent, a single specification will suffice for defining software interfaces on any language or platform environment. IDL interfaces support object-oriented designs as well as the integration of legacy software. Since the object management group is the only major standards consortium developing object-oriented standards specifications for software interfaces, IDL is synonymous with object technology open system.

IDL supports the integration of a diverse array of programming languages and computing platforms (Figure 2.10). With IDL one can specify software interfaces that are compiled and readily integrated to available programming languages. These capabilities are available commercially and support distributed communication in a general manner.

In this section, we have discussed how mainframe technology has evolved into client server technologies with middleware providing the distributed computing software capabilities. Because client server technologies have merged with object technologies, it is now possible to provide object-oriented capabilities that augment legacy systems across most or all programming environments. In addition, interoperability between CORBA and the Microsoft counterpart called COM+ enables the coverage of popular platforms on many

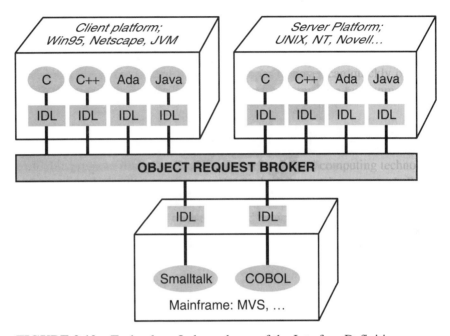

FIGURE 2.10 Technology Independence of the Interface Definition Language

organizational desktops. The vendors supporting open systems also support CORBA. The dominant Internet vendors are delivering CORBA and associated protocol stacks to numerous licensees. CORBA is the standard for object-oriented middleware. The products are available now as well as the horizontal services specifications that enable application development. The OMG is proceeding to develop the vertical specifications that will provide direct support for application-level interoperability.

The ISO has supported the designation of CORBA IDL as a standard for the definition of software interfaces across all computing environments.

Object orientation is a natural paradigm for modeling real-world information and business processes. Object technology supports the integration of heterogeneous and distributed information technologies that include legacy systems (Figure 2.11). Combining object orientation and component technology enables the creation of ambitious system concepts which are increasingly becoming the competitive advantage of application companies and end users.

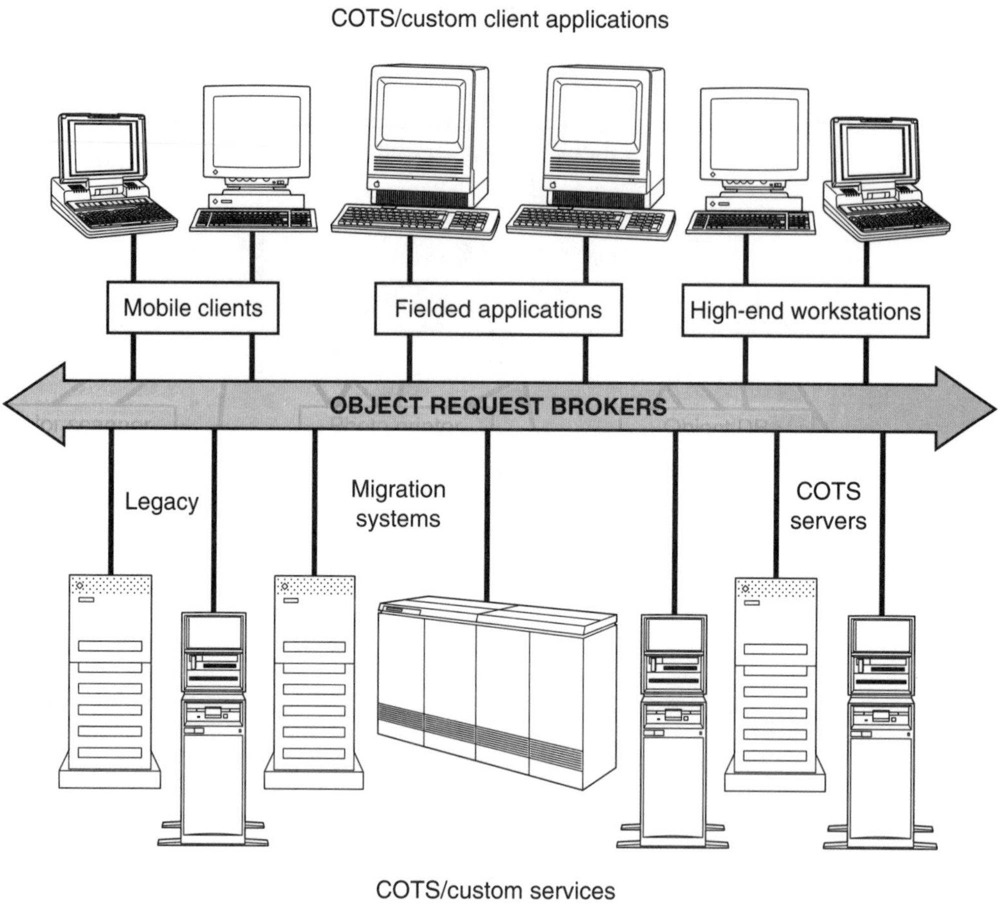

COTS/custom client applications

| Mobile clients | Fielded applications | High-end workstations |

OBJECT REQUEST BROKERS

Legacy   Migration systems   COTS servers

COTS/custom services

FIGURE 2.11   Interoperability Vision for Object Technology

2.4   Software Application Experience

In the commercial end-user environment, object technology has been applied to many important applications which enable business advantages. Examples include Fidelity Investments, one of the world's largest mutual fund companies, which as long as five years ago integrated its fund management workstations to support the integration of multisource information including decision-support capabilities that are crucial to the fund management business. The infrastructure they chose was an object request broker implementation conforming to the CORBA standard. Using CORBA, Fidelity Investments is able to customize the information gathering and analysis environment to the needs of individual fund managers. Many readers of this book probably have funds invested in one or more of the securities supported by CORBA. Wells Fargo, a large banking institution, has also applied object technologies to multiple applications to derive competitive advantages. One example is a financial transaction system which was developed and prototyped and deployed in less than five months based upon an object technology and CORBA implementation. In that system they integrated mainframe environments running IBM operating systems with minicomputer environments serving the on-line transaction terminals. In another Wells Fargo application, they integrated heterogeneous systems to support system management across a large enterprise. System management is one of the challenging and necessary applications which client server has created because the operation and management of information technology is no longer centralized and needs to be coordinated across many autonomous departmental systems as well as user desktops. Wells Fargo took advantage of object technology to implement such a distributed system management capability and greatly reduced their expense and response capabilities for system support challenges.

Another dramatic example of object technology was implemented by a large insurance provider. USAA had an auto claims system which was utilized by customer service agents to receive reports of damage claims over the telephone. USAA in addition to auto insurance has a number of other related product lines including life insurance and loan capabilities. By integrating their information technology using objects, USAA was able to provide the customer service agents with information about the full range of USAA product lines. When a customer called with an auto damage claim and the car was totaled and needed to be replaced, the customer services agents were able to process the insurance claim and offer a new car loan for the replacement of the vehicle. In addition, the customer service agent had information about customers such as the ages and number of children and was able to offer additional insurance coverages at the appropriate time frames during this same auto claim call. With these enhanced capabilities, essentially reengineering its customer service process, USAA was able to realize 30% increased revenue on its existing customer base by providing additional services to the customers who were calling USAA for auto claims purposes.

In the public sector, object technology has also been applied and delivered significant benefits. Several examples were implemented through the work of the authors on a project called *discus*, which is data interchange and synergistic collateral usage study. This project and its lessons learned are described in detail in another book, *The Essential CORBA*. One of the first lessons learned on discus was the power of using object technology to reuse design information. Once software interfaces were established and specified using IDL, it was relatively inexpensive to have contractors and commercial vendors support interoperability interfaces. The discus capabilities were defined before the Internet revolution, and when it became appropriate to integrate Internet capabilities, the same encapsulations were equally applicable to integrating new ways of viewing the data through Internet browsers. The existing legacy integrations implemented by discus were then used to extract information for viewing on Internet browsers.

Another case study implemented by the authors involved a set of information access services, which is a case study documented in another book, *Inside CORBA*. In this application, we discovered that the government had implemented a variety of systems with similar capabilities and the end users needed these systems to interoperate to support expanded access to information resources. The application we are describing does not differ in substance from the environment required by the Fidelity Investment Managers—in other words, gathering information from diverse resources in order to support important decisions. In order to resolve the users' needs, we conducted a study of existing systems that focused on the software interfaces supported through multiple technologies. By learning the details of the legacy system interfaces, we could formulate new object-oriented designs that captured the existing functionality in a manner that was common across the legacy system environment. By committing the new interface design to an IDL specification, we were able to work with other contractors to implement prototypes and forward the specifications through government standardization processes. Within two years, the interoperability concept evolved from ground zero to working software including a formal test sweep that assured conformance between multiple implementations of the specification.

There is an opportunity in many enterprises to realize these kinds of results. Because information technology in large enterprises is evolving from desktop and departmental information systems to interoperable enterprise systems, there is layer of enterprise architecture which does not exist in most organizations and can be implemented using distributed-object technologies in a manner that provides interoperability in a general way.

Let us summarize this section. Commercial organizations have realized many benefits from object technology that are directly relevant to their corporate competitive advantages. The authors' experiences in research and development show that design reuse is one of the most important concepts to apply in realizing these kinds of results. Given a proper software interface specification, it is relatively easy for software developers to understand the specification through training processes and then proceed to implement the specifications. A much more difficult problem would be to ask developers to integrate systems without this kind of guidance. In other words, reinventing a new custom interoperability link is significantly more difficult than if you give the developers a design for how the systems interoperate and they simply have to implement the code to implement that capability. In our research and development we found these kinds of benefits even at the smallest scales where only two or three subsystems were being integrated; as the scale of integration increased up to seven or ten or more systems, the benefits also increased.

Systems interoperability is achievable today through object technology, and these benefits are being realized in existing commercial systems and in system procurements in the public sector.

2.5 TECHNOLOGY AND APPLICATION ARCHITECTURE

Software architecture involves the management of both application functionality and commercial technology change. The kinds of benefits we just mentioned are not the direct result of adoption of a particular technology but involve exploiting the technology in ways that are most effective to realize the business purpose of the system. The simple decision to adopt CORBA or COM+ is not sufficient to guarantee positive business outcomes. One of the key challenges is managing the change in commercial technologies in a manner that supports long-term system life cycles and the ability to extend the system without substantial maintenance as the commercial technology evolves.

Figure 2.12 is an example of the class of technology challenges which must be managed by object-oriented architects. Figure 2.12 concerns the evolution of middleware technologies, starting with the socket technologies and evolving into remote procedure calls and distributed computing environment to the current Java 2 Enterprise Edition (J2EE) and ActiveX technologies. No one can reliably predict the future, but given what is known about proprietary technology evolution as well as open systems evolution, it is likely that many of the technologies that are becoming popular will eventually have their own life cycle, which has a distinct ending point based on when the software vendors discontinue their product support and move their attention to new product lines. This particular technology evolution in middleware has some dramatic effects on application software because the middleware is closely integrated with many of the emerging application capabilities. When a technology like ActiveX becomes obsolete

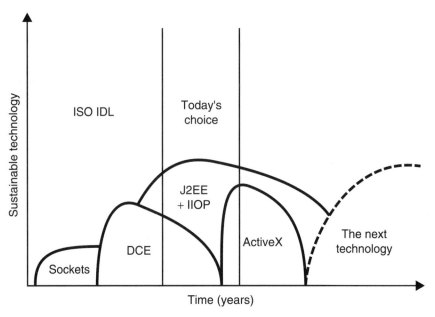

FIGURE 2.12   Managing Technology Change

has it then become necessary to upgrade application systems to the new technologies in order to maintain vendor support and integration of new capabilities. We can already see the demise of ActiveX on the horizon as COM+, a succeeding technology, will replace core elements of its technology. The software interfaces are likely to be quite different, especially because COM and COM+ are based upon an interface definition language, not the same one as CORBA, and COM+ doesn't have an interface definition language, at least in terms of current marketing information. It is important for the software architect to anticipate these kinds of inevitable changes and to plan the migration of application systems to the new technologies in a manner which doesn't mitigate the business purpose of current system development.

There are many challenges to the architect in the application space. Some of the most strenuous challenges involve the changing business processes which current businesses are undergoing. There is increasing competition from all sectors and a merger of capabilities through technologies like the Internet, newspapers, computer companies, cable television vendors, and telecommunications operators are starting to work in the same competitive spaces and are experiencing significant competitive pressure that is the direct result of information technology innovations and innovative concepts implemented in application systems. Even with previous generations of technologies it is fairly well known that requirements change a great deal. In fact, the majority of applications costs for software development can be traced directly to requirements changes [Horowitz 93]. For the first time in history, information technology budgets are exceeding payrolls in many organizations in industries such as financial services. Information technology is becoming synonymous with competitive advantage in many of these domains. However, the basic capabilities of system development are still falling far short of what is needed to fully realize competitive capabilities. For example, in corporate development, one out of three systems that are started end up in a project cancellation [Johnson 95]. These types of statistics represent inordinate risk for small and medium-size businesses, given the increasing cost and dependence upon information systems.

One of the fundamental rules of thumb of computing is that no technology ever truly goes away. One can imagine some early IBM minicomputers that are still faithfully performing their job in various businesses around the world. As information technology evolves, the need to integrate an increasing array of heterogeneous systems and software starts to become a significant challenge. As we integrate across enterprises and between enterprises using intranets and extranets, the architecture challenges become substantial. One problem is the current inadequacy of information technology infrastructure, including technologies like COM+ and CORBA which differ from the real application needs in some significant ways. As the challenges of information technology continue to escalate, there is another problem with the software skill base. In many industries, there are substantial shortages of software engineers. It is estimated that there is at least a 10% negative unemployment level in the United States in the software engineering profession. Some industries are much harder hit than others, including public sector systems integration contractors. In order to build systems with that challenge in mind, the object-oriented architect needs to plan the system development and control the key software boundaries in a more effective manner than has ever been done before.

Many critical challenges lie ahead for application systems developers and software architects. There is an escalating complexity of application system development. This is driven by the increasing heterogeneity of information systems and the need to integrate increasing scopes of systems both within and outside the company. In addition, the user requirements are increasing the user expectations, due to exposure to Internet technologies and other marvels of modern life and are driving software developers to take increasing risks with more complicated and ambitious systems concepts. The key role of the object-oriented architect is the management of change. Managing commercial technology innovation with its many asynchronous product life cycles is one area. Another area is managing the changing business processes which the information technology supports and implements. One area of potential solutions lies in the users influencing the evolution of open systems technologies, influencing software vendors to provide whole technology capabilities, and influencing legislators to put in place the appropriate guarantees of merchantability and fitness for purpose that underlie the assumptions in system architecture and development.

2.6   APPLYING STANDARDS TO APPLICATION SYSTEMS

In the adoption of object-oriented architectures and technologies, many common questions are raised which must be resolved in order to fully understand the implications. We have already discussed questions of defining object orientation and the component technologies which comprise object technologies. We have also touched on how object technologies compare with others, such as procedural technology.

Many other questions and requirements are crucial to certain categories of applications. Questions about performance, reliability, security on the Internet and how these technologies integrate with vendors that have significant market share are all important considerations in the adoption of these technologies. In the next few chapters we explain some of the fundamental concepts that describe the commercial and application sides of object-oriented architecture. We further make the case of the application of open systems technologies in object-oriented software development practice. We also address application development issues on applying object technology, integration of legacy systems, and the impact of these technologies on procurement and development processes.

It is important to understand that commercial technologies based upon open systems evolve according to certain underlying principles. These principles are clearly defined through a model developed by Carl Cargill that describes the five stages of standardization (Figure 2.13). To initiate an open systems standards process it is necessary to define a reference model. A reference model defines the common principles, concepts, and terminology that are applied across families of standards. These reference models also apply to object-oriented architectures and the integration of application systems. Reference models are an element often missing in software engineering processes that are addressing complex issues. Developing a formal reference model through a formal open systems process takes a considerable amount of effort from numerous people.

A typical reference model from the international standards organization may take up to ten years to formulate. Based upon a reference model, a number of industry standards can be initiated and adopted on a somewhat shorter time scale for formal standardization; this ranges up to seven years. Both reference models and industry standards are usually the intellectual product of groups of technology vendors. The standards represent the most general common denominator of technologies across the largest consumer base. In order to apply these technologies, it is necessary to define a number of profiles which serve the role of reducing the complexity of applying the standard within a particular domain or set of application systems (Figure 2.13).

There are two different kinds of profiles. *Functional profiles* define the application in general terms of a standard for a specific domain. Typical domains might include mortgage lending or automobile manufacturing. The functional profiles define the common usage conventions across multiple companies within the same industry. Functional profiles can be the product of information technology vendors but usually are a joint product between the users of technology and the vendors.

The next level of profiles is called *system profiles*. System profiles define how a particular family of systems will use a particular standard or set of standards. The family of systems is usually associated with a certain enterprise

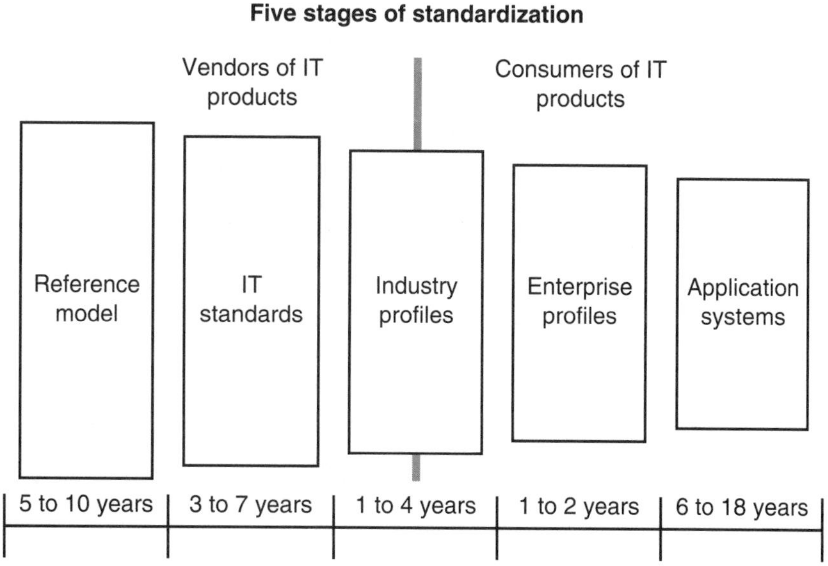

Five stages of standardization

Vendors of IT products		Consumers of IT products		
Reference model	IT standards	Industry profiles	Enterprise profiles	Application systems
5 to 10 years	3 to 7 years	1 to 4 years	1 to 2 years	6 to 18 years

FIGURE 2.13   The Five Stages of Standardization

or virtual enterprise. For example, a set of electronic data interchange standards for the Ford Motor Company define how the company and its suppliers for the manufacturing process can provide just-in-time inventory control so that Ford's assembly lines can proceed in an organized fashion without interruptions.

Above system profiles there are *application systems,* which are specific implementations. Even though the concept of profiles is new to many software engineers, profiles are implemented, perhaps implicitly, in all systems. Whenever a general-purpose standard or a commercial technology is applied, decisions are made regarding the conventions of how that technology is used, and those decisions comprise a profile. Unfortunately, many of the important profiles are buried in the implementation details of information systems. Notice that, in Figure 2.13, the time scales for developing each of the types of specifications is decreasing. The intention is that the reference models provide a stable architecture framework for all of the standards, profiles, and systems that are developed over a longer term. The industry standards provide the next level of stability and continuity, the profiles provide stability and consensus across domains and application families, and all of these mechanisms support the rapid creation of application systems on the order of half a year to a year and a half.

Figure 2.14 shows the breakout of reference models and profiles from the perspective of a particular vendor of information technology. In general, a vendor is working from a single reference model that spans a number of industry standards. The vendor implements technologies conformant with these standards and then works with various application developers and vertical markets to define the usage of the technology for valuable business systems. There is a multiplying factor for vendors in this approach in that for a small group of vendors there are potentially numerous customers that are enabled by the technologies that they supply.

Figure 2.15 portrays the concept from the perspective of the end-user application developer. We find this diagram somewhat amusing in a dark sense, but very representative of the kind of challenges that object-oriented architects in all kinds of information technology are facing today. For a given application system numerous standards and reference models are potentially applicable to the development of that system. A smaller number of functional profiles and system profiles can be obtained off the shelf to guide application system development. In general there is a gap between the application implementations and the industry standards in the area of profiling. Because profiling is primarily the responsibility of users, it's appropriate to say the users are to blame for this gap in guidance.

The model from the IT vendor's point of view

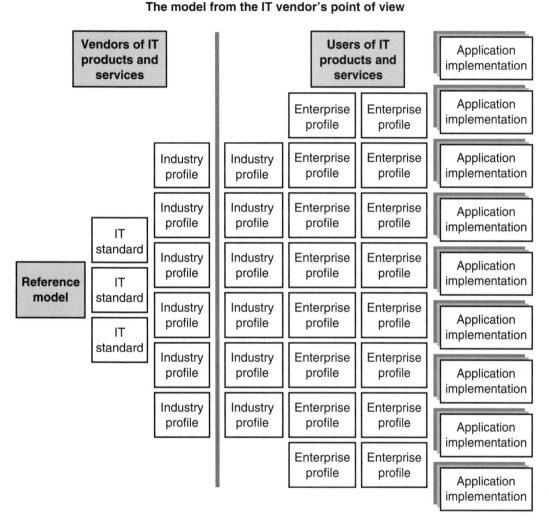

FIGURE 2.14   Standards from the Vendor's Perspective

When profiles are not agreed to between application system projects, the likelihood is that the systems will not be interoperable, even though they are using identical industry standards and even products from the same vendors. This can be a confusing and frustrating situation for application architects. It is necessary to understand these principles in order to resolve these kinds of issues for future system developments.

The model from the IT user's point of view

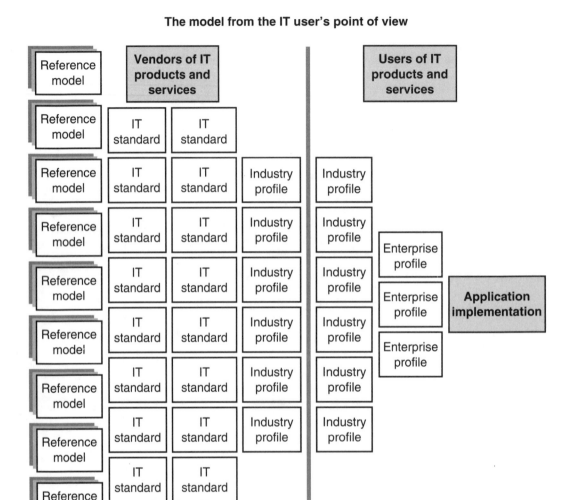

FIGURE 2.15   Standards from the User and Application Developer's Perspective

2.7   DISTRIBUTED INFRASTRUCTURES

Earlier, we introduced the concept of middleware that provided the software infrastructure over networking hardware for integrating server platforms with computing clients, which may comprise complete platforms in their own right.

Distributed infrastructure is a broad description for the full array of object-oriented and other information technologies from which the software architect can select. Figure 2.16 shows the smorgasbord of technologies available on both client server and middleware operating system platforms [Orfali 96]. On the client platform, technologies include Internet Web browsers, graphical user interface development capabilities, system management capabilities, and operating systems. On the server platform we have a similar array of technologies including object services, groupware capabilities, transaction capabilities, databases, and others. As we said before, the server capabilities are migrating to the client platforms as client server technologies evolve. In the middleware arena, we also have a fairly wide array of client server capabilities. These include a large selection of different transport stacks, network operating systems, system management environments and specific services. These technologies are described in significant detail in a book that we recommend by our friends Bob Orfali, Dan Harkey, and Jeri Edwards, *The Client Server Survival Guide* [Orfali 96].

Some of the key points to know about client server technologies include the fact that the important client server technologies to adopt are the ones that are based upon standards. The great thing about standards is that there are so many to choose from. A typical application portability profile contains over 300 technology standards. This standards profile would be applicable to a typical large-enterprise information policy. Many such profiles have been developed for the U.S. government and for commercial industry. The information technology market is quite large and growing. The object-oriented segment of

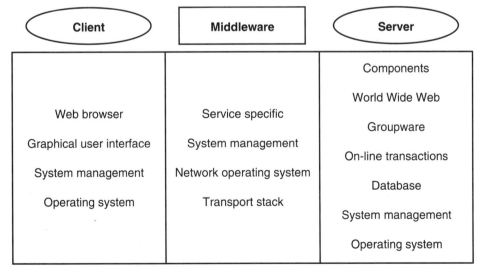

FIGURE 2.16 Infrastructure Reference Model

this market is still relatively small but is beginning to comprise enough of the market so that it is a factor in most application systems environments.

As standards evolve, so do commercial technologies. Standards can take up to seven years for formal adoption but are completed within as short a time as a year and a half within consortia like the OMG. Commercial technologies are evolving at an even greater rate, trending down from a three-year cycle that characterized technologies in the late 80s and early 90s down to 18-month and one-year cycles that characterize technologies today. For example, many vendors are starting to combine the year number with their product names, so that the obsolescence of the technology is obvious every time you invoke the program and users are becoming increasingly compelled to upgrade their software on a regular yearly basis. Will vendors reduce innovation time to less than one year and perhaps start to bundle the month and year designation with their product names?

The management of compatibilities between product versions is an increasingly difficult challenge, given that end-user enterprises can depend upon hundreds or even thousands of individual product releases within their corporate information technology environments. A typical medium-sized independent software vendor has approximately 200 software vendors that it depends upon in order to deliver products and services, trending up from only about a dozen six years ago. Figure 2.17 shows in more detail how commercial technologies are evolving in the middleware market toward increasing application functionality. Starting with the origins of networking, protocol stacks such as the transmission control protocol (TCP) provide basic capabilities for moving raw data across networks.

The next level of technologies includes the socket services which are available on most platforms and underlie many Internet technologies. These socket services resolve differences between platform dependencies. At the next layer, there are service interfaces such as transport-layer independence (TLI), which enabled a substitution of multiple socket-level messaging services below application software. As each of these technologies improves upon its predecessors, additional functionality which would normally be programmed into application software is now embodied in the underlying infrastructure. One consequence of this increasing level of abstraction is a loss of control of the underlying network details in qualities of services which were fully exposed at the more primitive levels. Beyond transport invisibility, the remote-procedure-called technologies then provide a natural high-level-language mechanism for network-based communications. The distributed computing environment represents the culmination of procedural technologies supporting distributed computing. Object-oriented extensions to DCE, including object-oriented DCE and

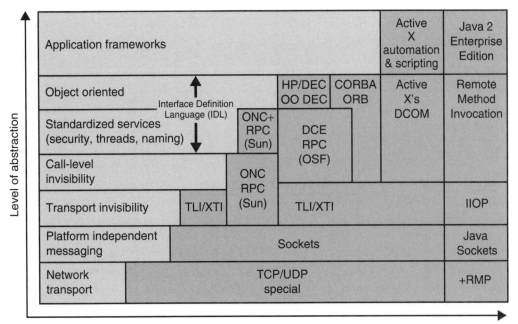

FIGURE 2.17   Evolution of Distributed Computing Technologies

Microsoft COM+, now provide mechanisms for using object-oriented programming languages with these infrastructures.

Finally, the CORBA object request broker abstracts above the remote
procedure's mechanisms by unifying the way that object classes are referenced
with the way that the individual services are referenced. In other words, the
CORBA technology removes yet another level of networking detail, simplify-
ing the references to objects and services within a distributed computing environment. The progress of technology evolution is not necessarily always in a
forward direction. Some significant technologies that had architectural benefits
did not become successful in the technology market. An example is the open
doc technology, which in the opinion of many authorities had architectural
benefits that exceed current technologies like ActiveX and JavaBeans.

Standards groups have highly overlapping memberships, with big companies dominating most forums. Groups come and go with the fashions of technological innovation. Recently Internet forums (W3C, IETF) have dominated,
as well as JavaSoft and Microsoft open forums.

Many networking and open systems technologies as well as other object-
oriented standards are the products of now defunct consortia. The consortium

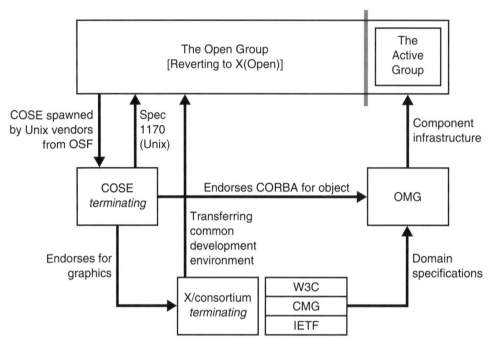

FIGURE 2.18   Commercial Software Technology Consortia

picture is dynamic. Some of the former consortia such as the Open Software Foundation and X Open are now merged to form The Open Group. Other consortia, such as the Object Management Group and the Common Open Software Group, are highly overlapping in membership. A recent addition to the consortium community has been the Active Group. The Active Group is responsible for publishing technology specifications for already released technologies developed by Microsoft (Figure 2.18). The Open Software Foundation originated the distributed computing environment which supports remote procedure calls as well as other distributed services. The distributed computing environment is the direct predecessor of the Microsoft COM+ technologies. Distributed computing environment represents the consensus of a consortium of vendors outside Microsoft for procedural distributed computing.

Along with CORBA, the distributed computing environment is a mainstream technology utilized by many large-scale enterprises (Figure 2.19). One important shortcoming of the distributed computing environment is the provision of a single-protocol-stack implementation. As distributed computing technologies evolve, it becomes increasingly necessary to provide multiple network implementations to satisfy various quality-of-service requirements. These requirements may include timeliness of message delivery, performance, and throughput, reliability, security, and other nonfunctional requirements. With a

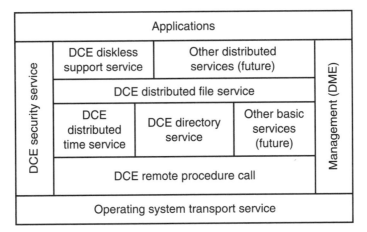

FIGURE 2.19   Distributed Computing Environment

single-protocol-stack implementation, the developers of applications do not have the capability to provide the appropriate levels of service. The technology gap described here is properly described as *access transparency,* a term defined by an international standards organization reference model that we cover in Chapter 9. Proper object-oriented distributed computing infrastructures do provide access transparency and give developers the freedom to select the appropriate protocol stacks to meet the application quality-of-service requirements.

Figure 2.20 shows the infrastructure technologies from the Microsoft COM+ and ActiveX product lines. The basis of these technologies for distributed computing came from the original OSF environment, but that technology was extended in various ways with proprietary interfaces that also support the use of C++ programs in addition to the C program supported by DCE. The ActiveX technologies have a partition between capabilities which support distributed computing and capabilities which are limited to a single desktop. The capabilities which are desktop specific include the compound document facilities. Compound document facilities support the integration of data from multiple applications in a single office document. When moving a document from desktop to desktop, there can be complications because of the lack of complete integration with the distributed environment.

Figure 2.21 shows some of the underlying details of how the component object model and COM+ model interface with application software. Application software is exposed to Microsoft generated function tables which are directly related to the runtime system from Microsoft Visual C++. The consequence of this close coupling between Visual C++ in applications software is that the mapping to other programming languages is not standardized

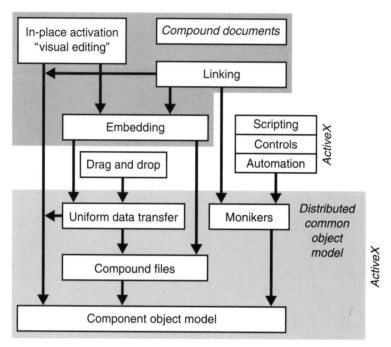

FIGURE 2.20   ActiveX Technology Elements

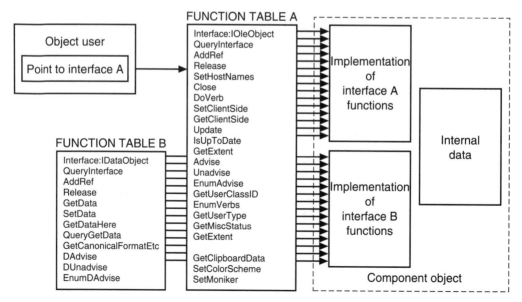

FIGURE 2.21   Component Object Model

and in some cases is quite awkward—for example, when ordinary C programs are applied with the COM+ infrastructure. The CORBA technologies provide a resolution of some of these shortcomings.

Figure 2.22 shows the basic concept behind an Object Request Broker (ORB). The purpose for an ORB is to provide communications between different elements of application software. The application software providing a service is represented by an object. This object may encapsulate software which is not object oriented. An application client can request services from an object by sending the request through the ORB. The CORBA mechanism is defined to help simplify the role of a client within a distributed system. The benefit of this approach is that it reduces the amount of software that needs to be written to create an application client and have it successfully interoperate in a distributed environment.

Figure 2.23 shows some of the finer-grained details from the CORBA model. Figure 2.23 relates to Figure 2.22 in that we are showing client and object software interoperating through an object request broker infrastructure. The part of the infrastructure which CORBA standardizes is limited to the shaded interfaces between the application software and the ORB infrastructure. CORBA does not standardize the underlying mechanisms or protocol stacks. There are both benefits and consequences to this freedom of implementation. Because different implementors have the ability to supply different mechanisms and protocol stacks underneath CORBA interfaces, a diversity of products support this standard and provide various qualities of service. Some implementations, in fact, provide dynamic qualities of service that can vary between local and remote types of invocations. The consequence of this freedom of implementation is that the mechanisms selected may not be compatible

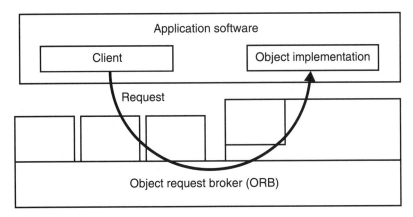

FIGURE 2.22   Object Request Broker Concept

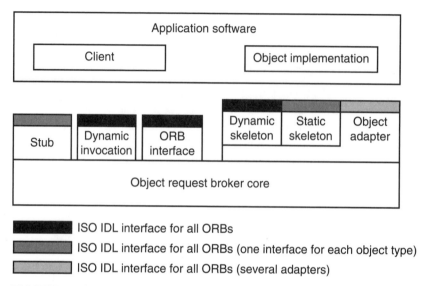

FIGURE 2.23   Key Interfaces in CORBA Architecture

across different vendors. An additional standard called the Internet Inter ORB Protocol (IIOP) defines how different ORB mechanisms can interoperate transparently. The implementation of IIOP is required for all CORBA products.

The CORBA infrastructure provides two different kinds of mechanisms on both the client and implementation sides of the communication services. On the client side, the client developer has the option of using precompiled stub programs that resemble ordinary calls to the application software. The use of static stubs minimizes the special programming which is required because the application is potentially distributed. The stub programs appear like local objects in the application environment, but the stubs represent a proxy for the remote object.

The client developer has the option of using dynamic invocation (Figure 2.23). Dynamic invocation is an interface that enables the client to call an arbitrary message invocation upon objects that it discovers dynamically. The dynamic invocation gives the CORBA mechanism extensibility which is only required in certain kinds of specialty applications. These applications might include program debuggers, mobile agent programs, and operating systems. The implementor of object services in the CORBA environment also has the capability to choose static invocation or dynamic invocation. The two options are generated as either static skeletons or dynamic skeletons.

The skeletons provide the software which interfaces between the ORB's communication infrastructure and the application program, and they do so in a way which is natural to the software developer. By using dynamic skeletons with dynamic invocation in the same program, interesting capabilities are possible. For example, software firewalls, which provide filtering between different groups of applications, can easily be implemented by these two dynamic capabilities.

Figure 2.24 shows the CORBA technologies in the object management architecture and how these technologies relate to the Cargill model that we discussed earlier. The object management architecture shown in Figure 2.9 provides a reference model for all the CORBA technologies. CORBA and the related standards, such as CORBA services and CORBA facilities, are examples of industry standards that apply broadly across multiple domains.

The CORBA domains comprise functional profiles in the Cargill model. In other words, the CORBA domain interface specifications represent domain-specific interoperability conventions for how to use the CORBA technologies to provide interoperability. Finally, the application objects in the object management architecture correspond directly with the application implementations in the Cargill model.

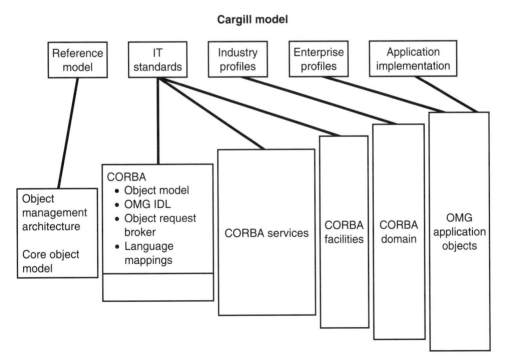

FIGURE 2.24   Extensions of the Object Management Architecture

Other initiatives (besides CORBA) have attempted to specify comprehensive standards hierarchies. First Taligent, then IBM in San Francisco attempted to define object standards frameworks, but neither garnered the expected popularity. Java J2EE has come closest to achieving the vision, and in our opinions represents outstanding progress toward completing the standards picture.

2.8   CONCLUSIONS

In this chapter we introduced the fundamental concepts of object orientation, open systems, and object-oriented architectures. We learned that object orientation helps to isolate changes in software systems by combining the data and processing into modules called objects. Object technology is a capability which is already present and entering the mainstream of software development. Object technology is broadly supported by commercial industry through software vending and by many mainstream end-user organizations in their application development.

We learned that the only sustainable commercial advances are through open systems forms of commercial technology. With proprietary technologies, the obsolescence of capabilities conflicts with the need to build stable application environments which support the extension of application functionality.

We learned that stovepipe systems are the pervasive form of application architecture but can be reformed into more effective component object architectures. In the next chapter we will describe object technologies and various reference models which make these technologies understandable.

In this chapter we talked about one of the key concepts in object-oriented architecture—the application of standards in software development. Proper understanding of how standards are utilized is very important to the successful exploitation of commercial technologies and the interoperability of application functions.

In this chapter we also described object-oriented client server technologies with a focus upon the underlying distributed computing capabilities and how they compare with related technologies from the procedural generation. We discovered that the companies supplying these technologies have highly overlapping interests which are expressed through commercial standards consortia and formal standards bodies. We discussed how distributed computing environments vary from the CORBA mechanism to the Microsoft technologies that are more closely related to remote procedure call. Finally, we described some of the details of CORBA infrastructure and how they relate to the Cargill model.

In conclusion, a wide range of open systems client server technologies support object orientation. These technologies enable the construction of a wide array of distributed systems based upon objects and components.

2.9   EXERCISES

EXERCISE 2.1   Assess the state of your current organization (or customer) with respect to the adoption of software paradigms. Prepare a short status assessment document containing recommendations for resolving any gaps in the current skill base.

BACKGROUND FOR SOLUTION: First look at the programming languages being used. Most procedural and OO organizations adopt single-language solutions. Then examine the training requirements. How much training is each developer required to have? We know of major IT organizations that require 9 weeks to as much as 26 weeks of training before they turn developers loose on the shop floor. At a bare minimum, we'd suggest 3 weeks. Suppose we're pursuing the OO paradigm. The recommended training is 1 week for "thinking objects," 1 week for OO programming, and 1 week for distributed systems development process and practice, e.g., experiencing systems building in a training environment. These are the recommended absolute minimums. Some of the smartest companies require much more.

EXERCISE 2.2   Assess the state of architectural control within your organization. Are you heavily dependent upon the architecture of a single vendor or set of vendors? What elements of the architecture do you control in a vendor-independent manner? Create a list of recommendations for resolving any discrepancies or shortcomings due to excessive vendor dependency.

BACKGROUND FOR SOLUTION: Ask people, "What is our architecture?" If the answer is Oracle or Microsoft, you should be concerned. These are honorable vendor firms, but in our way of thinking, what vendors do is not application architecture. Simple selection of a technology is not sufficient to resolve architectural forces. At a minimum, your enterprise architecture should describe the deployment of technologies and customization conventions for how products are used consistently across systems development. Ideally, your organization has its own APIs that resolve key interoperability issues, as well as rigorously maintained profiles for technology utilization.

EXERCISE 2.3   Assess the state of middleware technologies in your organization (or customer). Identify which technologies are utilized, and how effectively they are exploited.

> **BACKGROUND FOR SOLUTION:**   In our experience, there is a very high correlation between the technologies utilized and the architecture practices. If you are using several middleware infrastructures in a single application, you are most likely to have ad hoc architecture practices and relatively unmaintainable systems. In the era of CORBA enlightenment, begin to recognize the folly of this approach. Many organizations, being conservative, chose DCE as their corporate middleware solution. However, DCE remains a relatively brittle infrastructure (originating from the "C" procedural generation of technologies). Early adoptions of CORBA frequently resemble DCE-like solutions. As these organizations mature in their use of distributed computing, there is a corresponding flowering of architectural practices. Eventually, solid architecture frameworks like RM-ODP become quite attractive to these organizations, because they help architects think much more effectively about managing infrastructure.

EXERCISE 2.4   Describe a case-study experience for your organization as a useful lesson learned for other developers. Which products, versions, and platforms were utilized? How did you use and customize the applications to meet the needs of the application?

> **BACKGROUND FOR SOLUTION:**   A case study or "experience report" is quite different than a design pattern although they both share lessons learned. A case study is a specific instance of a successful solution. As you write this up, think about answering the questions that would be most useful to developers encountering a new architecture problem. What elements of the solution are most reusable, in a way that saves time and eliminates risk for readers about to define a new system architecture?

EXERCISE 2.5   Describe the infrastructure dependencies of one or more current applications in your organization. How would you re-architect these systems in their next generation to accommodate technology change more effectively?

> **BACKGROUND FOR SOLUTION:**   The worst case is if you are applying vendor technologies without profiling conventions and user-defined APIs. Unfortunately, the worst case is also typical of most organizations. Suppose a vendor provides 300 APIs to access its product. Your developers will use alternate sets of APIs for each project and even within a single system. If you want to migrate to something else, you have a supreme challenge. Consistency in use of product features can work wonders for enabling interoperability and

maintainability. The user-defined APIs, although proprietary, are very much under control and not likely to be vendor specific, e.g., CORBA IDL interfaces. To resolve these issues, you need to simplify the choices for how to utilize vendor products (i.e., using profiles) and clearly identify which aspects will be vendor independent. Reliance on standards is one step. Definition of profiles shows that you have sophistication in the use of standards and products.

EXERCISE 2.6   Which standards are being applied in your organization? Do they supply the desired benefits? Are there any profiles for these standards in your organization? Why or why not? Develop a plan, listing the recommended profiles of standards for your organization. Explain the rationale for why your organization needs each profile specification.

BACKGROUND FOR SOLUTION: Standards, while being one step away from vendor dependence, pose many of the same challenges as integrating with vendor-specific APIs. By definition, standards are very general purpose, applying to as many types of applications as possible. Therefore, the management of complexity is not an important goal for the standards writer. In fact, many standards are overly complicated in order to create barriers for vendor competition. Sophisticated application architects know this, and they plan to manage this complexity, e.g., profiles. We apologize for being so singled-minded about profiles, but this is a key solution concept that most organizations miss—with resulting negative consequences. In one of our favorite quotes, a senior executive laments that "We have created a set of fully standards-compliant stovepipes which can't interoperate." It's dead obvious why that's happened. You didn't read our book. Not that we created the concept, which is nearly as old as IT standards themselves.

EXERCISE 2.7   Describe the quality-of-service requirements for the distributed infrastructures in your organization (or customer). What qualities of service are readily supported today? What qualities of service could be usefully added? What distributed technologies would be applicable to meet these needs?

BACKGROUND FOR SOLUTION: A quality of service (QoS) is an important category of architectural requirements for distributed infrastructure. Do you need reliable communications, e.g., funds transfer? Do you need to support continuous media, e.g., desktop video teleconferencing? How reliable? How continuous? How secure? These are important questions that drive the selection of infrastructures, the migration plans of enterprises, and the practices of enterprise architects.

SOFTWARE ARCHITECTURE: GOING TO WAR

To be a software architect means that you must learn to think like an architect—in particular, a distributed systems architect. This is a substantial paradigm shift from thinking like an individual software developer writing one program. In this world of increasingly distributed IT systems, much of what you learned in your previous training can naively mislead you.

In order to go to war, you need to commit to a new mindset and a ruthless pursuit of architectural knowledge. Ignorance is our enemy, and knowledge is power on the architectural battlefield. We must erase mistaken assumptions and help you think about systems with much greater clarity, so that you can reason about the complex issues involved.

3.1   SOFTWARE ARCHITECTURE PARADIGM SHIFT

Unless you program telecommunications systems, video games, mainframe operating systems, or rigorously inspected software (e.g., CMM Level 5), almost every piece of software you will ever encounter is riddled with defects and, at least in theory, doesn't really work. It only *appears to work*—until an unexpected combination of inputs sends it crashing down. That is a very hard truth to accept, but experienced architects know it to be the case. In commercial software, nothing is real. If you don't believe this, invite a noncomputer user to experiment with your system. It won't take long for them to lock up one or more applications and possibly invoke the Blue Screen of Death.

In order to cope with this uncertain terrain, you need to begin thinking about software as inherently unreliable, defect ridden, and likely to fail unexpectedly. In addition, you need to confront numerous issues regarding distributed computing that aren't taught in most schools or training courses.

We have many things to learn and unlearn as we go to war. We begin by recognizing a key paradigm shift that leads to a deeper understanding of distributed computing and its pervasive consequences.

Traditional System Assumptions

The essence of the paradigm shift revolves around system assumptions. *Traditional system assumptions* are geared toward nondistributed systems—for example, departmental data processing systems. Under these assumptions, we assume that the system comprises a centrally managed application where the majority of processing is local, the communications are predictable, and the global states are readily observable. We further assume that the hardware/software suite is stable and homogeneous and fails infrequently and absolutely: Either the system is up or the system is down. Traditional system assumptions are the basis for the vast majority of software methodology and software engineering.

Traditional system assumptions are adequate for a world of isolated von Neumann machines (i.e., sequential processors) and dedicated terminals. The traditional assumptions are analogous to Newton's laws of physics in that they are reasonable models of objects that are changing slowly with respect to the speed of light.

Distribution Reverses Assumptions

However, the von Neumann and Newtonian models are no longer adequate descriptions of today's systems. Systems are becoming much less isolated and increasingly connected through intranets, extranets, and the Internet. Electromagnetic waves move very close to the speed of light in digital communications. With global digital communications, the Internet, and distributed objects, today's systems are operating more in accord with Einstein's relativity model. In large distributed systems, there is no single global state or single notion of time; everything is relative. System state is distributed and accessed indirectly through messages (an object-oriented concept). In addition, services and state may be replicated in multiple locations for availability and efficiency. Chaos theory is also relevant to distributed object systems. In any large, distributed system, partial failures are occurring all the time: network packets are corrupted, servers generate exceptions, processes fail, and operating systems crash. The overall application system must be fault-tolerant to accommodate these commonplace partial failures.

Multiorganizational Systems

Systems integration projects that span multiple departments and organizations are becoming more frequent. Whether created through business mergers, business process reengineering, or business alliances, multiorganizational systems introduce significant architectural challenges, including hardware/software heterogeneity, autonomy, security, and mobility. For example, a set of individually developed systems have their own autonomous control models; integration must address how these models interoperate and cooperate, possibly without changes to the assumptions in either model.

Making the Paradigm Shift

Distributed computing is a complex programming challenge that requires architectural planning in order to be successful. If you attempt to build today's distributed systems with traditional systems assumptions, you are likely to spend much of your budget battling the complex, distributed aspects of the system.

The difficulty of implementing distributed systems usually leads to fairly brittle solutions, which do not adapt well to changing business needs and technology evolution.

The important ideas listed below can help organizations transition through this paradigm shift and avoid the consequences of traditional system assumptions:

1. *Proactive Thinking Leads to Architecture.* The challenges of distributed computing are fundamental, and an active, forward-thinking approach is required to anticipate causes and manage outcomes. The core of a proactive IT approach involves architecture. Architecture is technology planning which provides proactive management of technology problems. The standards basis for distributed object architecture is the Reference Model for Open Distributed Processing (RM-ODP).

2. *Design and Software Reuse.* Another key aspect of the paradigm shift is avoidance of the classic antipattern: "Reinventing the Wheel." In software practice there is continual reinvention of basic solutions and fundamental software capabilities. Discovery of new distributed computing

solutions is a difficult research problem which is beyond the scope of most real-world software projects. *Design patterns* is a mechanism for capturing recurring solutions. Many useful distributed computing solutions have already been documented using patterns. While patterns address *design reuse*, object-oriented frameworks are a key mechanism for *software reuse*. To develop distributed systems successfully, effective use of design patterns and frameworks can be crucial.

3. *Tools.* The management of complex systems architecture requires the support of sophisticated modeling tools. The Unified Modeling Language makes these tools infinitely more useful because we can expect the majority of readers to understand the object diagrams (for the first time in history). Tools are essential to provide both forward and reverse engineering support for complex systems. Future tools will provide increasing support for architecture modeling, design pattern reuse, and software reuse through OO frameworks.

The software architecture paradigm shift is driven by powerful forces, including the physics of relativity and chaos theory, as well as changing business requirements and relentless technology evolution. Making the shift requires proactive architecture planning, pattern/framework reuse, and proper tools for defining and managing architecture. The potential benefits include: development project success, multiorganizational interoperability, adaptability to new business needs, and exploitation of new technologies. The consequences of not making the paradigm shift are well documented; for example, 5 out of 6 corporate software projects are unsuccessful. Using architecture to leverage the reversed assumptions of distributed processing can lead to a reversal of misfortunes in software development.

3.2   DOING SOFTWARE WRONG

After many years of brutal lessons learned, enterprise software development is moving out of the heroic programming dark ages and into an industrial-strength architecture revolution. The key is architecture-centered development, and most software experts agree that for complex systems *nothing else works*.

In this chapter we will explain the architecture-centered development process in some detail. But first, let's see why this software revolution is an inevitable necessity in enterprise development organizations.

This Old Software

To be successful, software must create an on-screen illusion that appears to meet end-user needs. But this illusion is temporary. In enterprise development, the internal structure of the software is also of great importance. In particular, the software architecture's ability to accommodate change will determine whether it provides ongoing value to the enterprise.

There are at least two unstoppable forces of change in enterprise software development: (1) requirements change and (2) technology change. In effect, our complex world is changing during system development and operational deployment.

Requirements change because the business environment changes, and because the end users' understanding of the requirements changes upon encountering realized system elements.

Technology changes are driven by relentless competition under the guise of innovation in the commercial software market. Vendor strategies are accelerating and enforcing change for software consumers. Currently, major vendors obsolete their own products every 6 to 18 months.

Because virtually every enterprise system relies on multiple commercial software suppliers, managing technology change is complex. Identifying, developing, and maintaining suites of integrated commercial products is an ongoing problem that every enterprise software organization must resolve for itself.

An Example: Doing Software Wrong

Here is a typical development scenario that is occurring in many enterprise software organizations today.

The enterprise needs a new software system. The target system is a replacement or consolidation of existing systems which do not support necessary changes to business processes. A project manager is appointed and a development team formed. The development team is a mixed group with some current and legacy skills (often with the balance toward legacy).

The project manager studies potential approaches and concludes that "object-oriented" (or other current buzzword) is the only paradigm that makes sense, given readily available, commercial technologies. In other words, the manager is led to believe that buzzword technology will make system success easy. Vendors encourage this illusion by claiming that their products can remake ordinary developers into programming stars. So the manager makes technology commitments and puts the development team through a product-specific programming course.

After that, nothing seems to happen. The team struggles to analyze, design, and program the system, without much measurable progress. The manager grows increasingly frustrated and worried, as the project schedule slips into political trouble with upper management and end users.

Statistically, the manager was doomed, almost from the start. According to reliable surveys, the brutal reality is that one-third of all corporate development projects are cancelled. Five out of six projects are considered unsuccessful and unable to deliver desired features. Even average projects have schedule and budget overruns nearly double the original project estimates.

Enter the Knight: Heroic Programmers

Heroic programmers can help a project to avoid short-term consequences, by delivering software that appears to meet end-user needs. Now that user interfaces are relatively easy to implement, the illusion of working software is increasingly easy to demonstrate. However, the complexities of developing a system that accommodates change is another matter. Heroic programmers are usually too close to the software problem to consider these longer-term consequences (Figure 3.1).

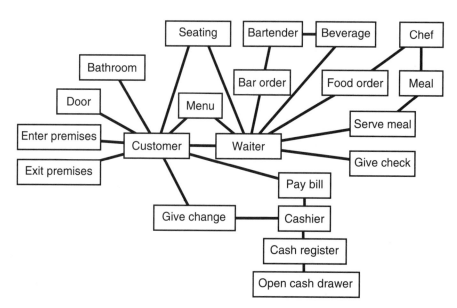

FIGURE 3.1   Heroic Programmers Often Fail to See the Bigger Dragon

With today's complex programming notations (e.g., C++) and distributed system capabilities (e.g., intranet, N-tier), it is widely understood that software modules are unmaintainable, except by the original programmer. Averaging at 30% annually in the United States, developer turnover can quickly obsolesce an undocumented, heroically programmed system into an unmanageable stovepipe system.

We believe that good programmers are absolutely necessary, but not sufficient, to ensure system success. Even in the most qualified of hands, the available program design methods, software tools, and computing technologies are surprisingly inadequate, compared to today's enterprise system challenges. Managing change and complexity requires much more than raw programming talent in order to realize a successful and maintainable system. Solutions to today's enterprise development challenges are possible through architecture-centered development—in other words, through working smarter, not harder, by doing software right.

3.3   DOING SOFTWARE RIGHT: ENTERPRISE ARCHITECTURE DEVELOPMENT

Solving complex problems with teams of people requires planning. For enterprise software systems, some of the most important planning is highly technical (i.e., planning system architecture).

Planning generates artifacts, but planning (as an activity) is much more important than project management plans, the typical artifacts. By this, we mean that document-driven process is not recommended because its priorities focus on paper artifacts, whereas the real product of any software development project is software. Instead, we view planning in a broader context, with multiple levels of formality and technical detail. For example, architecting is planning, and so are requirements analysis, design modeling, and generating plans. The level of formality should be tied to the longer-term usefulness of the documentation.

In architecture-centered development, planning is pragmatic (Figure 3.2). Project plans and design models are throwaway documentation because their accuracy is short lived. Once a plan or specification is out of date, it is essentially useless. For example, source-code changes can quickly obsolesce design models.

In addition software methods and standards should be treated as guidelines, not mandates. Project teams are encouraged to think for themselves and tailor the process to meet the project's needs.

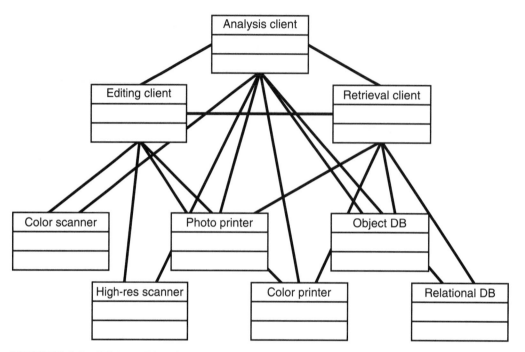

FIGURE 3.2   Without Planning, It Becomes Apparent That Many Individual Successes Are Not Sufficient for Overall Project Success

Pragmatics is a fundamental principle of software modeling: for requirements, architecture, and design. Every model has a purpose and focus, suppressing unimportant details. Models should document important decisions, based upon project assumptions and priorities. Deciding what's important is an essential decision skill that is part of being a competent architect.

Architecture-Centered Process

Figure 3.3 shows the 10-step process for architecture-centered development that covers the full system life cycle. This process is based upon key software standards and best-practice patterns proven in practice.

A key objective is to facilitate productivity in Step 7 for parallel iterative development (i.e., coding and testing). In this discussion, the activities preceding Step 7 are emphasized, because these steps comprise the architecture planning activities where we believe the key issues reside in current enterprise development.

We emphasize that this process is inherently iterative and incremental perhaps requiring revisions to artifacts from previous steps. However, the pre-

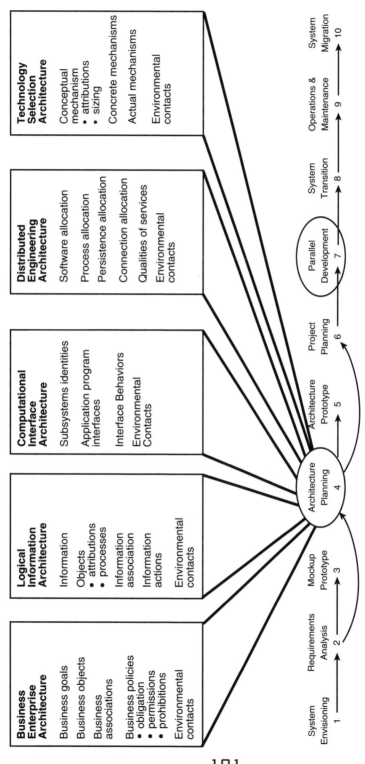

FIGURE 3.3 Architecture-Centered Development Process

development steps do have a waterfall progression, due to their interdependencies. The entire process is quality driven, with the ultimate goal of satisfying end-user needs by establishing a stable architecture description and a working software codebase that can accommodate change.

Step 1: System Envisioning

In discussing modeling, we mentioned the key words *purpose, focus, assumptions,* and *priorities.* These are all essential elements of a systemwide *Vision Statement.* If they change during system development, the project is at risk of obsolescing its own models. Therefore, the first step of architecture-centered development is to establish a Vision Statement, with the binding assumption that the Vision Statement cannot change, once development begins (Step 7). Any changes must be reflected in key project plans—in particular, the System Architecture (Step 3).

In effect, the Vision Statement is a binding agreement between the system developers and the system users. It should be short and to the point, typically less than 10 pages of text, depending on the system.

The Vision Statement establishes the context for all subsequent project activities, starting with requirements analysis.

Step 2: Requirements Analysis

The requirements should define the external behavior and appearance of the system, without designing the internal structure of the system. The external behavior includes internal actions (such as persistence or calculation) that are required to ensure desired external behavior. The external appearance comprises the layout and navigation of the user interface screens.

An effective approach for capturing behavioral requirements is through use cases. A use case comprises a top-level diagram and extensive textual description. A typical use case diagram is shown in Figure 3.2, for an information retrieval architecture. Use case notation is deceptively simple, but it has one invaluable quality: it enforces abstraction. Use case notation is one of the most effective notations ever devised for expressing complex concepts. Hence, it's great for ensuring simplicity and clarity in representing top-level requirements concepts.

For each circle in the diagram (called an individual use case), there is an extensive textual description of the relevant requirements. This write-up takes the form of a long list, containing a sequence of actions, described in domain-specific prose. The definition of use cases should be done jointly with domain experts. Without continuous involvement of domain experts, the exercise is a common antipattern called Pseudo Analysis, i.e., something to be avoided.

Use cases provide a domain model of the system for the purpose of defining architecture. Use cases also have a downstream role. In development, Step 7, use cases are extended with system-specific scenario diagrams. Eventually, these scenarios are elaborated into software tests.

The appearance, functionality, and navigation of the user interface is closely related to the use cases. An effective approach to defining the screens is called low-fidelity prototyping. In this approach, the screens are drawn out with paper and pencil. Again, the end-user domain experts are continuously involved in the screen definition process.

With the use cases and user interfaces defined, we have established context for architectural planning. In addition to generating documentation (including paper and pencil sketches), the architecture team acquires a deep understanding of the desired system capabilities in the context of the end-user domain.

A final product of requirements analysis is a project glossary which should be extended during architecture planning (Step 3).

Step 3: Architecture Planning

Architecture bridges the huge semantic gap between requirements and software. Because requirements notation is prose, requirements are inherently ambiguous, intuitive, and informal. It's right-brain stuff. Software, on the other hand, has the opposite characteristics. Software source code is a formal notation. Software is interpreted unambiguously by a machine, and its meaning is logically unintuitive (i.e., hard to decipher). It's left-brain stuff.

Architecture's first role is to define mapping between these two extremes. Architecture captures the intuitive decisions in a more formal manner (which is useful to programmers), and it defines internal system structure before it is hardwired into code (so that current and future requirements can be satisfied). Architecture is a plan that manages system complexity in a way that enables system construction and accommodates change. Architecture has another significant role: defining the organization of the software project. (See Step 6.)

Architecture planning is the key missing step in many current software projects, processes, and methods. One cause of this gap is the ongoing debate about the question: "What is architecture?" Fortunately, this question has already been answered definitively, by the software architecture profession, in a formal ISO standard for Open Distributed Processing (ODP).

ODP is a powerful way to think about complex systems which simplifies decision making (i.e., working smarter, not harder). It organizes the system architecture in terms of five standard viewpoints, describing important aspects of the same system. These viewpoints include business enterprise, logical information, computational interface, distributed engineering, and technology selection (Figure 3.4).

For each viewpoint it is important to identify conformance to architectural requirements. If conformance has no objective definition, then the architecture is meaningless, because it will have no clear impact upon implementation. ODP facilitates this process because ODP embodies a pervasive conformance approach. Simple conformance checklists are all that's needed to identify conformance points in the architecture.

In the following paragraphs we shall summarize each of these viewpoints. Using ODP, a typical architecture specification is concise, comprising about 100 pages, depending upon the system. Each viewpoint comprises 5 to 20 pages. It is expected that every developer will read this document, cover to cover, and know its contents. We suggest that the content be tutorialized (i.e., viewgraphs) and communicated to developers, in detail, through a multiday kickoff meeting. (See Step 7.)

Business Enterprise Architecture

The Business Enterprise Architecture (the enterprise viewpoint) defines the business purpose and policies of the system in terms of high-level enterprise objects. These business object models identify the key constraints on the system, including the system objective and important system policies.

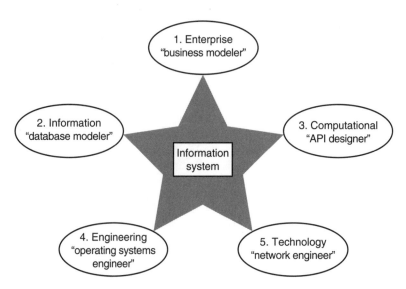

FIGURE 3.4   ODP Viewpoints

Policies are articulated in terms of three categories: (1) obligations—what business objects must do, (2) permissions—what business objects can do, and (3) prohibitions—what business objects must not do.

A typical Business Enterprise Architecture comprises a set of logical object diagrams (in UML notation) and prose descriptions of the diagram semantics.

Logical Information Architecture

The Logical Information Architecture (the information viewpoint) identifies what the system must know. This architecture is expressed in terms of an object model with an emphasis on attributes which define system state. Because ODP is an object-oriented approach, the models also include key information processes, encapsulated with the attributes, i.e., the conventional notion of an object.

A key distinction is that architectural objects are not programming objects. For example, the information objects do not denote objects that must be programmed. On the other hand, the architecture does not exclude this practice.

Architecture objects represent positive and negative constraints on the system. Positive constraints identify things that the system's software must do. Negative constraints are things that the system's software does not have to do. Knowledge of these constraints is extremely useful to programmers, because they eliminate much of the guesswork in translating requirements to software. The architects should focus their modeling on those key system aspects of greatest risk, complexity, and ambiguity, leaving straightforward details to the development step.

The information model does not constitute an engineered design. In particular, engineering analysis, such as database normalization, is explicitly delegated to the development activities (Step 7).

Computational Interface Architecture

Often neglected by architects, the computational interface architecture (the computational viewpoint) defines the top-level application program interfaces (API). These are fully engineered interfaces for subsystem boundaries. In implementation, the developers will program their modules to these boundaries, thus eliminating major design debates involving multiple developers and teams. The architectural control of these interfaces is essential to ensuring a stable system structure that supports change and manages complexity.

An ISO standard notation ODP computational architecture is the CORBA Interface Definition Language (IDL). IDL is a fundamental notation for software architects because it is completely independent of programming-language and operating-system dependencies. IDL can be automatically translated to most popular programming languages for both CORBA and Microsoft technology bases (i.e., COM/DCOM) through commercially available compilers.

Related techniques for defining computational architectures include architecture mining and domain analysis.

Distributed Engineering Architecture

Distributed engineering architecture (the engineering viewpoint) defines the requirements on infrastructure, independent of the selected technologies (Figure 3.5). The engineering viewpoint resolves some of the most complex system decisions, including physical allocation, system scalability, and communication qualities of service (QoS).

One of the key benefits of ODP is its separation of concerns (i.e., design forces). Fortunately, the previous viewpoints resolved many other complex issues that are of lesser concern to distributed systems architects, such as APIs, system policies, and information schemas. Conversely, these other viewpoints were able to resolve their respective design forces, independent of distribution concerns.

Many software and hardware engineers find this part of architecture modeling to be the most interesting and enjoyable. Fascinating decisions must be made regarding system aspects such as object replication, multithreading, and system topology.

Technology Selection Architecture

The technology selection architecture (the technology viewpoint) identifies the actual technology selection. All other viewpoints are fully independent of these decisions. Because the majority of the architecture design is independent, commercial technology evolution can be readily accommodated.

A systematic selection process includes initial identification of conceptual mechanisms (such as persistence or communication). The specific attributes (requirements) of the conceptual mechanism are gathered from the other viewpoints. Concrete mechanisms are identified (such as DBMS, OODBMS, and flat files). Then specific candidate mechanisms are selected from available technologies (such as Sybase, Oracle, and Object Design databases). Based upon initial selections from candidates, this process is iterated with respect to project factors such as product price, training needs, and maintenance risks.

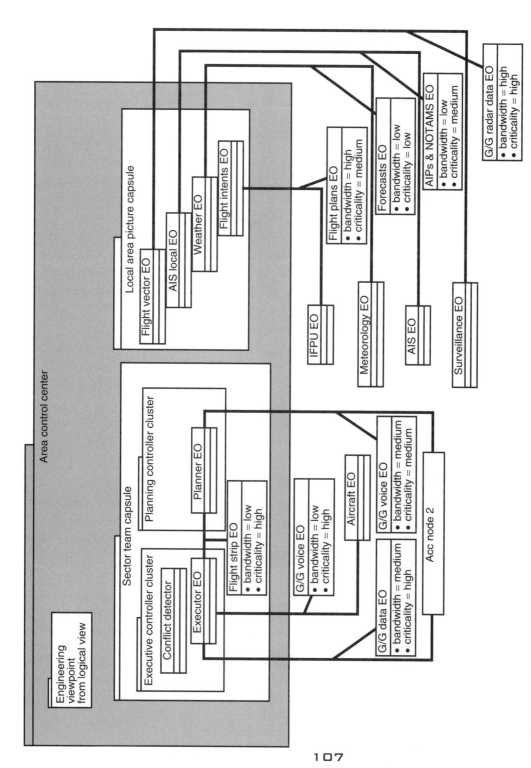

FIGURE 3.5 ODP Engineering Viewpoint

It is important to retain the rationale behind these selections, as it is important to record the rationale for all viewpoints as future justification of architectural constraints. This recording can be done in an informal project notebook maintained by the architecture team for future reference.

Step 4: Mockup

The screen definitions from Step 2 are used to create an on-line mockup of the system. Dummy data and simple file IO can be used to provide more realistic interface simulation in key parts of the user interface. The mockup is demonstrated to end users and management sponsors.

End users and architects should jointly review the mockups and run through the use cases (Step 2) in order to validate requirements. Often, new or modified requirements will emerge during this interchange. Generate screen dumps of any modified screens and mark them up for subsequent development activities. Any modifications to requirements are then incorporated by the other architectural activities.

Through the mockup, management is able to see visible progress, a politically important achievement for most projects. This step is an example of an external (or vertical) increment, which is used for risk reduction, both political and requirementswise.

With rapid prototyping technologies such as screen generation wizards, mockups can be generated in less than a staff month for most systems.

Step 5: Architecture Prototyping

The architecture prototype is a simulation of the system architecture. System API definitions are compiled and stub programs written to simulate the executing system. The architecture prototype is used to validate the computational and engineering architectures, including flow of control and timing across distribution boundaries.

Using technologies like CORBA, a computational architecture specification can be automatically compiled into a set of programming header files with distributed stubs (calling side) and skeletons (service side). Dummy code is inserted in the skeletons to simulate processing. Simple client programs are written to send invocations across computational boundaries with dummy data. A handful of key (e.g., high-risk) use cases are simulated with alternative client programs. Prototype execution is timed to validate conformance with engineering constraints.

Changes to the computational, engineering, or technology architectures are proposed and evaluated.

Step 6: Project Management Planning

As the final step in the predevelopment process, project management plans are defined and validated to resolve resource issues, including staffing, facilities, equipment, and commercial technology procurement. A schedule and a budget are established, according to the availability (lead time) for resources and project activities.

The schedule for Step 7 is planned in terms of parallel activities for external and internal increments. External increments support risk reduction with respect to requirements and management support (see Step 4). Internal increments support the efficient use of development resources—for example, the development of back-end services used by multiple subsystems.

Current best practices are to perform several smaller internal increments supporting larger-scale external increments, called VW staging. Ideally, several project teams of up to 4 programmers are formed, with 3-month deliverable external increments. In practice, this has proven to be the most effective team size and increment duration.

The architecturecentric process enables the parallel increments. Because the system is partitioned with well-defined computational boundaries, development teams can work independently, in parallel with other teams, within their assigned boundaries. Integration planning includes increments which span architectural boundaries.

The detail in the project plan should not be inconsistent. The plan should be very detailed for early increments and should include replanning activities for later in the project. This recognizes the reality that project planners don't know everything up front.

A risk mitigation plan is also prepared with identification of technical backups. The development team involved in mockup and architecture prototyping should continue to develop experimental prototypes with high-risk technologies in advance of the majority of developers. This is called the "run-ahead team" and is a key element of risk mitigation.

The final activity in project management planning is the architectural review and startup decision. Up to this point, the enterprise sponsors have made relatively few commitments, compared to the full-scale development (about 5% of system cost, depending on the project).

Executive sponsors of the project must make a business decision about whether to proceed with building the system. This executive commitment will quickly lead to many other commitments which are nearly impossible to reverse (such as technology lock-in, expenses, and vendor-generated publicity).

At this point, the system architects are offering the best possible solution and approach, in the current business and technology context.

If the system concept still makes business sense, compared to the opportunity costs, the enterprise is in an excellent position to realize the system because they're doing software right.

Step 7: Parallel Incremental Development

Development project kickoff involves several key activities. The developers must learn and internalize the architecture and requirements. An effective way to achieve this is with a multiday kickoff meeting, which includes detailed tutorials from domain experts and architects. The results of all previous steps are leveraged to bring the developers up to speed quickly and thoroughly. We suggest that the lectures be videotaped, so that staff turnover replacements can be similarly trained.

Each increment involves a complete development process, including design, coding, and test. Initially, the majority of the increments will be focused on individual subsystems. As the project progresses, an increasing number of increments will involve multiple subsystem integration. A project rhythm is established that enables coordination of development builds and tests.

For most of the software development activity, the architecture is frozen, except at some planned points, where architectural upgrades can be inserted without disruption. Architectural stability enables parallel development.

For example, at the conclusion of a major external increment, an upgrade to the computational architecture can be inserted, before the next increment initiates. The increment starts with an upgrade of the software, conformant with the changes. In practice, the need and frequency of these upgrades decreases as the project progresses. The architect's goal is to increase the stability and quality of the solution, based upon feedback from development experience. A typical project would require two architectural refactorings (upgrades) before a suitably stable configuration is achieved for deployment.

Step 8: System Transition

Deployment of the system to a pilot group of end users should be an integral part of the development process. Based upon lessons learned in initial deployment, development iterations might be added to the plan. Schedule slips are inevitable, but serious quality defects are intolerable for obvious reasons. Improving quality by *refactoring* software (improving software structure) is an important investment in the system that should not be neglected.

An important architect's role in this step involves system acceptance. The architect should confirm that the system implementation is conformant with the specifications and fairly implements the end users' requirements. This task is called architectural certification.

In effect, the architect should be an impartial arbitrator between the interests of the end users and those of the developers of the system. If the end users define new requirements which impact architectural assumptions, the architect assesses the request and works with both sides to plan feasible solutions.

Step 9: Operations and Maintenance

Operations and Maintenance (O&M) is the real proving ground for architecture-centered development. Whether or not "doing software right" was effective will be proven in this step. The majority of system cost will be expended here. As much as 70% of the O&M cost will be due to system extensions—requirements and technology changes that are the key source of continuing development.

Typically, half of a programmer's time will be expended trying to figure out how the system works. Architecture-centered development resolves much of this confusion with a clear, concise set of documentation: the system architecture.

Step 10: System Migration

System migration to a follow-on *target architecture* occurs near the end of the system life cycle. Two major processes for system migration are called big bang and chicken little. A *big bang* is a complete, overnight replacement of the legacy. In practice, the big bang seldom succeeds; it is a common antipattern for system migration.

The *chicken little* approach is more effective and ultimately more successful. Chicken little involves simultaneous, deployed operation of both target and legacy systems. The initial target system users are the pilot group (as in Step 8).

Gateways are integrated between the legacy and target systems. Forward gateways allow legacy users to have access to data that is migrated to the target system. Reverse gateways allow target system users to have transparent access to legacy data. Data and functionality are migrated incrementally from the legacy to the target system. In effect, system migration is a continuous evolution. As time progresses, new users are added to the target system and taken off the legacy environment.

In the long term, it will become feasible to switch off the legacy system. By that time, it is likely that the target system will become the legacy in a new system migration. The target system transition, Step 8, overlaps the legacy system migration, Step 10. In the chicken little approach, Steps 8, 9, and 10 are part of a continuous process of migration.

3.4   BOTTOM LINE: TIME, PEOPLE, AND MONEY

As a general rule, enterprise software projects requiring more than a year for delivery should be avoided. In a one-year development, at least 3 to 6 months should be allocated to the architecture phases (Steps 1 through 6).

The architecture phases require only a minimal staff. The architecture team includes a project manager and a set of one to four architects depending on project complexity. A part-time Run-Ahead Team augments the architecture staff, for implementation exercises, including the Mockup and Architecture Prototype (Steps 4 and 5). A part-time Domain Team assists in drafting the requirements and user interface design. The Domain Team also validates the architecture and the mockup from the end-user perspective.

The development phase is scalable to fit the project complexity and delivery schedule, through small functional teams of developers (ideally teams of 4 developers on 3-month increments).

The schedule breaks down as follows: approximately 50% for system planning and 50% for development. The development efforts would be split about 25% for actual coding and 25% for testing and training. These allocations are conformant with best practices for project management, which work in multiple domains, including software projects.

Cost estimates include an empirically verified 70% to 30% partition between development and O&M. In addition, we estimate that a typical project requires less than 5% of the system budget for the architecture phases.

3.5   CONCLUSIONS

Architecture-centered development is doing enterprise software right. The process detailed in this chapter is called the ODP+4 process; it is based upon widely utilized architecture standards and best-practice patterns. It is called ODP+4 because it generates an Open Distributed Processing architecture as well as other formal and informal artifacts, including: (1) the Vision Statement, (2) the use-case-based requirements, (3) the rationale, and (4) the conformance statements.

Architecture-centered development is pragmatic. Modeling focus is given to those decisions that are architecturally important. Not every artifact is required. Document formality is selective.

From experience, we have seen so many projects doing software wrong, that it's no wonder five out of six projects are unsuccessful. The age of the heroic programmer is coming to an end, and the age of the professional software architect has begun. Driven by escalating user expectations, business changes, and technology innovations, many organizations now realize that proper system planning generally translates into system success, and improper planning leads to system failure.

Finally, the role of the software architect is relatively new in many project cultures. What has been called architecture, informally, needs to become conformant with standards and best-practice patterns, if consistent development success is desired.

3.6   EXERCISES

EXERCISE 3.1   Which mistaken traditional systems assumptions are commonly applied by your organization in software development? How would you remedy this situation?

BACKGROUND FOR SOLUTION: Much of what people learn in school (e.g., computer science courses) can be viewed as negative training with respect to this paradigm shift. Not everyone in the organization needs to embrace the paradigm shift completely. At a minimum, the architects of the system do have to have a solid understanding of these concepts and need to define system boundaries that mitigate the consequences of the actions of wrong-thinkers.

EXERCISE 3.2   Are there obvious AntiPatterns which your organization continually repeats in development after development? What alternatives would you recommend to avoid these recurring mistakes and/or refactor the results of existing solutions?

BACKGROUND FOR SOLUTION: Please refer to our book *AntiPatterns* for a full disclosure on this sensitive topic [Brown 98]. In our experience, AntiPatterns are more prevalent than patterns of success. One of our good friends mused that if people would simply avoid the most obvious mistakes, software development would be much more successful, as an industry. In other words, our friend thinks that you may not need a new set of good practices, as long as you avoid the practices that are known not to work.

EXERCISE 3.3   How does the process of Enterprise Architecture Development compare with your current organizational practices for building large systems? Do you have an explicit architectural phase before hordes of programmers join the effort? Do you use Lo-Fi screen design and architectural prototyping to reduce risks? Do you have a run-ahead team? Is your architecture prework defining effectively organizational interfaces that enable parallel development?

BACKGROUND FOR SOLUTION: Sophisticated architecture practices are rare indeed, in today's software industry. The one-man heroic programming team is still a commonplace fixture in many shops. Not surprisingly, some of the best-known products in today's software market are the result of one-man development teams. It works for some commercial organizations that can tolerate the release of extremely deficient products. Not so, in most application development shops. We know that it is brutally difficult to attempt to think and work architecturally, when every manager is under extreme time pressure to deliver results. First they have to understand that there is a problem. Lending them a copy of our book *AntiPatterns* is one way to move forward. We wrote it specifically for people who have difficulty admitting that there is a problem, when it's incredibly obvious to most other people.

EXERCISE 3.4   What is your organizational process for architecting and developing a system? Are there conventions for how much time is devoted to system planning (e.g., architecture) versus programming and other tasks? If you had a magic wand, how would you refactor your organizational practices to improve system successes and reduce unnecessary commitments and risks?

BACKGROUND FOR SOLUTION: On a typical project (in many shops), a large group of developers (perhaps 30 or 50) join the project on day one. These people are rapidly allocated into a human organization before there is an architecture available to guide these decisions. Once in place, these organizations are almost impossible to change. Then there is a long period of negotiations as these groups struggle to define the system architecture to be conformant with their organizational boundaries. The architect has lost control. Ideally, what should happen resembles the Enterprise Architecture Development process that we describe in this chapter. Commitments for developers and equipment are delayed until adequate planning has occurred. Irreversible decisions are not made until the organization fully understands what it wants to accomplish.

SOFTWARE ARCHITECTURE: DRILL SCHOOL

In order to provide technical leadership, an architect must have mastered several fundamental areas of software design and aspects of the overall software development process.

Most software architects would agree that software design involves multiple levels of abstraction. The notion of design levels originates from the hardware design levels proposed by Bell and Newell in 1971. Design levels help to simplify hardware design because they provide a separation of concerns. In design patterns terminology, design levels provide a separation of "forces."

By limiting the sets of forces that need to be resolved in each design decision, we simplify design problems. This simplification is possible because not all design forces are equally important at all levels. Design levels are defined in terms of a reference model. The reference model partitions and allocates the major design forces so that each force is resolved at an appropriate level.

The separation of design levels is an important, but missing, element in most object technology practice. Design levels are particularly important for the creation and understanding of object-oriented architecture.

4.1   ARCHITECTURE VERSUS PROGRAMMING

Software design levels has been a topic of academic discussion. Representing the software architecture research community, Shaw and Garlan propose a three-level model, comprising:

1. machine
2. code
3. architecture

The machine level comprises unmodifiable binary software, including the operating system and linkable modules. The code level is modifiable source code. The architecture level is a higher level of abstraction. In their model, architecture comprises software partitioning, software interfaces, and interconnections.

The three-level model establishes a useful frontier for academic research on software architecture. However, it does not have enough levels to provide a sufficient separation of design forces. In addition, this model cannot explain key object-technology benefits, such as interoperability and reuse. Interoperability and reuse require at least one more level in the model: *The Enterprise,* an architecture of system architectures.

The Fractal Model of Software

Another way to view software levels is in terms of scale (Figure 1.9). Objects and classes are the finest grain level. This is the level defined by programming languages (C++, Java) and infrastructures (e.g., CORBA, J2EE). The next level comprises microarchitectures, which are simple configurations of objects. This is the level addressed by most design patterns. Configurations of microarchitectures form frameworks (in the Taligent sense). Groups of frameworks form applications (or subsystems). Groups of applications form systems.

The idea for the fractal model was proposed by Richard Helm, co-author of *Design Patterns: Elements of Reusable Object-Oriented Software* [Gamma 94]. A missing element from the fractal model is the separation of concerns (or forces).

Major Design Forces

There is surprising agreement about the major design forces on the part of various communities of software researchers. Much of the work is driven by a single major force at a particular design level, although the particular force and design level vary by group.

Many identify adaptability as the key design force. Adaptability is alternately called "management of change" or variation-centered design. Others focus on management of complexity. Management of complexity is the major driving force of the academic software architecture community, as well as much of the software metrics community.

The Effect of Scale on Forces

Management of change is one of the major design forces in object-oriented architecture. Its importance varies greatly with the scale of software and design level. As the scale of software increases, so does the frequency of change.

For example, an individual application may need to be upgraded only occasionally. A system may comprise many applications, each requiring upgrade. The effect of change is cumulative. At an enterprise level, change is very frequent, with new applications, systems, peripherals, and employees moving every day.

There is a similar effect of scale on other major design forces. This realization leads to a separation of forces between design levels.

Software Design Levels

The Software Design-Level Model (SDLM) builds upon the fractal model (Figure 1.9). This model has two major categories of scales, Micro-Design and Macro-Design. The Micro-Design levels include the finer-grain design issues from application (subsystem) level down to the design of objects and classes. The Macro-Design levels include system-level architecture, enterprise architecture, and global systems (denoting multiple enterprises and the Internet).

The Micro-Design levels are the most familiar to developers. At Micro-Design levels, the key concerns are the provision of functionality and the optimization of performance. At the Macro-Design levels, the chief concerns lean more toward management of complexity and change. These design forces are present at finer grains, but are not nearly of the same importance as they are at the Macro-Design levels.

An interesting boundary in the SDLM model is between the enterprise and the global levels. Forces that are important to resolve inside the enterprise are very different than the forces that are important externally. Inside the enterprise, control of information technology and resources is challenging, but feasible. At the global level, issues of technology transfer, control of intellectual property (licensing), and security are key issues between enterprises (and individuals).

Using Design Levels

Design levels are an important and useful intellectual tool. Design levels help to simplify design problems by separating design forces. Each design level limits the number of forces that need to be resolved by any given design decision. Design levels have been in use for dozens of years in digital hardware engineering, and it is time for object technology to adopt a similarly effective conceptual discipline.

Design levels are a key issue for object-oriented architecture because they define the problems and forces that architecture must resolve.

4.2   MANAGING COMPLEXITY USING ARCHITECTURE

One of the key skills of any software architect is the management of software complexity. Software complexity is the one of the key characteristics of all nontrivial software systems which must be managed. Successful management of complexity leads to improvement in many system qualities such as understandability, maintainability, and modifiability.

Complexity is an interesting phenomenon because it arises from the aggregation of many small design decisions. For system-level interfaces, the effects of complexity are multiplicative, because multiple parts of an integrated system are affected by each design addition. For example, it may seem very reasonable to add a few attributes and operators to a subsystem interface. If this uncoordinated practice is repeated on multiple subsystems, the result will be excessive complexity and brittle interdependencies. Another key factor is interpersonal: It is easier to reach consensus on design disagreements by adding complexity, rather than by eliminating overlapping details. This is the chronic failing of formal standards groups which produce "designs by committee."

Creating Complexity

Many key qualities of software systems are directly related to complexity, including cost, maintainability, extensibility, and so forth. In practice, successful management of complexity is rare. Poor management of complexity has several causes, including:

▶ *Lack of Priority:* Many software practitioners do not appreciate how critically important management of complexity is to the success of any software architecture and system implementation.

▶ *Lack of Architectural Sophistication:* Design patterns for managing complexity are not commonplace in software education, training, and practice.

Many software projects fail to manage complexity because they do not consider control of complexity to be part of architecture. System-level design details are often delegated to multiple developers, who readily produce unique, uncoordinated designs. Other projects inherit excess complexity from the architecture of a proprietary product. Vendor architectures emphasize flexibility to satisfy the widest possible consumer market. For vendors, management of complexity has low priority, implicitly delegated to application developers.

In order to successfully manage complexity, one needs to understand and apply a number of architectural options. The following sections summarize some of the key techniques for managing complexity in software architectures.

For present purposes only, I have labeled these options in terms of familiar analogies. These architectural options are not exclusive. In each analogy, "It" refers to complexity:

▶ Sweep It Under a Rug (Encapsulation)
▶ Hide It in a Crowd (Repository Architecture)
▶ Ignore It (Horizontal Architecture)
▶ Slice It (Layered Architecture)
▶ Dice It (Vertical Architecture)

"Do not slide through regions where high rates of information exchange are required" [Rechtin 97].

Complexity comprises implementation details derived from the domain and the technology. By managing complexity, we reorganize these details in a beneficial way. By organizing complex details, we eliminate unnecessary dependencies and other factors that compromise system quality.

Option 1: Sweep It Under a Rug

Encapsulation is an obvious way to hide implementation details behind an interface. As one of the fundamental properties of object-oriented (OO) environments, encapsulation unifies the software's data model and procedural model into object abstractions.

Encapsulation using language-specific mechanisms is not always as effective as we might hope. When an implementation changes, there are unforeseen impacts on related objects, which must also be modified.

Industrial-strength encapsulation, using CORBA Interface Definition Language (IDL), is a way to increase the effectiveness of encapsulation. Users of X11R6 Fresco experienced the enhanced encapsulation benefits of IDL even in a single-language, nondistributed environment.

Option 2: Hide It in a Crowd

One of the most effective ways to manage complexity is to use a repository architecture. In most cases, the repository is a database, but there are other forms, such as a blackboard. Repository architecture is a design pattern that is highly applicable to system-level architecture with documented benefits and consequences. It is interesting that many software architects and developers fail to utilize this pattern when appropriate, exposing large numbers of fine-grain object instances across system-level boundaries.

A repository architecture manages complexity by consolidating access to many objects through query languages or accessor methods. One query-language statement can consolidate messaging to thousands of objects. An object or relational repository schema provides a common model and access protocol for management of large numbers of objects.

Option 3: Ignore It

By ignoring nonessential differences between complex objects, we can define common interface abstractions that provide many benefits, such as interoperability, adaptability, substitutability, and isolation. The concept of "common interface" has many synonyms in the software literature: design reuse, variation-centered design, standards, and so forth. As one of the gang-of-four states: "The structure of most design patterns is similar." A metapattern for this similar structure is the Common Interface.

Because the Java language supports interfaces as a language feature, some software gurus are just discovering the benefits of common interfaces. Java interfaces allow flexible substitution of multiple classes supporting a common interface protocol. Distributed object practitioners have enjoyed the benefits of language-independent, common interfaces for years.

Option 4: Slice It

A layered architecture defines levels of abstraction in a system, allowing application software to be isolated from low-level details.

Layering defines sets of horizontal services with common interface abstractions. These services are reused by multiple application objects and higher-level service objects. Layering is a basic form of software reuse which provides interoperability and portability benefits, in addition to managing complexity.

Layering is a flexible concept which takes many forms. Layering is frequently applied in object wrapping, operating systems, networking, frameworks, standards profiling, and application architectures.

Option 5: Dice It

Layering defines *horizontal* interfaces and partitions that manage complexity. Definition of *vertical* partitions is also useful. Vertical partitions can isolate complexity into independent subdomains. Each subdomain can support unique vertical frameworks. Vertical dependencies can be limited to objects in the vertical partition. Cross-domain dependencies (such as interoperability) should be handled through horizontal interfaces.

In practice, most systems contain many unique vertical interfaces. Good architecture has a healthy balance between horizontal and vertical interfaces. Without horizontal interfaces, vertical partitioning is ineffective. Horizontal interfaces enable vertical partitions to interoperate without unnecessary dependencies.

"The first line of defense against complexity is simplicity of design"
[Rechtin 97].

4.3   SYSTEMS INTEGRATION

We extend our discussion of architectural issues related to client server systems integration by covering a number of additional areas from which many important questions arise. Handling tough questions about your architecture is one of the key skills which we hope you will learn in our drill school. You may have detected an attitude of skepticism in some of the previous remarks which we believe is appropriate for a mature understanding of technology capabilities and how they apply to system development. Object-oriented architects are responsible for developing the technology plans that manage these underlying technologies in a way that supports the full system life cycle, which may range up to 15 years for systems in the public sector.

The key concepts for technology management allow us to predict that technologies in today's configurations will be evolving into new technologies which may obsolesce many of today's current interfaces and infrastructure assumptions. One approach for mitigating this inevitable commercial technology change is by defining application software interfaces which the architect controls and maintains to isolate application technologies from the majority of commercial infrastructure which are subject to rapid innovation. We have covered these concepts and the details of how to implement them in significantly more detail in some of the authors' writings; please refer to the bibliography.

"Use open architectures. You will need them once the market begins to respond" [Rechtin 97].

Taking a somewhat cynical view of open systems technologies, one can conclude that the developers of standards in both formal and consortium organizations represent the interest of technology suppliers. There are significant differences in quality between the kinds of specifications which are created and utilized for the general information technology market, comprising the vast majority of object technology specifications and the specifications used in particular mission-critical markets such as telecommunications. For general information technology specifications, there are many cases where the standards do not support testing. In fact, only about 5 or 6 percent of formal standards have test suites which are readily available. The majority of testable standards are compilers such as FORTRAN compilers, PASCAL compilers, and so forth. The CORBA technology market has taken a direction to resolve this issue, at least in terms of the base specifications for CORBA technologies. Significant additional work needs to occur to enable general information technology standards to truly meet the needs of object-oriented architects.

What about the Internet? The integration of Internet technologies is a capability that has high priority in many organizations. The use of intranets and extranets is becoming a mission-critical capability for large and medium size enterprises. There has been substantial research and development in this domain. Figure 4.1 shows some of the kinds of interfaces which have been created to support the integration of object technologies to the Internet. Commercially supplied products which tie CORBA technologies directly to the Internet, such as HTTP, are readily available. The implementation of ORB

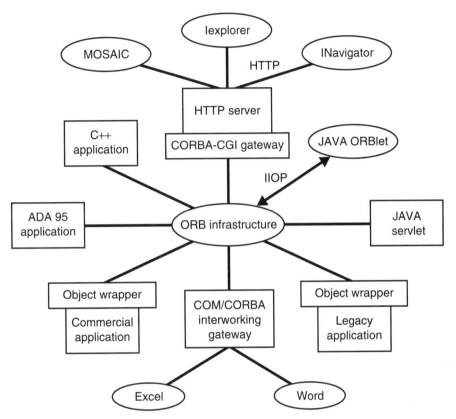

FIGURE 4.1   Integration of Multiple Technology Bases

technologies in an Internet-ready fashion has occurred—for example, with the implementation of Java language based ORBs which are integrated with browser environments. The use of object-oriented middleware is an important and revolutionary step in the evolution of the Internet. Object oriented middleware represents the ability to rapidly create new types of services and dynamically connect to new types of servers. These capabilities go well beyond what is currently feasible with technologies like http and the Java remote method invocation, which is a language-specific distributed computing capability.

Figure 4.2 addresses the question of integration of Microsoft technologies with other object-oriented open systems capabilities. Based upon industry-adopted standards, it is now possible to integrate shrink-wrapped applications into distributed object environments supporting both CORBA and COM+. The definition of application architectures can implement this capability in several

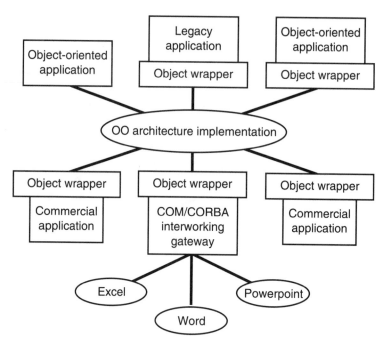

FIGURE 4.2   Systems Integration with Object Wrapping

ways. One approach is to adopt the shrink-wrapped defined interfaces into the application software architecture. In this way the application's subsystems become directly dependent upon proprietary control interfaces, which may be obsolesced at the vendor's discretion. The alternative approach is to apply object wrappers to profile the complexity of the shrink-wrap interfaces and isolate the proprietary interfaces from the majority of the application subsystem interactions. The same level of interoperability can be achieved with either approach, but the architectural benefits of isolation can prove significant.

What about security? Computer security is a challenging requirement that is becoming a necessity because of the increasing integration and distribution of systems, including intranet and the Internet itself. One reason why security is so challenging is that it has frequently been supplied to the market as a niche-market or nonstandard capability. For example, the COM+ technology and its ActiveX counterparts do not have a security capability. When one downloads an ActiveX component on the Internet, that component has access to virtually any resource in the operating-system environment, including data on the disk and system resources which could be used for destructive purposes. The implication is that it is not wise for anyone to be using ActiveX and

COM+ in Internet-based transactions and information retrieval. The object management group has addressed this issue because of end-user questions about how this capability can be supplied. The group adopted the CORBA security service, which defines a standard mechanism for how multiple vendors can provide security capabilities in their various infrastructure implementations. Computer security has been implemented in selected environments. An understanding of the CORBA security service and how to apply it will be important in the future to enable organizations to satisfy this critical requirement.

What about performance? Object-oriented technology has suffered criticism with respect to performance. Because object technology is providing more dynamic capability, there are certain overheads which are consequential. In the case of OMG and CORBA specifications, it is fair to say that the CORBA architecture itself has no particular performance consequences, because it is simply a specification of interface boundaries and not the underlying infrastructure. In practice, CORBA implementations have similar underlying behaviors with a few exceptions. In general, CORBA implementations can be thought of as managing a lower-level protocol stack which in many cases is a socket-level or TCP/IP layer. Because the CORBA mechanisms provide a higher level of distraction which simplifies programming when an initial invocation occurs, the ORB infrastructure needs to intelligently establish communications between the client program and the server program. For the initial invocation, certainly additional overhead and handshaking are required to perform this purpose. This handshaking would have to be programmed manually by the application developer without this infrastructure.

Once the ORB establishes the lower-level communication link, the ORB can then pass messages efficiently through the lower-level layer. In benchmarks of ORB technologies, some researchers have found the CORBA technologies are actually faster in some applications than comparable programs written using remote procedure calls. Part of the reason is that all of the middleware infrastructures are evolving and becoming more efficient as technology innovation progresses. On the second and subsequent invocations in an ORB environment, the performance is comparable to remote procedure calls and in some cases faster. The primary performance distinction between ORB invocations and custom programming to the socket layer is involved in what is called the *marshaling algorithms*. The marshaling algorithms are responsible for taking application data, which is passed as parameters in an ORB invocation, and flattening it into a stream of bytes which can be sent through a network by lower-level protocols. If a machine generates the marshaling algorithms with custom marshaling, it cannot be quite as effective as a programmer who knows how to tailor the marshaling for a specific application.

Because of the increasing speed of processors, the performance of marshaling algorithms is a fairly minuscule consideration overall compared to other performance factors such as the actual network communication overhead.

Proper distributed object infrastructures give you additional options for managing performance. Because these infrastructures have the access transparency property, it is possible to substitute alternative protocol stacks underneath the programming interfaces which are generated. Once the application developer understands and stabilizes the interfaces required, it is then possible to program alternative protocol stacks to provide various qualities of service. This approach is conformant with best practices regarding benchmarking and performance optimization. The appropriate approach is to first determine a clean architecture for the application interaction, next to determine the performance hot spots in the application, and then to compromise the architecture as appropriate in order to perform optimizations. Within a single object-oriented program, compromises to the architecture are one of the few options that one has. In a distributed object architecture, because the actual communication mechanisms are transparent through access transparency, it is possible to optimize the underlying communications without direct compromises to the application software structure. In this sense, the use of distributed object computing has some distinct advantages in terms of performance optimization that are not available under normal programming circumstances.

What about reliability? Reliability is a very important requirement when multiple organizations are involved in various kinds of transactions. It is not reasonable to lose money during electronic funds transfers or lose critical orders during mission-critical interaction. The good news is that distributed object infrastructures, because of their increasing level of abstraction from the network, do provide some inherent benefits in the area of reliability. Both COM+ and CORBA support automatic activation of remote services. CORBA provides this in a completely transparent manner called *persistence transparency,* whereas COM+ requires the allocation of an interface pointer, which is an explicitly programmed operation that also manages the activation of the services, once that operation is completed. If a program providing CORBA services fails, CORBA implementations are obligated to attempt to automatically restart the application. In a COM+ environment, one would have to allocate a new interface reference and reinitiate communications.

An important capability for ensuring reliability is the use of transaction monitors. The object management group has standardized the interfaces for transaction monitors through the object transaction service. This interface is available commercially through multiple suppliers today. Transaction monitors support the so-called acid properties: durability, isolation, and consistency.

Transaction monitors provide these properties independent of the distribution of the application software. Use of middleware technologies with transaction monitors provides a reasonably reliable level of communications for many mission-critical applications. Other niche-market capabilities that go beyond this level can be discovered through cursory searches of the Internet. In conclusion, what is needed from commercial technology to satisfy application requirements is quality support for user capabilities. This includes quality specifications that meet the user's needs and products that meet the specifications.

In order to ensure that these capabilities are supported, new kinds of testing and inspection processes are needed that are able to keep pace with the rapid technology innovation occurring in consortium and proprietary vendors today. The end users need to play a larger role in driving the open systems processes in order to realize these benefits. In terms of application software development it is necessary to have on each development team one or more object-oriented architects who understand these issues and are able to structure the application to take advantage of the commercial capabilities and mitigate the risks of commercial innovations that may result in maintenance cost. The use of application profiles at the system profile level for families of systems and the functional profile level for the mains should be considered when application systems are constructed. It is also important for software managers to be cognizant of these issues and to support their staffs in the judicious design, architecture, and implementation of new information systems.

4.4   MAKING THE BUSINESS CASE

Software architecture has many potential benefits. Many of these are not realized by some adopters of the architectural practices. We believe many of these shortfalls are due to inadequate practice of architecture principles and disciplines. Some key benefits of software architecture include various forms of reuse, which can provide benefits such as reduced risk, reduced cost, and reduced time to market. Another important benefit of an architectural approach is interoperability. Interoperability can only be realized if the computational architecture is managed appropriately for application system development across an enterprise. We covered some significant success stories for object orientation and object technology in Chapter 3. In addition, many other documented studies show how the technology can provide benefits if it is applied properly.

One of the best collections of object technology success stories is Paul Harmon's book, *The Object Technology Case Book Reference* [Harmon 96]. It documents 18 case studies of projects that were award winners in an annual com-petition sponsored by *Computer World.* Some examples include a SmallTalk ap-plication by Allied Corporation where they realized a 2400-to-1 reduction in operational cycle time. In other words the cycle time for performing their task was reduced from nine weeks down to nine minutes through the use of an object-oriented information system. In addition this application reduced the required personnel from seven down to one, and the qualifications of that person were re-duced to a novice level, whereas formally they needed experts. In addition, be-cause of the reduction in staff there was a corresponding reduction in the amount of capital required to perform this application capability.

Other examples from the case book include several systems at Boeing, one of which reduced the time to market by 30% and reduced the time on some tasks by up to a factor of ten. In another Boeing case study, they reduced the production costs up to 20% on their applications. The general results for re-use benefits are fairly consistent, in that the primary benefit is through the reduc-tion in system development time, which can be as large as 70%. The actual cost savings, if you include the development of the reusable software usually hovers around the 10% to 15% level, because the development of reusable software does require extra effort.

Another consideration is that most of the documented success stories for software reuse are based upon companies developing software for commercial applications and applying that software to multiple commercial applications, instead of applying the software to internal applications.

Simplify designs by minimizing the number of interface operations.

In Figure 4.4 we describe the primary paradigm shift at the architectural level for how new systems can be constructed using object technologies to

Interoperability within vertical specialty market areas

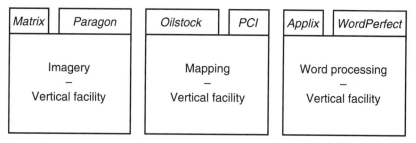

FIGURE 4.3   Vertical Domain-Based Integration

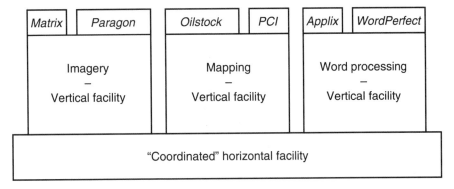

Extend vertical approach with a cross-domain interoperability using a horizontal facility

| Matrix | Paragon | | Oilstock | PCI | | Applix | WordPerfect |

| Imagery – Vertical facility | Mapping – Vertical facility | Word processing – Vertical facility |

"Coordinated" horizontal facility

FIGURE 4.4 Hybrid Horizontal and Vertical Integration

provide enhanced benefits in system extensibility and reduced complexity. Figure 4.3 is an example of this paradigm, showing how many of the available standards only provide interoperability among vertical functions of the same kind. It is in the interoperability across vertical functions in a horizontal sense that the true benefits occur.

In Figure 4.4 is a revised architectural concept which adds the horizontal capability to the vertical integration. Figure 4.5 shows the potential benefits of a hypothetical environment using the various kinds of architectural approaches. If the traditional approach called custom integration is applied, the types of systems that are constructed resemble the stovepipe configuration and quickly escalate in complexity, such that the benefits of interoperability are overcome by the cost of creating and maintaining the integration solution.

With highly coordinated integration, it is possible to reduce the complexity and cost of extension down to almost constant factors. However, this level

	#1 Custom	#2 Coordinated	#3 Vertical	#4 Hybrid
Baseline	$N \times N$	2N	$N \times N$	2N to $N \times N$
Extend	2N + 1	2	2N + 1	2 to 2N + 1
Replace	2N – 1	2	N – 1	2 to N – 1
Merge	$2N \times N + N$	No New I/F	No New I/F	No New I/F

FIGURE 4.5 Comparison of Architectural Options

of coordination is not possible or practical in most organizations today. With vertical types of standardization the benefits do not vary significantly from custom integration, so there is a category of vertical architecture standards which does not provide significant leverage across a wide variety of applications. In the fourth column in Figure 4.5 the hybrid architecture approach allows a variation in the level of benefits that can be controlled by the application architect. Further details of how this approach is implemented are given in our book *The Essential CORBA* [Mowbray 95].

Figure 4.6 translates these concepts into dollar figures for a hypothetical enterprisewide system integration project. In order to achieve interoperability across this organization with 20,000 users and 50 applications, the potential cost is as high as a billion dollars, or $50,000 per seat. The numbers are based upon experiences and lessons accrued over the last ten years. In order to extend the system with custom integration the cost could be as high as $40 million in order to tie one new application into the existing 50. If you had to merge two companies, which is not an unusual occurrence these days, the cost of integrating two companies that have already performed custom integration across the board could be as high as $2 billion. If you apply a proper architectural approach to systems integration, the cost can be substantially reduced. If you could define a common architectural solution that applied across all 50 applications, the cost of integration could be reduced to $500 per seat. The addition of a new application could be reduced as low as $10 per seat, and if two organizations supported the same coordinated specifications, it might already be the case that their internal systems would interoperate without modification.

Architect a small horizontal interface supported by all components.

This section has discussed several aspects of the business case for object technology. Paul Harmon's *Object Technology Case Book* [Harmon 96] in-

	Custom Integration	Cost per Seat	Coordinated Integration	Cost per Seat	Potential Savings
Achieve Interoperability	$1,000,000,000	$50,000	$10,000,000	$500	99%
Add Application	$40,400,000	$2,020	$200,000	$10	99.5%
Integrate Agencies	$2,020,000,000	$50,500	Already Integrated	Already Integrated	100%

FIGURE 4.6   Potential Benefits of Architectural Coordination

cludes many examples of how object technology has helped organizations reduce costs in time to market. In Chap-ter 2 we gave several additional examples of what is possible. The key to applying object technology effectively is the proper application of architectural principles and practices. Through these principles, it is possible to achieve some dramatic kinds of results in integrating systems across large-scale enterprises. These results scale down to small application configurations as well, as our experience shows.

4.5   ARCHITECTURE LINKAGE TO SOFTWARE DEVELOPMENT

If we apply proper architectural principles to create and maintain software structure, potential cost saving could be 50% or greater [Horowitz 93]. Good software structure is a function of the overall application architecture, the software interfaces or what is called confrontational architecture, and the implementation itself (Figure 4.7).

Computational interfaces may be the key enabler for improved software structure. Software interfaces as specified in IDL define boundaries between modules of software. If the software interfaces are coordinated architecturally, it is possible to define the boundaries for application programmers so that the intended structure of the application becomes its implemented structure. In practice we have found that the specification of software interfaces provides an actual benefit to the programmers, because they then have a guideline for how

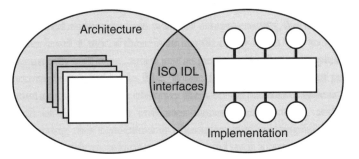

Good software structure = architecture + interface + implementation
Good architecture supports management of change and complexity

FIGURE 4.7   Computational Specification Links Architecture and Implementation

to implement software independently of other application developers. When developers share the same specification, their software can then interoperate, even though the applications are developed separately.

Figure 4.8 describes the overall process for how these kinds of results can be achieved. Starting with a set of enterprise requirements for a community of users, a business object analysis process can define the overall structure and characteristics of the application environment. Business object analysis is an object-oriented analysis in which both end users and object-oriented modelers and architects participate in defining new information technology capabilities which satisfy the needs of the business and the constraints of the technology implementation process. Once the business object analysis has produced object models, there is a further step, a drill-down exercise to define the common interface definitions. The common interface definitions are the software interfaces which define the actual internal software boundaries for the system. This is a drill-down exercise because these interfaces will specify the actual operations and parameters which are passed throughout the software system.

The common interface definitions must be coordinated with individual software projects in order for the appropriate lessons learned and legacy-migration considerations to be incorporated into the designs. As the common interface definitions mature and are applied across multiple projects, these

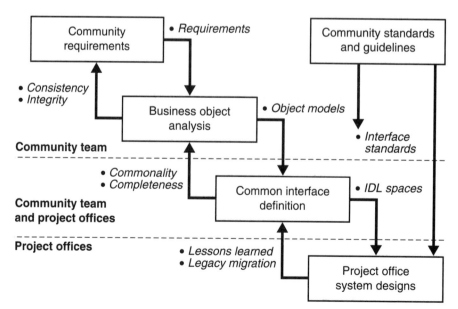

FIGURE 4.8   Sample Architecture-Driven Process

definitions can become localized standards and profiles for the community of developers. These can provide useful information for new developers and commercial vendors that may want to participate in the interoperability solutions. It is not sufficient for interface specifications to stand alone. One important lesson learned that has been repeatedly discovered is that no matter how precise a specification is, the definition of how applications use this specification is required to assure interoperability. This requirement is equivalent to the profiling concept that we introduced in Chapter 2.

Figure 4.9 shows how a set of specifications both horizontal and vertical can be constrained with respect to a profile, so that application developers will be much more likely to provide interoperability between separate implementations. There is a distinct difference between specifications and profiles, which needs to be incorporated into software process. A specification such as an IDL definition should be designed so that it can be reused across multiple applications or families of systems. The profile information, on the other hand, should correspond to specific applications and families of systems, so that the conventions can be specialized without compromising the reusability of the overall specification. Specifications can be standardized either locally within the organization or on a more global scale through organizations like the object management group. However, profiles should remain fluid. Profiles in their best case are documented developer agreements for how standards specifications are used in specific instances.

Identifying the appropriate categories of specifications to be standardized is a challenge that many organization never overcome. The process which has been applied repeatedly to achieve this purpose is shown in Figure 4.10. The problem for many individual software development projects and end users is understanding the need for commonality and how that need is distinguished

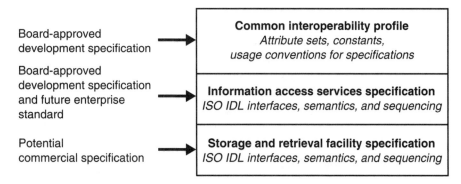

Board-approved development specification → **Common interoperability profile** *Attribute sets, constants, usage conventions for specifications*

Board-approved development specification and future enterprise standard → **Information access services specification** *ISO IDL interfaces, semantics, and sequencing*

Potential commercial specification → **Storage and retrieval facility specification** *ISO IDL interfaces, semantics, and sequencing*

FIGURE 4.9 Interoperability Profile

Enterprise architecture process
Full-scale process for coordinating architecture

1. SURVEY: Requirements, technology, and architecture inputs
   to all technology suppliers and consumers

2. BRAINSTORM: Candidate interoperability interface facilities

3. DIAGRAM: Categories of facilities, to produce strawman
   architecture reference model

4. DEFINE: Candidate facilities in a prose template format

5. REVIEW/EDIT: Iterate to improve quality and consensus

6. APPROVE: Formalize architectural decisions and initiate
   configuration control

7. TUTORIALIZE: Ensure support through understanding

FIGURE 4.10   Large-Scale Architecture-Driven Process

from the actual design and architecture of specific applications. The same problem arises in identification of common data elements when commonality of information architecture is desired. The first step in the process is to basically survey the available requirements and technologies and other kinds of input which provide stakeholder impact on the selection of common functionality. Given that a broadly based survey across the scope of the enterprise is impossible, a smaller group of architects can get together and brainstorm some of the candidate facilities for interface coordination.

It is important to abstract the selection of these facilities in an architectural block diagram to display how some facilities play roles that are horizontal in relationship to some of the others. It is also important to define a diagram extraction in order to communicate the structure of an architecture of this scale to multiple stakeholders in these deliberations. In Step 4, the individual facilities identified earlier are defined and documented as to their scope and basic functionality. This definition is necessary in order to constrain the drill-down process, which will be necessary in order to drive out the details for the interface definitions or data element definitions. In Step 5, a review process allows the various stakeholders in the architecture to verify that their needs are being met and also to build consensus across the enterprise for funding the reusable assets which will be defined when the interfaces are created.

Step 6 in the process is to slow the pace of architectural decision making and stabilize the architecture. After multiple iterations of the architecture document and review among all of the potential stakeholders, it is necessary to conclude the exercise and publish the document. It is then appropriate to tutorialize this information and make sure that there is a thorough understanding of it across the developer community. This final step of communicating architectural vision is often overlooked in many organizations, because once approval is obtained, many architects assume that potential developers will be constrained by the organizational decision and they assume that it is an appropriate transfer of responsibility to individual developers to understand what has been documented.

There is a key distinction between what happens in Steps 1–6 and what happens in Step 7. In Steps 1–6 the design of the architecture is being delivered and there is open discussion of potential extensions and changes, particularly among individual architects who are highly cognizant of the design implications. In Step 7 the assumption is that the architecture has been stabilized and that individual elements of the architecture are no longer the subject of debate. It is not possible to properly disseminate the architecture if the perception is that the debate is continuing. This phenomenon is the downfall of some significant and otherwise well-conceived architectures.

Figure 4.11 shows the overall prices for architecture migration. The migration process starts with some preexisting software including legacy applications,

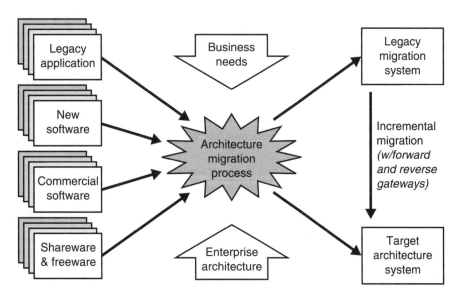

FIGURE 4.11   System Architecture Migration

commercial software, and the possible use of shareware or freeware. Mixed into this is the creation of new software which will be implementing many new capabilities within the target system. The architecture migration process is influenced by business needs and by the definition of enterprise architecture that we described earlier, with a focus on the computational interfaces which are the real keys to controlling software boundaries. Once the target architecture is defined, then there is a continuous process of migration.

The process of migration may take many years to realize and may never truly be completed. The kind of migration that we recommend is sometimes called chicken-little migration because it does not assume that on any specific date the legacy system will be shut down and the new system turned on at potentially substantial risk to the organization if the new system is not perfect. In chicken-little migration the capabilities of the legacy which already provide business value in the capabilities of the target system can be brought on line or transferred as the target system takes form. Figure 4.12 shows one of the key concepts in how the target system is realized by leveraging legacy applications. The legacy application will have one or more mechanisms for transferring information. At a minimum a legacy system maintains some files on disk or perhaps a database, and the legacy implication may have more than that; for example, it may have some application program interfaces that are documented or other types of command-line interfaces.

Legacy applications may comprise a majority of commercial software having the same kinds of mechanisms available for the purpose of integration. In our experience with object-oriented integration we found a different set of mecha-

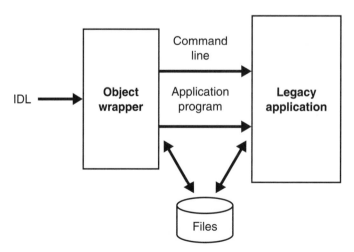

FIGURE 4.12   Legacy Object Wrapping Approach

nisms for virtually every legacy and commercial package that we encountered. The purpose of the object wrapper is to map from the preexisting interfaces to the target architecture interfaces which may be defined using IDL. In addition to providing a direct functional mapping, there are capabilities of the target architecture which should be considered and will reside in the resulting object wrapper. For example, a distributed object architecture typically has one or more directory services to enable applications to dynamically discover other applications in the environment without hardwired programming of point-to-point integration. The support for metadata director services is one of the new functions that the object wrapper can provide. Other kinds of functions in the wrapper include support for security, for system management, and for data interchange.

Object-oriented technology enables the creation of significant applications. Through survey research we have discovered some of the key challenges to the migration to object technology. The key challenge is the difficulty in establishing an architecture for the information system for the enterprise. To quote one of our sources, people start in the middle of the software process, immediately begin development without doing their homework, with no vision, no business process, and an incomplete architecture. Another challenge is in management of the object-oriented process, which differs in some fundamental ways from how software processes from previous paradigm were managed. To quote one of our sources, people are solving tomorrow's problems with today's technology and yesterday's methodology. Another challenge that we frequently encountered was a difficulty in sustaining an architecture during development and maintenance, once an architecture had been established. To quote our sources, it is easier to scope and start over rather than to figure out what they did. Another source noted that requirements evolve during design implementation, leading to hack design.

Other types of challenges were perceived as smaller obstacles than one might expect. For example, technology requirements were accorded a fairly low priority in the migration to object technology, compared to architectural and management issues.

4.6   ARCHITECTURAL SOFTWARE NOTATION

In this section we will convey a basic familiarity with software notations that is essential for all architects. If you are very experienced with software design and the Unified Modeling Language (UML), you can safely skip this section. Understanding these notations enables you to understand the business implications of information technology. This section uses a subset of the UML including those features which are commonly used and commercially supported in computer-aided software engineering tools today. We recommend that your organization adopt UML in order to facilitate communication in general computer literacy for interpreting architectural documentation.

Before UML, there existed a large number of proprietary information technology diagrams and notations (Figure 4.13). In fact, every authoritative practitioner of object orientation and other information technologies had their own notation—for example, Booch notation, Odell notation, object modeling technique (OMT) notation, and so forth. It was a general consensus that approximately 70% of the concepts that were being modeled through these various notations were overlapping. It took the industry many years to discover how to unify notations in these common areas and provide a way to extend the common notation to capture their specialized extension.

The unified modeling language is a consensus standard of the Object Management Group. UML is a unique standard because it is also supported by the Microsoft Corporation, which participated actively in the OMG process. It captures the common concepts from the proprietary notations in a uniform manner, and it is designed for extensibility, so that particular kinds of extensions can be defined consistent with the standard. In particular the UML standard includes extensions for business modeling and for objectory process. UML contains and represents common notational conventions for information

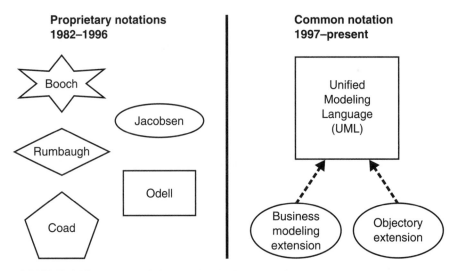

FIGURE 4.13 Object-Oriented Modeling Notations

systems models. These include object-oriented models as well as more general business process models in other forms of information representation. Authorities such as David Harel have described the creation of UML as an industry standards achievement as significant as Algol 60. Today, UML is enthusiastically supported by most object-oriented software authorities and major vendors including IBM and Microsoft.

The UML standard includes several sections. The UML notation guide is the specification that is most likely to provide benefits. The diagramed notation is defined along with a minimal set of semantics that defines the meaning of the notation. There also exists a much more elaborate semantic description of UML called the UML meta-model, a standard that provides additional details about the fine-grained issues of diagram meaning. In addition, UML includes an object constraint language, which is a textual notation using first-order logic that enables rigorous description of diagram-based constraints.

There are two categories of UML diagram types, as shown in Figure 4.14. Static diagrams represent the logical structure of information objects. Dynamic diagrams represent the behavior and activities of these objects. The static diagram types include use case diagrams, static structure diagrams, and implementation diagrams. Use case diagrams are used for enterprise viewpoint modeling and other kinds of top-down analysis to discover the key functionality of information systems. Static structure diagrams are used for information viewpoint objects as well as other important descriptions, because they identify exclusive objects and define constraints on those objects, including the object attributes, the object operation, and other characteristics. Implementation diagrams enable the description of the computational components as well as the technology objects and how they are deployed and allocated.

"Modeling is a craft and at times an art" [Rechtin 97].

UML Diagram Types

Static	Dynamic

1. Use case diagrams	4. Interaction diagrams
	  – Sequence diagrams
	  – Collaboration diagrams

2. Static structure diagrams	

3. Implementation diagrams
  – Component diagrams
  – Deployment diagrams
	5. State chart diagrams
	  – Activity diagrams

FIGURE 4.14   UML Diagram Types

Dynamic UML diagrams include interaction diagrams and state charts. Interaction diagrams represent the time-based behavior of groups of objects exchanging object-oriented messages. State chart diagrams are usually used to represent the internal states and transitions of individual objects.

Figure 4.15 represents a running example that we will use to help explain the capabilities of UML notation. In this example we are modeling various characteristics of a purchasing system. This is a contrived example, and we will only define aspects of this system which are useful for describing the features of UML. In this purchasing system we have employees who engage in the acquisition of capital equipment. We have corporate buyers who have the authority to conduct purchasing transactions, and we have vendors that manufacture and market capital equipment that the employees need.

Figure 4.16 is an example of packages, used to represent the key architecture viewpoints. A package is used to represent any grouping of UML modeling elements, much as parentheses are used to group words in sentences. In modeling tools, packages are used to represent subsidiary diagrams. Wherever a package appears, there is yet another more detailed diagram, viewable on another modeling screen or page.

Figure 4.17 is a use case diagram representing the top-level functionality of the procurement system. In this diagram we have represented the boundary of the procurement system as a UML package. UML packages appear as file

A modeling example: purchasing system

Employee users

Capital equipment

Corporate buyer

Vendor

FIGURE 4.15   Purchasing System Modeling Example

Example: Packages

Purchasing system architecture

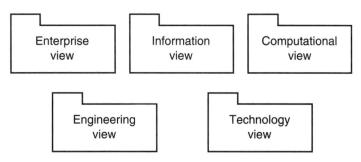

FIGURE 4.16 Example of UML Packages

folders in diagrams and usually represent the existence of an embedded diagram within a particular viewpoint. In a case tool, clicking on a package will reveal a more detailed diagram from that viewpoint of the system. In our use case we have a number of stick figures which represent actors that participate in using the system. Actors are analysis objects which in most cases are

Example: Use Case Diagram

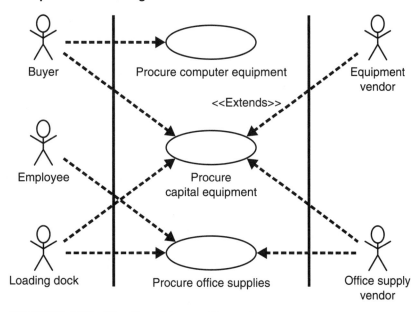

FIGURE 4.17 Use Case Diagram Example

external to the system. Each of the use cases is represented by an oval in the diagram and represents some major function of the system which can be detailed later as analysis and design progresses. Dependencies between actors in use cases are represented as arrows in this diagram (Figure 4.17). The power of use case analysis is that the diagrams are simple representations of what the system does. Use case analysis forces the modelers to focus on the highest priority capabilities of the system that provide value to the users.

The second type of diagrams in UML are called static structure diagrams. Many people call them class diagrams. The purpose of static structure diagrams is to identify the concepts and constraints that are structural within the information system. Static structure diagrams contain two types of entities including classes and objects. Classes represent a specific category of behavior. Objects represent specific instances of classes. Classes and objects are represented with rectangles in the UML. Objects are distinguished because the name appearing in the top cell of the rectangle will be underlined. Whenever we have this underlined element in a UML diagram, we generally mean that we are representing an instance of that entity.

Figure 4.18 is a static structure diagram for the purchasing system. In this case we have a package which represents the purchasing communities and we have various information objects that represent various kinds of documents involved in the purchasing process. For example, there are purchase requisition documents, procurement checklist documents, and purchase order documents. Relationships between the classes are represented by lines. These lines are called associations. Another common notation shown in Figure 4.21 is a comment or note, which is represented by a rectangle with the top right corner folded in. A note is attached to one or more model elements and specifies additional constraints or semantics for the diagram.

Figure 4.19 is another static structure diagram showing the employee type class and various subclasses including employee contacts and purchasing contacts. The unique kind of association that represents inheritance is shown in Figure 4.19 as a line with an open-ended arrow. This is called a generalization association. Figure 4.20 shows major forms of associations appearing in UML. The purpose of associations is to show relationships between model entities. These relationships may be one-to-one, one-to-many, or other types of cardinality constraints. Most associations in UML diagrams are plain lines between objects and classes. An association can have a name attached to it and an identification of roles at each end of the association. Each of the roles can be identified by numbers or ranges of numbers. If the asterisk symbol is used, this means *many,* which denotes any number from zero to infinity.

Static Structure Diagram

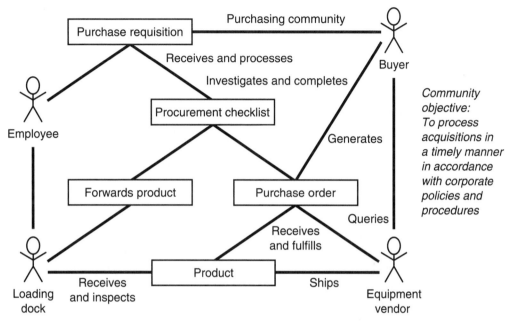

FIGURE 4.18   Structure Diagram Example

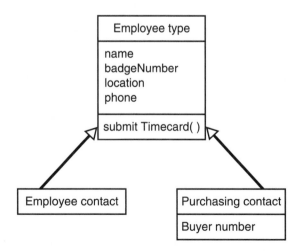

FIGURE 4.19   Generalization Relationship Example

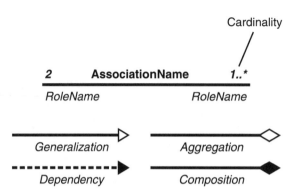

FIGURE 4.20   Representation of Object Associations

Other types of associations include *generalization* for representing inheritance, *dependency* for showing general kinds of change relationships, *aggregation* for showing part–whole relationships and collections, and then *composition,* which is a stronger form of aggregation that implies that the life cycles of the related objects are tightly coupled. In other words, in composition, if the aggregate object is deleted, all of the objects that are part of that composition are also deleted (Figure 4.20).

Figure 4.21 is yet another static structure diagram and shows more of the details of associations and attributes and operations that UML can represent. When particular elements of UML are not explicitly represented, such as operations and attributes, that does not mean that these constraints do not exist. It simply means that in this particular model for this purpose it was not necessary to represent that constraint. Figure 4.21 shows several objects with explicit representations of attributes and operations. If the class element is represented explicitly, it has by default three compartments. The top compartment is the name of the class; the second compartment is a list of the attributes of the class. Each attribute represents state information, which may be public or private. The state information can include representation of data type and default initial values. The third compartment contains operations by default. The operations are identified by their visibility, whether they are public or private, the operation name, a parameter list, and a return type. All of these may be optionally included except for the operation name, which is required.

The static structure diagram is the most important part of UML to understand properly, because it is the richest set of descriptive features in UML and is useful for virtually any application of modeling static structure and constraints. Component diagrams are another type of static representation.

Static Structure Diagram

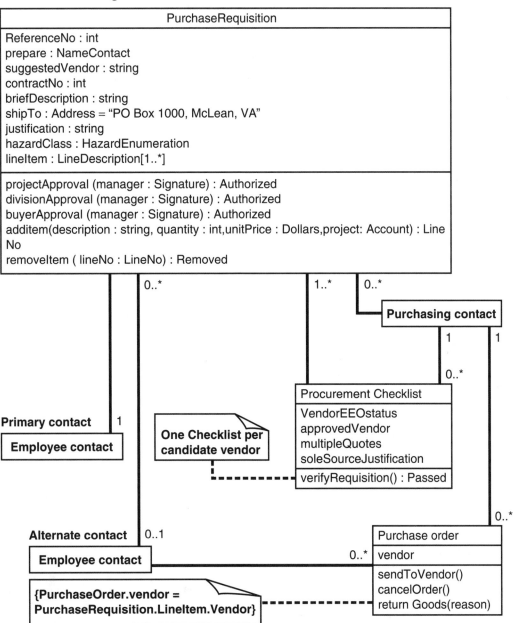

FIGURE 4.21 Structure Diagram: Purchase Requisition Detail

Figure 4.22 is an example showing various components and dependency relationships between them. Component diagrams are analogous to the computational viewpoint objects that we described earlier. Component objects are software modules that have interfaces and dependencies upon other computational objects. Figure 4.22 shows the computational objects as rectangles with interface components.

Deployment diagrams are another form of structural representation. They are very simple and may not be sufficiently sophisticated for many of your modeling needs. We recommend the use of static structure diagrams when complex constraints need to be represented. Deployment diagrams include processor symbols, which represent independent computing elements, and device symbols which represent dependent computing elements such as peripherals. Figure 4.23 is an example of the deployment diagram. The processing

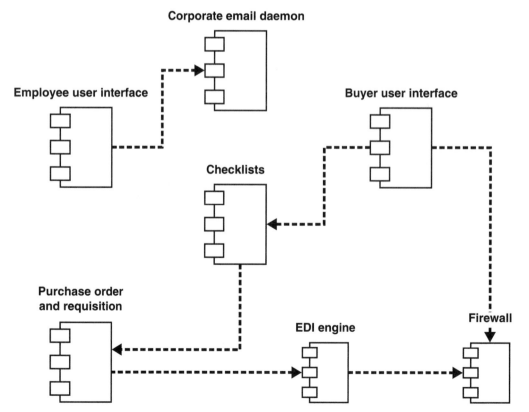

FIGURE 4.22   Component Diagram Example

Deployment diagram

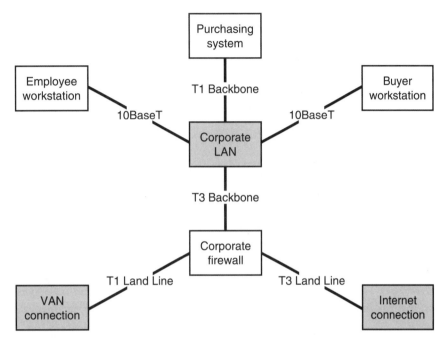

FIGURE 4.23 Deployment Diagram Example

elements have shaded surfaces and the device elements do not. There are associations between these deployment objects that represent various kinds of physical connections. Dynamic modeling diagrams include state chart diagrams and interaction diagrams.

Interaction diagrams come in two flavors, and these diagrams are isomorphic. In other words, for any given collaboration diagram, there is an equivalent sequence diagram which contains the same information represented differently. This applies in the reverse direction as well. Collaboration diagrams resemble ordinary static structure diagrams except that we are representing the dynamic time-base behavior of a set of objects which is executing. Within these diagrams we have ordinary UML objects, which have underlying names and messages that are directed associations between these objects.

Figure 4.24 is an example showing an execution sequence and the order of messaging of this information exchange between the object and the purchasing system. The order of object message transmission is indicated by a numbering sequence, one, two, three, and so forth. These imply a time-based dependency between these messages and how they interact with the information objects.

Example: Collaboration Diagram

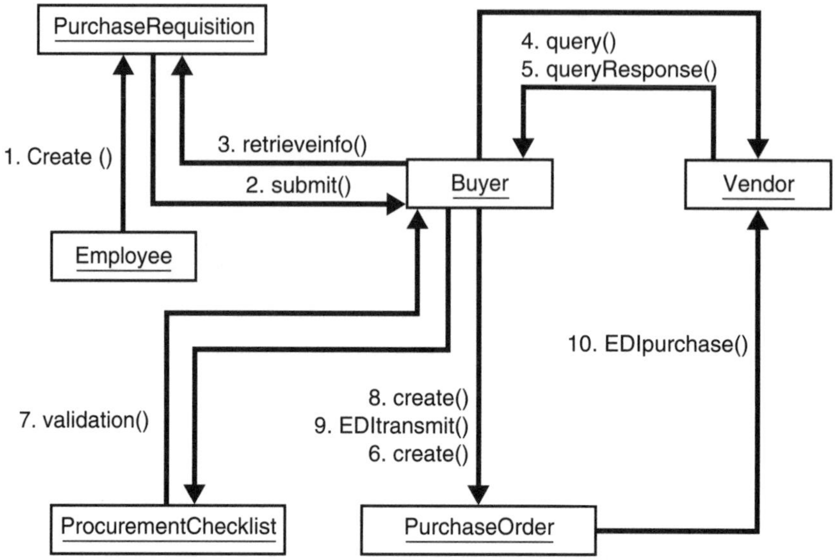

FIGURE 4.24   Collaboration Diagram Example

Sequence diagrams, another very important form of UML notation, are used to convey the details of use cases and how use cases will operate as well as showing the description of the system in a manner that is readily interpreted by most users.

Sequence diagrams, like collaboration diagrams, contain objects which are rectangles with underlying names in the notation. Figure 4.25 is an example of the sequence diagram showing the purchasing system completing a purchase transaction. Notice that the messages and objects in Figure 4.25 correspond exactly to the transaction that we represented in the collaboration diagram in Figure 4.24. Each object has a dashed line extended from it which runs down the paper. This is the *object life-cycle line* and represents the time when the object is actively processing a particular message. The object life-cycle line runs down the page in increasing time so that we see a chronological progression of messaging between the objects.

The final type of UML diagram is the state chart. State charts represent control flows that cause state transitions. Typically, state chart diagrams represent the state of a single object and the transition between these states as the object executes. Figure 4.26 is an example of a state chart diagram for our purchase system example. In this case we are representing the states of the buyer object. The state chart represents several decision points and their representa-

Example: Sequence Diagram

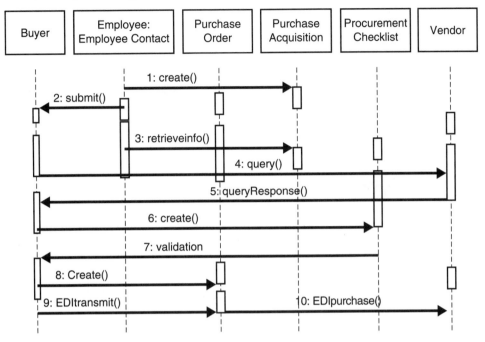

FIGURE 4.25 Sequence Diagram Example

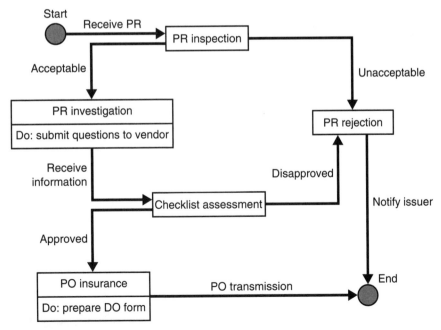

FIGURE 4.26 State Chart Example

tive states which are significant to the object's functioning. These states can be used to determine the overall structure of the source code for this object.

"If you can't explain it in five minutes, either you don't understand it or it doesn't work" [Rechtin 97].

4.7   CONCLUSIONS

We began this chapter with a discussion about managing software complexity, and we end it with a drill school lecture on software modeling. Software architects must know the fundamentals as well as be able to use them creatively to achieve architectural goals.

If your organization has not yet adopted a standard notation. and your developers are not literate in it, UML provides an opportunity to introduce new modeling practices. UML is a standard notation from the Object Management Group, an ISO-affiliated organization. UML is an industry consensus supported by most of the major authorities in object-orientation. UML's key benefit is its clarity of description, since it is relatively devoid of cryptic symbols, such as "crows' feet" used by precursor notations to represent cardinality. UML is the first object-oriented modeling notation which is widely recognized and understandable by the majority of software practitioners.

4.8   EXERCISES

EXERCISE 4.1   Managing Complexity Using Architectural Options

Consider one approach to a distributed collection management service. You could model it after the approach used by many C++ tools vendors and specify interfaces for numerous collection types (bag, list, keyset, etc.), operations to provide type-specific operations such as a comparison between objects, and commands for executing processes on objects stored within the collection. (See Figure 4.27.) Assume the distributed collection management service takes each of these characteristics to the extreme. Use the architectural options described to refactor the design into a more manageable set of interfaces.

BACKGROUND FOR SOLUTION:

Step 1: The management of elements in a collection is fairly straightforward and can be implemented using various design tradeoffs. Collection types

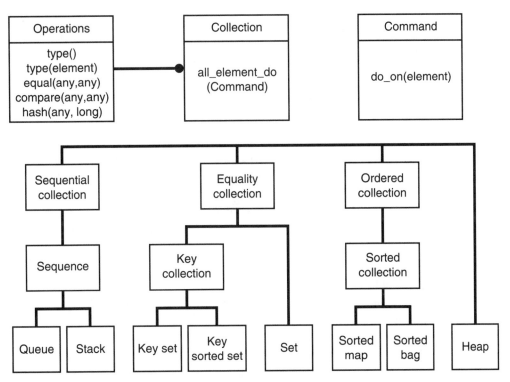

FIGURE 4.27   Distributed Collection Management System

such as bag, list queue, etc., are different ways to implement collection management behaviors. *Sweep it under the rug and ignore it* directs us to abstract the collection management behavior to a higher level of abstraction and not expose the specific implementation details to client applications.

Step 2: The distributed collection management service described handles three separate responsibilities: element management, type-specific comparisons, and commands. Such a design can be sliced into three simpler interfaces, each of which focuses on just one area of responsibility. Separate out the notion of generically managing collection elements, as generic elements, into a single interface which hides the details of the collection implementation. Define a separate command interface which operates on a list of objects rather than a collection. The command and collection interfaces should not have any dependencies between them. This approach to design is strictly superior to other approaches where the collection expects a command and iterates over its elements, executing a command on each item. In the new design, the responsibilities are sliced so that each command decides how to iterate over the set of elements provided rather than the collection. The collection no longer needs to know about the command interface, and the command does not know about the collection.

Step 3: The *dice it* architectural option is used to define the third interface which separates out the vertical type-specific behavior from the horizontal capabilities of element management. Commands can have a standard interface which can support both horizontal commands, operations which do not refer to the specific object subtype, and vertical capabilities, where operations depend on the contents of the object. Horizontal commands would include generic operations which refer to the interface repository or perform general logging. Vertical commands would include operations which require inspection of the object contents, such as sorting and data transformations. The third interface should be a standalone version of the operation's interface which may be used in the implementation of a command. Most frequently, it may be appropriate to collocate the type-specific operation's implementation with the command sets which require it.

The new design produced by applying these architectural options would be more component oriented and capable of supporting a greater variety of applications. However, it is less object oriented in the traditional sense, as the collection itself no longer encapsulates as much functionality. However, it provides a better base for building fully encapsulated objects, which delegate to the new collection components rather than reimplement such behavior in a new object.

LEADERSHIP TRAINING

There are some definite benefits to being a soldier—the rush of being a part of something larger than yourself, having a well-defined role which is important and vital to the success of great enterprises, the camaraderie of fellow soldiers, and the belief that if everyone performs as well as you, victory will soon be at hand. However, the reality of a battlefield is that not all soldiers are equal. Some troops are well trained, well equipped, disciplined, and possessed of a great deal of combat experience; others are recently thrust into battle straight from civilian work, lacking knowledge, discipline, experience, and even the will to compete against hostile enemy forces. Similarly, in the software industry, there is a great degree of difference in productivity between the best and worse performers. For the most part, raw recruits in the software industry frequently have the will and a fair degree of knowledge but need a proper environment to acquire the discipline and experience required to excel. Therefore, more experienced and disciplined developers are forced to leave their comfortable foxholes to assume the greater responsibility of leading a team of developers with diverse development experience into the greener pastures of effective software development.

5.1   LEADERSHIP IS A NECESSARY, LEARNABLE SKILL

It is rare that a talented developer can immediately excel when first thrust into a leadership role. Furthermore, close examination of those who are successful typically reveals a history of informal leadership activity such as mentoring and assuming responsibility for tasks such as configuration management, which already affects a large number of fellow developers. Fortunately, leadership, while being a necessary part of an architect's skill set, is also a learnable skill.

Special characteristics of architectural leadership must be emphasized in order to maximize a software architect's chance for success. They are vision, integrity, and decisiveness. *Vision* provides a concrete goal for a development team to focus upon. Without having a vision, it will be difficult to justify the rationale for the many technical decisions which are made throughout the development life cycle. A high standard of *integrity* is essential for motivating team members to look beyond their own self-interest and consider the various issues from the viewpoint of what is best overall rather than easiest for them. Finally, an architect needs to be *decisive,* both to facilitate progress and to maintain the confidence of the team that the technical issues are understood well enough to be quantified and acted upon.

It is the job of the software architect to clearly articulate a compelling vision for the software project. The vision provides the motivation for the team and provides the basis for making tradeoffs in order to accomplish the overall vision. This is extremely vital in software, where success can be realized through a variety of methods, each with its own unique set of tradeoffs and consequences. The architect's vision becomes the software project blueprint, the clear path through which the overall concept of the software is realized in an actual software product.

It is absolutely essential that the software architect is honest and has the absolutely highest standard of integrity. With software, the product is extremely malleable, lending itself to a tremendous number of approaches for accomplishing any particular task. As the technical leader, the architect has to advocate a particular approach as the most desirable technical solution. If the architect's actions are perceived as being motivated by other than technical reasons—for example, to appease various political forces in an organization—it undermines the trust of team members who are expected to preserve the architectural vision.

Finally, the most vital attribute a software architect must have is decisiveness. When a technical issue arises which requires the architect to make a decision, more likely than not the worse decision is to avoid making any decision at all. Doing so impedes, rather than facilitates, progress, and it frustrates people who can be far more effective once the decision is made. Remember that failing to decide something is also a decision, just one that is unlikely to result in any sort of resolution and may run an increasingly high risk of magnifying the problem. Not being decisive demonstrates to others both a lack of urgency and a lack of confidence in resolving technical issues. Either of these is sufficient to compromise the architect's ability to serve in a leadership role, but the combination is a recipe for the certain alienation of other team members who do possess these vital qualities. If the architect does not exhibit a determination to have the development effort succeed in its goals, then other team members will question whether the team and their role within it are meaningful and whether the team goals are worth pursuing.

5.2   THE ARCHITECT AS TEAM BUILDER

The software architect leads by bringing the team together. As the most visible and technical of the management staff, the architect is in a position to turn the mindsets of the team members in a common direction. All but the most dysfunctional of teams want to be successful. However, where people differ is on the details of what it means to have a successful outcome as well as the best means of achieving it. To correct the first of these issues, the architect must continually communicate the vision of what the final outcome of the development team can be if the management and technical plans are followed. This creates a willingness in team members to give the day-to-day decisions the benefit of the doubt as long as they believe that the end goal is sufficient to satisfy their own personal criteria for project success.

Once a team is on the same page as to the overall vision and desired outcome, the common view of where the team is going serves to lessen the contention about what is the best means to achieve it. Rather than suspecting that the motives of other team members are different from their own, people are more willing to consider various solutions and defined objectives on their technical merit. In a software project, any time the discussion can be converted into a purely technical discussion rather than one based on personality and ego management, it is a major win in moving toward the project goals.

One important lesson software architects must learn is to trust the skills and talents of other people on their team. A common mistake of new software architects is to micromanage other team members. This results in one of two predictable outcomes. (1) The other developers may become resentful of your lack of trust and confidence in them, resulting in a significant negative impact on their productivity with regard to the team goal and overall project vision. (2) Even worse, the developers may eagerly allow the architect to assume the bulk of the project responsibilities. This creates the illusion of working in the short term, but it breaks down quickly as the reality sinks in that the architect cannot work as effectively on his/her own as with a high-performance team of dedicated developers focused on accomplishing the same outcome. Therefore, having trust in other team members to execute tasks independently is critical for the overall success of the team. Yes, this involves undertaking risks which some people, in hindsight, may claim are unnecessary. However, taking the long view, it is important that others accept and live up to their individual and team responsibilities in order to maximize the overall output from a development team.

A software architect is sometimes required to mediate between conflicting demands of project management and higher-level stakeholders in a development project. Often the demands on the software developers were made higher up in the management chain than the software architect without detailed knowledge of the development staff that will be responsible for delivering on whatever claims and expectations were formulated. In order to be effective, a software architect focuses first and foremost on the needs of the development staff. At some level, every project plan ever made is a fantasy. It is the flesh-and-blood developers who must feel respected and motivated enough to produce the concrete project deliverables. The software architect must be aggressive in serving the needs of developers through communicating with management, overseeing the purchase of productivity-enhancing tools and COTS products, ensuring proper recognition for the team, etc. After all, the ultimate value the architect adds is to ensure that the developers are efficient and effective in performing their tasks.

5.3   ALWAYS INSIST ON EXCELLENCE IN DELIVERABLES

A responsibility of the software architect is to review developers' work products. Inevitably, in the early stages of a new effort, it is likely that several of the work products (use cases, designs, test plans, etc.) are going to fall short of the architect's expectations. Most likely, the disconnect between the architect's expectations and the work produced is due not to malice or a lack of effort but rather to a lack of understanding of what precisely the architect's standards are. It is in these early stages where detailed review is essential and where the architect must insist on excellence in the work products produced. This should be done professionally and politely, however; the quality and level of effort must not be compromised. If the architect does not insist upon excellence in the early development process, it is unlikely that it will ever be achieved in future iterations.

An architect should expect some resistance the first time any experienced developer has to undergo a work review. Typically, the architect will receive arguments about the worth of producing deliverables which satisfy the standards, about whether the task description was clear enough to sufficiently describe the desired deliverables, and a thousand or so similar variants, most of which blame the standards and the architect rather than the developer. The software architect's best course of action is to be gracious and accept full blame and responsibility, but insist that the additional work required to achieve the desired deliverable is performed in a timely manner. If this is done well, the most avid detractors of the initial standards will eventually become their staunchest defenders, once their value has been demonstrated later in the development process. When integration time is reduced by two thirds by having clear and very specific design documents, no one on the team will want to proceed to implementation and integration without them ever again.

The software architect must be versatile and set an example for the rest of the development team to follow. For example, if the project is at risk of being delayed because a critical design is missing, frequently the best contribution the architect can make is either to sit down with the group and jointly develop the design, or sometimes, particularly if the subsystem slipped through the cracks at task assignment, to produce the design independently. In either case, the architect should adhere to the same process, in terms of documentation guidelines and reviews, that everyone else on the team adheres to. Similarly, if integration is delayed because of problems in debugging tricky parts of the source code, ideally the architect will sit with the developers and, if all goes well, assist in rapidly resolving the obstacles. Not surprisingly, this aspect of being a software architect frequently comes easily to new architects, as it was a responsibility also assumed by them as experienced developers. The more difficult part is finding the time to continually develop the architect's skill set so he can be equally versatile after several years as a software architect.

However, there are a few pitfalls which must be avoided. As the software architect, you have the most visible technical role. Like it or not, you are also the technical role model for the team and your actions directly impact their actions and mentality. Therefore, if you take or suggest shortcuts and kludges to quickly resolve a development issue, like it or not, you are implicitly advocating that others use similar means to resolve issues which they find problematic. Also, rest assured that less experienced developers will encounter many more things which are problematic than will the architect, and they will be more than content with adding numerous kludges to source code rather than asking for help in resolving the problems according to the known architectural principles. Similarly, if your code lacks a unit test or is not related back to the requirements specification, you will immediately discover several developers who automatically are following your lead. Therefore, as the architect, you must conduct your efforts exactly as you expect others to conduct their own behavior. It is far easier to start off with a good example and maintain it, than it is to explain why you didn't and yet still expect others to conform to your stated standards.

ETIQUETTE FOR SOFTWARE ARCHITECTS

As silly as it may sound, an investment in a book on general etiquette and the time it takes to read and absorb it will always pay off handsomely for a software architect. Most of the problems which will hurt the productivity of a development team are people problems rather than technical ones. Etiquette can frequently head off the people problems before they escalate into major obstacles. For the one or two individuals who are too foolish to heed the above wisdom, here are a few of the most basic techniques, strictly etiquette related, which will help you succeed as a software architect:

▶ Before you criticize work anyone else has produced, start the conversation off by identifying a few things you liked about the work.
▶ Generalize criticism into a heuristic, using specific cases as examples of the heuristic not being followed, rather than immediately criticizing specific instances.
▶ Do not talk to people only when something is wrong. Let people know when you like their work and efforts. Sometimes, just ask how things are progressing and how you can improve upon your efforts.

Just as serving as an example to the development team comes easily to most new software architects, having confidence and courage when first appointed as the architect typically does not. At a minimum, a software architect's courage should take two forms. *First,* no technical question should ever be feared by the architect. The decisions of the architect should be made based on his best technical knowledge. Not every decision is popular, but they are all based on understanding the various tradeoffs in making use of various technologies and design approaches. Any question should either be answerable by recapping the known tradeoffs or be a source of information which may require that an existing tradeoff be reevaluated. Neither case reflects badly upon the architect, since honestly considering questions and hearing new information, even from critics, is a perfectly valid technique of information acquisition! A software architect should welcome both types of questions without getting agitated, as they both provide practice in articulating the project's architectural vision and may lead to cases where the vision is further refined in light of new information. *Second,* the architect should never be afraid of making a concrete decision.

One constant in software development is that good software architecture never just happens. It must be planned, monitored and defended over the lifetime of the software. If, as a software architect, you are not constantly monitoring the execution of software processes to verify that the architectural principles and guidelines established at the outset of the project are adhered to and maintained, then you are failing in your role. A software architect cannot be effective without actively seeking out the real progress and direction of the project from the developers who are performing the actual work.

As a software architect, you have knowledge and information which frequently exceed that of many team members. As a general rule, the architect should be willing to share information with other team members and trust them to use it constructively. For example, if the team is incorporating a technology with known limitations, such as the CORBA marshalling delays with complex data types, then it should be willing to acknowledge the problem and discuss why the benefits of the technology are sufficient to overcome its limitations. While information sharing may occasionally be damaging—for example, by bringing up the limitations to higher-level management who may be unable to adequately understand the technical tradeoffs—in the long run it builds trust among team members and enables them to develop solutions rather than waste time rediscovering known problems. An environment where the cumulative knowledge of the entire team can be brought to bear, both in solving problems and in seeking out still more knowledge, is the most ideal for software development. Little is more disappointing than seeing a talented architect attempt to horde information, which typically becomes obsolete at a faster rate than it can be stockpiled.

SEVEN HABITS OF HIGHLY SUCCESSFUL SOFTWARE ARCHITECTS

Keep it simple. When communicating to team members various architectural concepts or software mechanisms, resist the temptation to provide a complete and detailed explanation of how things work or a detailed comparison against all the alternatives in front of a group. Instead, say enough to communicate the idea at a high level, just low enough to be understood in principle, and let individuals do their own homework or meet with you individually to address their specific concerns.

Let others defend the architecture. It is always preferable to have someone else respond to a technical concern rather than have the software architect appear to be the sole source of knowledge. It reinforces teamwork, provides the architect insights from people who agree as well as disagree, is a key aspect in mentoring others, etc.

Act, don't argue. Arguing technical points in a meeting wastes time, hurts feelings, and seldom if ever fully resolves any technical issues. When such an argument starts, act—either assign people to get or verify the relevant information, set up a meeting specifically for resolving the debated topic, or, if time requires an immediate course of action, lay down the law explaining why the time constraints force an end to the matter.

Keep an eye on the prize. Always be aware of the end goal. It is easy to be distracted by tasks and smaller technical issues, and frequently other team members will succumb to one form of tunnel vision or the other. However, it is vital that the architect is always focused on the overall vision of the system and can relate every task or technology to how it contributes to the end goal.

Be willing to change, but never too much at once. After the initial bootstrapping of a software development effort, be wary of implementing too many process improvements all at once, as there is a risk of compromising the effective parts of the process.

Learn where to stop. Resist the temptation to go into too many details and to micromanage design decisions. For example, it would typically be enough to specify that caching is required in client applications and that the caching code should be reused throughout the application. However, detailing the specific caching algorithm used or writing the caching pseudocode is probably overkill. Learn to trust other team members to provide design and implementation details and let them come to you in case of difficulties.

Know how to follow. If there is a lead architect you report to, or even if you delegate the responsibility for an issue to someone else, avoid publicly confronting others on major design issues. This is accomplished by knowing ahead of time what is going to be discussed and the reasons for the various decisions. This is a key aspect to developing a focused, high-performance team.

The software architect serves as a technical mentor to other developers on a project. Often the architect is asked to help resolve technical problems or mediate a technical dispute between two parties. Rather than simply resolving the technical problem or deciding between the two alternatives, the software architect should go the extra mile. In the case of technical problem solving, the architect should walk the developer through the steps necessary to resolve the problem at a level of detail low enough that the developer can resolve similar problems in the future without additional aid. In mediating technical disputes, the architect should articulate the issues and design tradeoffs which make a particular alternative more desirable in a particular case than the competing alternative. If possible, the architect should figure out the concerns being addressed by the inferior alternative, and point out what elements are missing in the current case which, if present, would make that alternative more desirable. Ultimately, team members should feel that interacting with the architect is a learning experience. Furthermore, if the same technical issues are brought to the attention of the software architect, take the developer to task and ask why he/she doesn't feel comfortable resolving such problems without your assistance. Eliminating road blocks to applying new knowledge is an easy way to improve the efficiency of a development team.

A software architect should always be willing to hold team members accountable for their lack of productivity. If a design is overdue, it is reasonable to ask for the reason for the delay and a description of where the elapsed time has been spent. Similarly, if a coding task is delayed, getting specific details about whether the delay was caused by problems in the design, debugging a tricky section of code, or unforeseen complexity in the implementation is vital. Such information can lead the architect to gain productivity increases across the board by conducting debugging tutorials or by improving design review procedures. Also, always make it clear that as soon as delays are anticipated, developers have an obligation to let the project manager know so tasks can be replanned accordingly.

Most development efforts, even ones with mature processes and an experienced team, cannot avoid some degree of chaos. Left unchecked, the unexpected technical and organizational issues could occupy just about all of the software architect's time. However, any software architect needs to ensure that the bulk of his/her time is devoted to issues internal to the development team. An effective architect must always be available on relatively short notice to attend to the team's internal details, which may delay development if not attended to promptly. These issues include resolving disputes over interfaces between various subsystems, weighing in on problems caused by product upgrades, or providing verification that certain design approaches aren't in violation of the architect's vision of the system.

5.4   ARCHITECT'S WALKTHROUGH

A number of development milestones occur that require the attention of the software architect. Unless the architect is available, the development team may be faced with either waiting for approval—the kiss of death for rapid development—or making assumptions that may not always be accurate. Correcting these incorrect assumptions at a later date is always substantially more expensive and difficult than getting them right initially. Therefore, an architect must give the impression that he/she is always available with the expectation that the internal demands of a development team will be greatest early in the development process through the design process, tapering off somewhat during implementation, testing, and deployment. The best way to be available is to walk around periodically and talk to people about their progress. If any significant issue comes up, set up an appointment between the two or three people most involved and discuss it at some time separate from that devoted to the walkthrough. This limits the time spent during the walkthrough and gives the people involved a chance to work things out on their own before the meeting. If the meeting continues to be necessary, everyone will be prepared to focus on a specific problem, which, if properly facilitated, can lead to a short, highly productive meeting.

Another benefit of the walkthrough is that you get a lower-level understanding of the project details than you would from just meeting with the team leaders. Restraint is required to remember that the primary objective of the architect in a walkthrough is to listen and understand the problems rather than immediately to attempt to resolve every issue. In fact, the less direct guidance given in a walkthrough, the better. Rather, think about the problem and make suggestions to the appropriate team leader. This will keep the team leader in the information loop, allowing him/her freedom in incorporating your suggestions into the overall team direction. In addition, it will provide you with greater insight into team dynamics in future walkthroughs, when you can gauge to what extent your suggestions were accepted by the overall team. The architect should avoid making too many suggestions directly to team developers, as these suggestions are frequently taken as mandates, regardless of the direction set by the team leaders. Without fail, the political and organizational problems resulting from such actions will overshadow any short-term technical benefits. In general, the architect should always be willing to listen, but direct action, and even suggestions, must be performed with care, taking the needs of the entire development effort into consideration.

So after nine months or so with the same team, you realize that there are still hotly debated topics, people who just don't like each other, and a project that is falling behind schedule. The issue most new architects face is evaluating whether their efforts have actually made a difference on a particular software project. Fortunately, there are a few heuristics which are effective for recognizing when you are succeeding as an architect. Unfortunately, the ultimate metric, repeatedly delivering high-quality software on time within the estimated constraints, typically takes several years to establish.

Heuristic 1: Arguments within a team are over increasingly trivial subject areas.

With any group of software professionals of diverse backgrounds, there will always be disagreements of some kind or another. Early in a project new to software architecture, the typical disagreements focus on whether or not XYZ is the right thing to do. Later, if the architect is successful, there is an implicit agreement on what to do, and the developer battleground shifts to arguments about how to accomplish XYZ. These arguments will be just as heated and impassioned as the previous wave of disagreements, but the debated issues are at a lower level. Later, if there is an implicit buy-in on how to accomplish XYZ, new arguments will arise, again just as heated, on what an implementation of how to accomplish XYZ looks like. While the volume levels and passion may be constant and to an outside observer the internal problems appear unchanged, it is the shift of focus which indicates vision, architectural, and design consensus. Achieving this consensus is a monumental accomplishment and eliminates a slew of problems which would arise did such a consensus not exist.

Heuristic 2: When it appears that there is no *consensus initially, consensus is easy to achieve* after *listening to all sides.*

Frequently, when establishing the overall vision and defining the architecture for a project, complete consensus is nearly impossible to achieve. For whatever reasons, there will always be a few people who will need concrete evidence of the benefits of the approach on their own personal level, before they will accept any vision save their own. Later, if a consensus is established, there will be roughly the same number of disagreements. However, most frequently, one side or the other is mainly motivated to ensure that its concerns are acknowledged and known to the team and is not actually demanding that all of its issues are addressed immediately. An architect should recognize such concerns for what they are and allow them to be presented to the team. Typically, when the minority side has been convinced that it has been heard and understood, it will not object to a more popular alternative plan which satisfies the architectural vision and project objectives.

Heuristic 3: Other developers are willing to argue the merits of the architecture.

When this occurs, it indicates team buy-in for the system architecture. Note that if the software architect considers himself the sole defender of the architecture and is always the first to rise to its defense, the architect will never realize that this architectural buy-in has occurred. Therefore, the architect should be patient and give others the opportunity to comment when architectural issues are challenged. If the architect is exceptionally successful, several meetings will pass where consensus is reached in accordance to the architectural principles of the project without the architect's saying anything. Of course, when this occurs in several consecutive meetings, the architect is obligated to bring donuts to subsequent similar meetings.

Heuristic 4: There is an implicit willingness to delegate development issues to teams.

As the subjects of many meetings degrade in quality, fewer of the team members will care about how many of the development issues (configuration management trees, coding conventions, utility modules, etc.) are resolved. In such cases, it is beneficial to everyone to delegate an issue to a group of two or three people. This group can meet independently, come to an agreement on the issue, and present the agreed-upon solution to the development team at a later date. In fairness, it is important that everyone agree to accept whatever solution is agreed upon by the smaller group. Otherwise, interested parties will not join the group in hopes of overriding the group's decision later, thereby wasting the efforts expended by the developers who possessed the initiative to join the smaller group.

Heuristic 5: The software architecture becomes less obvious.

There is an implicit acceptance that adhering to the architectural principles has some value, so that there is no longer any need to debate it or even talk about it except when mentoring new developers or presenting to new stakeholders. Design and code reviews rarely turn up areas which reflect a lack of understanding regarding the software architecture. They may take just as long but now focus on lower-level issues, such as variable naming, or lack of reuse.

Conversely, you know when you are not succeeding as a software architect when the opposite of these heuristics are true—for example, if various fundamental aspects of the architectural vision are questioned throughout the development life cycle, or achieving a consensus on meaningful issues is increasingly more difficult to obtain. If a consensus is developing against the architectural vision, then it is necessary to understand the opposing arguments and discover why they are so compelling to the developers on the team. Sometimes, gaining insight into the compelling nature of the opposing arguments may result in modifying the architectural vision to one which can achieve buy-in from the development team. At other times, the software architect needs to present a better case as to why the proposed architecture is better than the available alternatives. Frequently, this may require educating the team on technologies and industry trends which they may not otherwise be aware of. This education process, along with everything else that is required to achieve vision and architectural buy-in, is a prerequisite for a successful development project and for a software architect to be successful in his/her role.

It is important to differentiate between architectural leadership and management. The most obvious difference is that the software architect is responsible for creating and articulating the technical vision of the development effort. Frequently, the architectural vision is not limited to a single effort but provides a blueprint of what the organization can accomplish in the long run. The success of the current project validates the architectural vision and provides greater confidence that the long-term architectural vision is achievable through similar methods. Management, on the other hand, is focused on the success of a short-term project with limited, well-defined objectives. For example, an architectural vision could be a component-based enterprise framework which may be used to produce scalable applications in several domains. A manager's goal is to produce a workflow management system for logistics in nine months with a team of twelve developers. Similarly, a manager has to ensure that a specific set of agreements are satisfied and often has to interact with external stakeholders to verify that what is being produced matches their expectations. Any changes in direction, such as new requirements or procedures, are communicated from external stakeholders to project management, whose responsibility is to communicate the changes to the team. The architect, however, is focused more internally and communicates why the work is meaningful and the purpose of doing things in the prescribed manner. It is not uncommon to have the software architect advocate taking more risk and adopting radical changes if he is expected to produce a technically superior product without involving too many additional resources. Management, on the other hand, tends to be more cautious and more willing to repeat technical approaches which have been successful in the past rather than gamble on state-of-the-art techniques. All but the most routine of software development efforts require both a software architect and a project manager.

5.5   CONCLUSIONS

The software architect has a unique leadership role in the software development effort. The architect educates the development team on technical issues when time permits, sells them on the defined vision when there isn't enough time to educate, and relies on the cultivated trust between the architect and the team in the remaining cases. Regardless of the method, the architect keeps the team focus on the overall technical vision and has the difficult tasks of verifying that the team is on the same technical page based on work products and of communicating with the team. The architect must serve as the technical role model to team members and maintain their respect on technical issues in order to effectively guide the project toward the desired technical goals.

5.6   EXERCISES

EXERCISE 5.1   As an architect, mentoring your team is of utmost importance. For each person on your existing project, list the behaviors which he/she could improve upon. Afterward, write down a list of concrete steps which you can take to help the person improve in these areas. Develop a concrete plan specifying whom you will work with, how often, and how you can assist each person. Finally, execute the plan. Repeat at regular intervals for the best long-term results.

SOFTWARE ARCHITECTURE: JUMP SCHOOL

In the military, jump school is used to prepare soldiers for landing in enemy-occupied terrain. Without adequate intelligence, paratrooping soldiers can find themselves in the middle of a village dung heap, a minefield, or a camouflaged enemy camp. Similarly in software, when the architect joins an organization or project team without adequate intelligence information, there is no telling what they are getting into. An architect can be doomed from the start due to existing organizational or interpersonal problems among team members. Conversely, you may discover a team that is already well organized, where you have the luxury of devoting the majority of your time to technical rather than process and team-building activities. This chapter is not about intelligence gathering; rather, it is about making the best of whatever situation you encounter when assigned as the architect of a software development team. The information on software process and team building will provide the tools for building an environment where the architect can successfully transfer architectural principles throughout a team and ensure that they are realized in the software development process.

6.1   PROCESS

In order to have a specific software architecture produce a worthwhile design and a useful implementation, an effective software process needs to be in place. A good software process will detail the steps necessary to repeatedly produce a software product which satisfies a set of requirements or a design objective.

Unfortunately, many emerging architects lack the luxury of an existing, proven software process. In such cases, it is the responsibility of the software architect to work with the project manager in defining and executing the software processes necessary for success.

PROCESS PREREQUISITES

The process prescription described in this section is designed to meet the needs of the middle 80% of software organizations. There are more sophisticated guidelines for more mature organizations, for example, the Capability Maturity Model (CMM) approach defined by the Software Engineering Institute (SEI). An extremely dysfunctional organization—for example, one in which people are afraid to tell the truth—is unlikely to benefit from this approach or any other.

There is an important prerequisite to the insertion of software process which is a key challenge for many organizations. In order to effectively utilize a software process, the organizational skill base must be sufficiently high in the areas covered by the process to make it effective. It is much easier to adopt software processes from a book, consultant, or product (e.g., *The Unified Software Development Process* [Jacobson 99]) than to train the skill base to perform that process. Many organizations make this mistake and struggle mightily to overcome their capabilities shortcomings.

For example, when adopting object-oriented technologies, the development team needs to have some knowledge and experience of the technology before progress is feasible. First, people need to be trained to think in terms of objects. This is a simple thing technically, but a very difficult transition for some people. Many will never succeed in adopting the paradigm shift. Second, people need to be trained to develop with an object-oriented programming language. Competence in using the programming syntax is not the key training objective. What's more important is that people use the object-oriented language properly as an object-oriented language, and not as if they were using a language designed for some other paradigm. It's a very common problem that causes serious problems in object-oriented projects.

Finally, the people need experience with the new paradigm so that they apply common sense and mature engineering judgment. The fact that you have transitioned to objects does not mean that you can ignore common sense and machine limitations. We have seen many designs from otherwise competent engineers that have unwarranted levels of resources and complexity for otherwise simple tasks. This maturity of judgment often goes beyond what you will find documented in textbooks and courses. Instilling this practicality in the development environment is one of the important contributions that architects can contribute to a project. We are amazed that, a decade after the initial popularity of object orientation, many organizations are still in the early phases of transition and experiencing the age-old problems mentioned here.

Every military campaign is executed according to a thoughtfully crafted set of plans. Similarly, in software architecture, a detailed plan is needed to effectively capture requirements, produce designs which satisfy the requirements, manage the configuration of software, and test software artifacts to ensure their quality and consistency with the requirements and designs. Admittedly, it is frequently easier to discuss the need for improved software processes than to establish a plan for creating organizational processes and effectively implementing them for a particular team or organization. However, a well-kept secret among veteran software architects is how to create effective software processes. Before detailing the steps in process creation, there are a few golden rules which every software architect must know.

First, a software process which is not defined cannot be repeatable. If a process is not written down, then there is no basis to claim whether the same steps were truly executed according to a preconceived plan. When a team member has a skill at executing a particular process, there is frequently a resistance to documenting and detailing the steps executed to achieve the goal. Regardless of where the resistance comes from, be it a fear of being replaced or a desire to maintain control over future executions of the process, it must be overcome in order to mature the organization to the point where benefits from an architecture-driven approach can be realized.

Next, a software process needs to be tracked. Specifically, every software process must have concrete, definable deliverables. For example, a quality initiative which involves only a series of lectures cannot be considered a process. This is not to say that lectures and seminars are bad, but rather that without mechanisms to capture feedback and to measure how presented information is actually applied, it will be difficult to determine the impact of such activities. Generally, it is best to break deliverables down so that some portion can be completed every two or three days. A longer period between deliverables does not provide the feedback necessary to ensure that the deliverable is satisfying expectations. Project management that waits weeks or months for a tangible demonstration of progress is guaranteed to receive excuses and radical misinterpretations of the original goals. Just as military leaders rely upon continuous battlefield assessments to measure the progress of a campaign, a software architect needs a steady stream of concrete measures of development progress to assist project management in their frequent replanning efforts and to quickly identify problem areas on a project.

Also, all processes must have a clear progression. Even ongoing processes should define the progression through each cycle. For example, a defect tracking process is typically an ongoing process in an organization supporting multiple products with varying release dates. However, how an individual defect is identified, documented, and resolved must be clearly specified in the process. The consequence of failure to do so is that often a process is defined but its execution falters or occurs sporadically, frequently resulting in a state where outcomes are unreliable—which defeats the point of having a process at all.

A Basic Component Framework Software Design Process

This section begins our definition of a lightweight process for component software architecture and development. Compared to heavyweight approaches to architecture-centered development (e.g., ODP+4), this process is much more compatible with object-oriented approaches that your developers may already be familiar with. If you are working with a small team of developers, and you don't have complex distributed-systems issues to contend with, this process may be right for your project. Architects should carry a big bag of tricks with flexible notations and processes to meet the demands of the terrain.

Given the increasing popularity of component software, it may be beneficial to present a single design process which is effective in coping with the unique issues related to this emerging development approach. The assumption is that the system being built is of reasonable complexity and spans across several distributed heterogeneous systems.

A component-oriented design process is used to define how to implement the requirements for a project so that reuse is maximized from existing framework components and services, and to provide a distributed, scalable enterprise platform for the domain model and future system extensions. The basic approach used is a top-down design methodology which clearly defines the software boundaries, component responsibilities, and system collaborations. In addition, the external interfaces to COTS packages and the existing component base are specified in the design documents.

The design process presented has three distinct stages:

▶ *Conceptual design phase*: Specifies at a high level the goals and specific responsibilities of a component

▶ *High-level design phase*: Documents the classes, methods, and attributes for the subsystem

▶ *Detailed design phase*: Defines the precise semantics for the attributes and methods and the IDL, which provides a well-specified transition into implementation

Most component architectures define four architectural layers (Figure 6.1):

▶ Foundation layer
▶ Domain layer
▶ Application layer
▶ User interface layer

Each design falls within one of these architectural layers. The foundation layer defines the infrastructure components used throughout the system. It contains classes to manage database access, object-oriented querying, collections, basic object services, and object primitives used to compose more complex objects.

The domain layer defines the components which are recognized in and are unique to a particular domain. Components in the domain layer represent either specific business entities or specific business processes. Typically, domain components provide minimal, coarse-grained methods to access their underlying data representation. This is necessary because domain components are used throughout a particular enterprise and are typically distributed, requiring remote access. By defining a coarse-grained interface, network latency is reduced, with the application layer caching the information to provide a finer-grained method of accessing information to service view components.

The application layer provides the application logic for a set of views. It contains specializations of domain components which are tailored to perform a precise set of tasks. The coordination of object services in the foundation layer and domain components from the domain layer typically occurs in the application layer. Additionally, optimizations such as caching and conversions from domain types to user interface types occur in this architectural layer.

Finally, the user interface layer contains the user interface components that interact with the user and the application layer to provide a complete application from the user's standpoint.

The *conceptual design* focuses on high-level design issues. It defines the overall scope of the design subsystem and the limits of the responsibilities of the subsystem. Part of the process is to examine the requirements being ad-

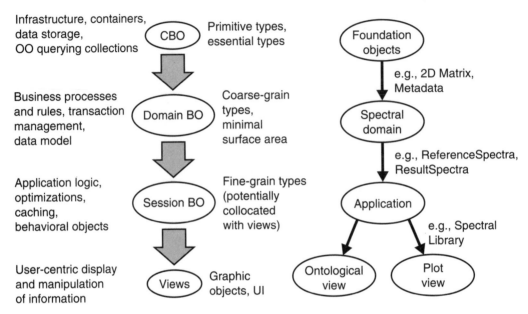

FIGURE 6.1   Layered Architecure for Distributed Component Development

dressed from different angles to ensure that the design resolves the design issues in such a manner as to let it be reused in other similar situations in other subsystems. Also, the design must handle the use case scenarios naturally and smoothly without unnecessary complexity. The deliverables for the conceptual design stage are:

▶ A one-sentence goal of what the design does
▶ A list of the responsibilities of the subsystems
▶ A clear statement of the architectural level the component is developed for

The document also gives the classes and objects initially identified for the subsystem and a description of what the class semantics and relationships are. This enables an early discussion on how the design satisfies a specific set of project requirements. Specifically, the conceptual design document can be used to discuss how the use cases in the requirements document are satisfied by the conceptual design.

The *high-level design* provides the details on precisely how the classes which make up the conceptual design are specified. The standard modeling notation in the industry is the Unified Modeling Language (UML), and the high-level design uses the static class diagrams to describe the static model of the classes in the subsystem. The dynamic model is provided in UML sequence diagrams in the detailed design stage. In the high-level design there are three key deliverables:

► Screen mockups of the component being designed
► The static class diagrams
► A document which provides information on the expected dependencies of the subsystem

Specifically, the document describes how the subsystem collaborates with other parts of the framework, what third-party tools and other components will be used in implementing the subsystem, and also the representative use cases which will be used in detailed design for providing detailed sequence diagrams of the selected scenarios. The static class model provides the classes, attributes, and methods for subsystem objects and explicitly identifies the relationships between them. The high-level design is the absolute minimum which must be completed before any amount of implementation can begin.

The *detailed design* provides the component specification for distributed components in the system (typically in OMG IDL); sequence diagrams for one or more use cases which are satisfied by the subsystem, either entirely or collaboratively with other subsystems; and detailed prose descriptions of the precise semantics of all attributes, methods, and data structures for the subsystem classes. The interface specification also includes the possible exceptions for a component, and the prose details when they occur and how they will be handled.

The sequence diagrams illustrate a use case scenario by tracing through the object model and showing by what method signatures are invoked and on what classes in order to satisfy the use case. An explanation of how system data is produced and what transformations are performed by libraries and nonobject portions of the system is also provided.

The combination of the conceptual, high-level, and detailed designs forms the design document deliverable for a subsystem. Together, the document contains the conceptual overview for the subsystem, detailed UML diagrams of the classes, screen mockups, sequence diagrams showing system dynamics, and a detailed prose description of the semantics of each of the subsystem components.

The component development methodology incorporates a concurrent design process where each of the subsystems is designed and managed by its own design process. The subsystems with the fewest dependencies are designed and implemented first, with subsystems with a higher number of dependencies being designed later. This provides the ability to stage the design process (Figure 6.2) so that concrete incremental progress can be validated with both design and software deliverables. In addition, the components which support the greatest amount of dependencies benefit from more iteration, creating a more robust, reliable platform for application components.

In Appendix B, a set of design templates defining the deliverables for this process and a sample set of designs documented according to the templates are provided.

Finally, process deliverables must be defined well enough to establish clear expectations as to what the document will contain and how it will be

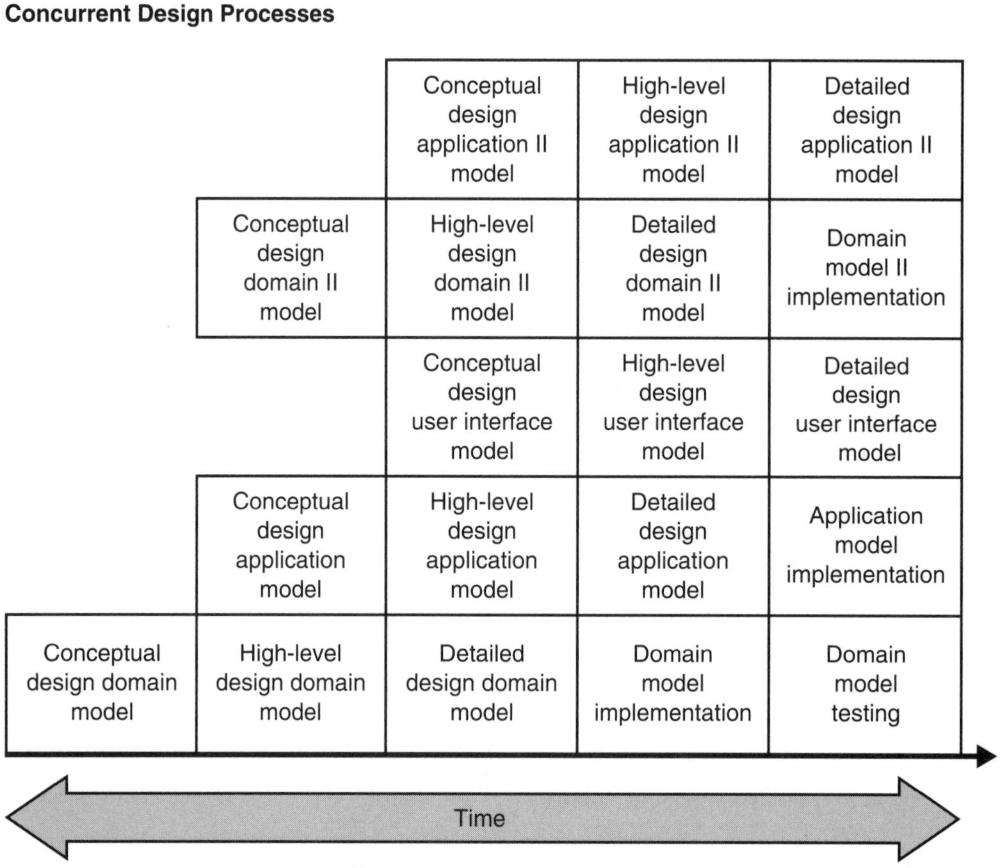

Concurrent Design Processes

		Conceptual design application II model	High-level design application II model	Detailed design application II model
	Conceptual design domain II model	High-level design domain II model	Detailed design domain II model	Domain model II implementation
		Conceptual design user interface model	High-level design user interface model	Detailed design user interface model
	Conceptual design application model	High-level design application model	Detailed design application model	Application model implementation
Conceptual design domain model	High-level design domain model	Detailed design domain model	Domain model implementation	Domain model testing

Time

FIGURE 6.2   Component Development Methodology Facilitates Concurrent Design of Subsystems

presented. Specifying how a process deliverable is to be presented is a recurring weak point for many processes, the predictable result being that the process deliverables vary significantly depending on the people executing the process or on other inconsistent factors.

6.2   CREATING NEW PROCESSES

Specifically, the detailed process for creating processes is defined as follows:

1. *Define the goals of the process explicitly.* There should never be any doubt about what a particular process is expected to accomplish.
2. *Explain the current organizational context, which illustrates why a process is needed.* This provides a basis for later discussing whether the process is still needed when an organization changes.
3. *List a brief outline of the process, which covers the process steps and how the process progresses.* Each step in the process should have a concrete completion point. Even ongoing tasks should have some well-defined completion point, for example, a single cycle. The steps of the process should provide measurable progress toward the completion of a process deliverable.
4. *Make sure the process deliverables and timetable are explicitly stated.* Ideally, the specifications for the deliverables include how the product is to be formatted as well as the information it contains.

Next, it is important to know when it is necessary to define a new process. There are two key indicators: (1) a major disruption or problem occurred which could have been prevented if a process was in place, or (2) an opportunity exists for improved outcomes if a process is put in place. So either a new process prevents or eliminates bad outcomes, or it creates desirable outcomes or improves existing outcomes.

Finally, maintain a high standard for how a process is defined. Processes which are vague, open-ended, and do not satisfy or exceed the criteria listed above for a process will create a false sense of security in an organization and will ultimately waste valuable time and resources, as critical process elements are endlessly debated and redefined.

In a brand-new software development effort, an architect should ensure that processes exist for at least the standard stages of the software development process, i.e., requirements, design, configuration management, testing, etc. Over time, processes will need to be created to improve software quality, including a code review process, defect tracking process, etc. Again, it may not be the role of the architect to define and execute all of these processes; however, he does have the responsibility of ensuring they are in place and sufficient for the project needs. Without these processes, it will be extremely difficult for the architect to have a direct input on how the software architecture is realized in the designs and actual implementation.

For development environments where existing processes are in place, new processes are developed to solve particular recurring problems. It is critical that the existing context, which determines the need for the process as well as the process details, is communicated to those affected by the process. In addition to developing buy-in, it allows process participants to provide critical feedback either into how the process can be improved or on other issues which also need to be addressed to effectively accomplish the process goals.

A common mistake of a novice software architect is to assume responsibility for tracking too many of the various processes required for the project to be successful. While there are times when a software architect needs to assume some process execution duties, a more effective approach is to delegate the majority of such responsibilities to the project manager or other members of the development team. The architect's responsibility is to ensure that the processes are being tracked and that the software artifacts (design models, documentation, code, etc.) are in accordance with the guidelines and heuristics dictated by the software architecture. Properly done, documenting how to make architectural tradeoffs and verifying that the artifacts are in compliance will dominate the bulk of the software architect's schedule. It is the time-consuming process execution which frequently overwhelms novice architects and impedes their effectiveness in controlling the architectural consistency throughout a project.

6.3   TEAMWORK

One frustrating aspect of becoming a system architect is realizing that you probably could not build a large software system entirely by yourself in a reasonable time frame. And even if you could, you probably could never convince an organization that allowing you to do so is in its best interest. Therefore, it is nearly inevitable that you will have to interact with a team of individuals in order to design and develop software.

It is difficult to create a well-designed system without an understanding of the domain model which the system supports. The key elements of a well-described domain model follow.

Domain Model Requirements

1. *A discussion of the domain business problem the domain model supports and the context in which it provides meaningful solutions.* The domain business problem should not refer to software constructs but to the objectives of the business and various users of the system. For example, in banking, a business problem would state that a customer uses a bank to save money, write checks against funds in the accounts, borrow funds at an agreed-upon interest rate, and transfer funds between accounts.

2. *A discussion of the domain business objects which comprise the model and the relationships between them.* For example, a banking system would define the types of accounts supported, the relationships between the accounts, the business rules governing account ownership, and how funds may be transferred between accounts.

3. *The business processes which the system either automates or facilitates.* The business process definitions must include the purpose of the process, the specific inputs and outputs of the business process, and any records or side effects produced. For example, it may not be possible for the system to perform a higher-level task such as analysis. However, it may facilitate analysis by executing algorithms, which are a single step in the analysis, and presenting the intermediate results to the analyst. Defining the concrete steps and decision points by which an analyst performs the business function of analysis allows a design to accommodate automation without depriving the user of the control and configuration needed to achieve the desired results.

4. *A discussion of the various roles which the system supports and how the roles are acquired and released in various scenarios.* Each role should be clearly defined with a concrete and limited set of responsibilities. For example, a bank may define the roles of teller, office manager, loan officer, and customer. Even if the customer may want the appearance of creating a new account, the domain model may require the system to play the role of a teller or office manager in order to complete the transaction rather than have the customer assume a new role.

5. *A discussion of the various ways information is organized in a domain.* For example, in banking there may be an employee organization starting with the board of trustees and bank president and ending with the security guards. Another organization may be the staffing arrangement on a typical day with M number of tellers, N number of guards, X number of account managers, etc. Yet another way to classify the organization may be with respect to signature authority. Having information about the various classification schemes used in the domain provides a basis for later

abstractions. Frequently, the abstractions are frozen prematurely, and the precise domain classifications, which justify the design abstractions and modularization of functionality, are lost.

An important role of software architects on a team is to ensure that the highest-quality software can be delivered within a certain set of constraints. Even in the face of intense time constraints, the role of an architect includes an awareness that compromising too much on software quality will eventually extend the time to delivery rather than shorten it. Knowing your role on a development team is essential, both for maintaining personal focus, for team confidence, and for demanding essential concessions (time, tools, expertise) from other stakeholders who may possess different agendas, for example, marketing departments, human resources, etc.

Unfortunately, the word *quality* has become greatly abused throughout corporate America, and especially in the software development industry. For an emerging architect, leading a team in developing software, quality involves adhering to basic principles. A key principle is to avoid rework of existing code. This is most effective when a second principle is followed: strive to reduce the amount of code required overall to accomplish the system objectives. For any two designs which accomplish identical functionality, the minimal design which leads to the simplest implementation is preferable. This does not mean the simplest design is always preferable, as frequently a small design means the problem has been overabstracted and a large amount of significant implementation details are undocumented. Obtaining a feel for the complexity of the implementation is crucial to really understanding the true simplicity of a proposed solution.

Just as the software architect has a well-defined role on a development team, there are a few other roles which must be satisfied by individuals other than the software architect. A project manager is necessary to fulfill the vital and time-consuming tasks of tracking the progress of the development effort and providing updates, both to the higher-level stakeholders and to the development team who evaluate progress against their predetermined goals. As new information arrives which affects the schedule, the project manager solicits information for replanning and updates the involved parties. Additionally, there will be team members who will be responsible for executing one or more individual software processes. For example, there may be a build manager who ensures that configuration management is actively used and that the software can be built regularly. Someone else may be responsible for code versions or bringing new team members up to speed and arranging mentors. A requirements analyst may be tasked with ensuring that design and implementation tasks and deliverables are traceable back to stated or derived requirements.

Under some rare circumstances, an architect is given the opportunity to assemble a new development team from scratch. When this occurs, recognize and appreciate what a rare opportunity you possess and resolve to make the most of it. Although team formation is usually a management function, the architect often plays an influential role. Obtain a big-picture view of what the project entails and identify the processes and skill sets required to be successful. Don't allow the team to become too unbalanced in a specific skill. For example, most software applications require fairly sophisticated interactive user interfaces, which may be difficult to achieve with a team of relational database experts. A good mix is desired not only for their ability to perform their specialty but more importantly to provide a unique viewpoint and to educate fellow team members about the benefits and limitations of their technical areas. In choosing the size for a team, keep it small. If the work requires a team of more than 5 people, create subteams, with the understanding that the subteam structure exists primarily to make communication manageable. Enforce this by ensuring that team leader selection is based on their ability to effectively communicate with team members and the architect, rather than on purely technical skills or experience.

Even in the case where the architect is assigned to a team, the same guidelines on team balance and team size apply. It does not matter how many people a team has if the right mix of skills and experience is not already present on the team. In the past, training and time allocated to get team members up to speed on a particular skill set was sufficient. However, with the radical decrease in development cycle times, many companies hire people having the skills demanded by a particular project, either as new employees or consultants, rather than train existing staff. In such cases, failure to utilize the new employee or consultant as a mentor to existing employees with different skill sets is a common mistake.

Once the membership of a team is established and the development process begins, the architect must immediately decide and communicate how design and implementation tradeoffs will be made and what is the intended quality level of the software. This must be decided carefully, as it is difficult and expensive to change either of these after the project kickoff. Often, some architectural planning is useful, before team formation, in order to guide these decisions. If performance is a top priority, then the architect should make it clear that all design and code are expected to maximize performance over space, maintenance, and robustness. In effect, the architect should define the design force priorities for the team. Concepts such as design by contract and caching should be reviewed and their existence validated in design and code reviews as well as reflected in the test plans. If quality is a high priority, then more time needs to be allocated to review and test processes. These tradeoffs must be documented explicitly for the team. Ideally the guidance would be broken down into specific design and implementation heuristics for individual developers to follow.

Starting from the project kickoff, the architect should maintain a continuous flow of information to team members. If design by contract is used, circulate articles about its effectiveness and how other people coped with its disadvantages. If developing a product, provide information about comparable products or off-the-shelf solutions which may help shorten development time. If you hear that someone is struggling with a particular design, stop by for a chat and lend him Arthur Riel's design heuristics book, for example [Riel 96]. The architect cannot be effective by walking around and talking all the time (i.e., hallway management) or by hiding in an office and waiting to be called upon. Rather, his role is to provide technical guidance, receive technical feedback (including project deliverables), and ensure that all team members have whatever information they need to be successful, from both internal and external information sources.

A key part of the architect's role is to maintain a continuous interest in all parts of the project. Early in a software project, everyone's interest is high, as there are a lot of possibilities. If the process is successful, decisions will be made which constrain the possibilities, and as parts of the system begin to get implemented, real-world problems are encountered affecting schedule, performance, and resource constraints. It is typical to see interest in any effort decrease once it is actually under way. However, in the early stages, the architect is identified as the key person who understands and decides technical matters, At a high level, the actions of the architect and fellow team members are seen as potentially affecting all aspects of the system. As the system is further decomposed, some problems become more interesting than others to the architect, either due to their complexity or because they coincide with the technical areas of personal interest. If the architect constantly spends time on the areas of most personal interest, team members will feel their own areas are viewed as less important. If these feelings persist, team members in a particular subarea will tend to psychologically distance themselves from the team as a whole. They will feel the architect and other team members do not respect their work and will tend to focus solely on their tasks, independent of the concerns of the system as a whole. The architect can prevent this by making a constant effort to allocate time to all areas and to ask questions and probe into the technical challenges in all aspects of the system. In addition to maintaining the morale of all the subteams, frequently the knowledge gained provides a better holistic view of the system and opportunities for synergy which would not otherwise be apparent. Furthermore, the architect is setting an example of the kind of cross fertilization high-performance teams demand. When possible, have regular meetings where all team leaders are allowed to voice concerns and get feedback on looming technical challenges. Ensure that everyone fully understands how each subgroup contributes to the overall project objectives. Be prepared to ask specific questions to draw out crucial status information, if subteam leaders are reluctant or decline to provide sufficiently detailed information.

In most projects, there are a few critical dependencies whose prompt completion is essential for other tasks to proceed. As an architect, frequently one or more of these tasks are either already on your desk or well on their way to your desk. It is vitally important that critical dependencies are recognized and that steps are taken to minimize the external factors which hinder their completion. Frequently, such tasks include senior developers who are also solicited to mentor other less experienced developers. Working with the project manager, the architect must intervene to protect people working on critical tasks by temporarily suspending or reassigning routine responsibilities and to ensure that enough quality time is spent bringing critical tasks to completion. Few things are as detrimental to a schedule as having several teams unable to proceed because they need the results of a team that is behind schedule, especially when the slippage occurs from doing important work, but not work as important as removing the dependency.

Most software development teams work best with a flexible work environment. Most professionals in the industry are honest enough that, given a chance to arrive later at work by an hour or two when no morning meetings are scheduled, they will diligently work the same amount of time or more later to compensate. However, this is not always the case, and major team morale problems arise when benefits such as flexible work hours are abused. No leader, architect, or manager should tolerate repeated and blatant abuse of flexible work policies. If someone claims to work excessive time in the evenings, then it is reasonable to expect tangible results from the time spent, especially given the lower frequency of interruptions and office distractions. The team members should be judged on their results, and when the results do not measure up to the expectations of the team, either the project manager or the architect is responsible for finding out why and ensuring that a cooperative team environment is maintained.

EXPLAINING INCREMENTAL DEVELOPMENT
TO UPPER MANAGEMENT

Upper Management to Software Architect: "Hey, these UML diagrams look different than the ones three months ago. Why do you keep changing your architecture?"

If you are doing your job as an architect well, eventually one or more of the stakeholders will confront you with the above statement. Keep calm; don't panic. There are a few common misconceptions you need to quickly dispel in order to resolve this situation. First, there is an industry confusion about the difference between software design and architecture. In order to clarify the distinction in the minds of people having various, and frequently less intensive, technical backgrounds, the following real-world analogy is recommended:

"Say, do you know what Gothic architecture is? You know, with the medieval cathedrals and intricate designs and all. What about Ionic architecture, like the Romans used to build the Pantheon? You know, buildings with the rows of columns and fancy murals. What about modern architecture, with the rectangular shaped buildings and windowpanes and so on? Well, just because you have a building's architecture, it doesn't mean you have its blueprints. You still have to decide for each and every building how many rooms are needed, what their dimensions are, where the doors are, and a thousand other critical details.

"The architecture may tell you that if you need to support a ceiling, you do it according to a particular set of guidelines. It does not tell you the precise amount of support required or where to put the light switches. A building can be built an infinite number of ways using the same architecture. Similarly, software architecture does not provide a set of design blueprints. Working with a particular software architecture will still require incremental design and development.

"As more is known about the problem space and as new functional or derived requirements are discovered, it is okay that designs evolve to handle new classes or problems. However, that does not mean that the architecture is changing. In fact, it is the presence of a good software architecture which allows individual designs to change without causing cascading changes throughout the system. So rather than view the changes in individual designs as a weakness in the architecture, we either fix the processes which allow the new requirements to be introduced in the course of actual implementation or address how a particular subsystem was designed, rather than architected."

6.4 CONCLUSIONS

In this chapter we have introduced a lightweight component-oriented development process which is suitable for most organizations and projects. Given that an ideal team size is 4 developers working for 3 months, this sort of process compares favorably with heavyweight approaches introduced elsewhere in this book, such as RM-ODP and the Zachman Framework.

It is important to note that good software architects are very pragmatic. Our goal is to produce a working software system that satisfies stakeholder needs. We are not in the business of creating piles of papers or mind-numbingly extensive requirements specifications. We recommend what's necessary and prudent to achieve the result, avoiding unnecessary make-work whenever possible.

We usually favor lightweight approaches over heavyweight ones, but we are cognizant of each approach, and its strengths and weaknesses. And we are equally capable of fulfilling the system needs, regardless of methodology. We skip unnecessary steps, bypass irrelevant viewpoints, and add those viewpoints and techniques that are appropriate, even if they go beyond the scope of a particular framework.

6.5 EXERCISES

EXERCISE 6.1 Define a code review process for a small development team with an approximately equal mix of experienced and inexperienced software developers. Follow the process template.

BACKGROUND FOR SOLUTION: Here is one possible solution for a code review for a small development team.

SMALLCORP SOFTWARE INSPECTION PROCESS

PROCESS RATIONALE: There are several issues in the current software development process which could be mitigated by regular code reviews. Currently, the software is sometimes unable to satisfy all use cases or provide all of the functionality its interface would suggest. There has been a lack of reuse of client access code, which creates several unnecessary maintenance points for code of sometimes significant complexity. The actual naming and coding standards differ from the corporate coding standards. Frequently, the software contains several defects which are not discovered until integration or, in some cases, deployment. Additionally, maintaining code has been difficult when people leave due to a lack of comments and esoteric coding practices. For example, people introduce third-party libraries to solve a particular problem without telling anyone or even documenting the vendor source of the library. Regular, systematic code reviews are expected to significantly reduce such incidences.

PROCESS GOALS: The software inspection process has three main goals. The first is to improve software quality. What is meant by "improve software quality?" Improve in relation to what baseline? The baseline is a process with the same timeline, but no inspection process. Thus, the baseline consists of a process with a small amount of additional time for all the other development activities. We expect to improve quality by discovering and correcting inadequate comments, poor design, and errors early in the software life cycle. The second goal is to create and disseminate recommended code solutions for solving specific, recurring technical problems. The third goal is to facilitate maintenance and enhancements by increasing uniformity of software styles.

PROCESS OUTLINE: The software inspection process has three main phases: before the software inspection meeting, during the meeting, and after the meeting.

BEFORE THE MEETING: The inspection process is based on three-person round-robin teams. Figure 6.3 illustrates the concept. Teams can be self-appointed or assigned, but everyone with new code should be on a team, and teams should change membership from one round to the next. Each team member chooses one or more major classes to be inspected and distributes them to each member of the team. Each member reviews the code written by one other member before the meeting starts and brings the annotated code to the meeting for discussion.

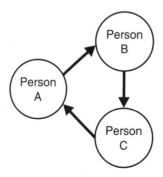

FIGURE 6.3 Three-Person Round-Robin Inspection

A software inspector should look for the following kinds of things. The most obvious are errors such as failing to take account of all cases, dividing by zero, failing to check array bounds, failing to check for null pointers, etc.

Also, make sure that the basic purpose of a class is documented and that complex code, e.g., code involving third-party software such as Objectstore, is explained in comments.

Still another type of comment is just checking that all requirements are met and that the code matches the documented design.

As for software style standards, e.g., indentation and naming, Eidea Labs has adopted Scott Ambler's Java coding standards. All inspectors should be familiar with these standards.

See http://www.ambysoft.com/javaCodingStandards.html for more information.

DURING THE MEETING: Here is an example of how three-person round-robin inspection should work. Suppose that Vick, Christy, and Zhian are on a team. First, the team decides who will review whom. Each reviewee selects some new code that needs review and tells the reviewer where it is. For example, Zhian reviews Vick's code, Vick reviews Christy's code, and Christy reviews Zhian's code. Each team member brings three copies of reviewed code with annotations including suggested improvements and highlighting of possible problems.

The flow of the meeting will look something like this:

> ~40-minute review of Vick's code
> Break
> ~40-minute review of Christy's code
> Break
> ~40-minute review of Zhian's code

Let's keep the meetings from taking forever, and let's prevent review of one person's code from taking up all of the time allocated for the remaining reviews. If time runs out, time runs out. Move on to the next person's code. Take the rest offline.

During the meeting, a reviewer hands out the annotated code. The reviewee narrates his/her code by stepping through one thread of execution in methods of a class, or through an important thread in client code. Both of the other participants ask questions and give suggestions. The reviewer makes sure that all his/her comments are covered. The third person needs to watch the clock! The third person should help to keep the meeting on track, try to resolve disputes, and take notes of cool techniques and sneaky bugs. The group should reach consensus on changes that need to be made to code under review, and the reviewee should record his/her own action items for those changes.

AFTER THE MEETING: The participants of an inspection meeting are expected to produce several deliverables. Of these, software revisions according to the meeting recommendations are the most important. In addition, one person from the review documents the meeting with a note containing at least the following information:

- ► Line of code reviewed
- ► How long the meeting lasted
- ► Number of errors identified (no author data; missing comments not counted)
- ► Recommended solutions to recurring problems (with code samples as appropriate)

A physical file with a copy of all annotated code and the meeting document will be created. The files will be organized by date and the names of all participants. These files will serve two purposes. First, they can be used to verify that participants complete meeting action items. Second, they can be used to establish a longitudinal record for evaluating the benefits of the software inspection process itself.

PROCESS DELIVERABLES: This section provides a simple checklist of all the deliverables produced during the process:

- ► Annotated code (annotations from before and after the meeting) from each participant
- ► Corrected code from each participant
- ► Meeting document
- ► Folder containing all of the above

PROCESS TIMETABLES

SINGLE SOFTWARE INSPECTION TIMETABLE: The timetable for one round of a software inspection process is as follows. Choose a team and pass out code. Allow three or four days between everyone's receiving the code and the meeting. The meeting should take about two hours, as mentioned above. Fixes recommended during the review should be performed immediately. The amount of time required for these fixes depends greatly on their nature. Redesign might take a week, while adding comments may take only an hour. The results note should be written and sent by close of business (COB) the following day.

SOFTWARE INSPECTION CYCLE: From a longer-term perspective, software inspections should take place every two weeks during the implementation phase of the life cycle. After each inspection, each participant will require approximately one day to make changes according to action items and to create the meeting document.

SOFTWARE INSPECTION IN THE SOFTWARE DEVELOPMENT LIFE CYCLE: Where in the overall software development life cycle should the inspection occur? The code should be inspected during unit test and before integration. Once code from multiple authors has been integrated, it is far more labor intensive to isolate and correct errors. By inspecting the code before this phase, we can eliminate many time-consuming integration-phase problems.

REFERENCES: Abstracts of several papers on software inspection are available at these URLs:

http://www/ics.hawaii.edu/~johnson/FTR/Bib/category-metrics.html
http://www.ics.hawaii.edu/~johnson/FTR/Bib/urls.html

SOFTWARE ARCHITECTURE TIP: PRACTICAL MVC USE

In Basic Training you were introduced to the MVC and Observer design patterns. Many of the constructs in the Java language require the implementation of one or more interfaces to use preexisting view components with a particular data model. So what do you do when you have several different views, each of which demands a particular data model interface implementation? See Figure 6.4 for one approach.

Do *not* create a "manager" class to coordinate the disparate models. Such an approach is unwieldy and error-prone. Each data model would possess its own copy of the data, and extensive code would be needed to keep the models in sync. In addition, adding in a new representation would require changing existing methods in order to accommodate the new data model and its classes. Instead, consider the motivation behind the MVC design pattern: "to have a single model which supports multiple views. The view should know about the model but not the other views." With that in mind, Figure 6.5 presents a cleaner, more effective approach.

Here you have a single model which controls all the data needed by the various views. The model has the responsibility of implementing all required interfaces so that they all use the single data set. Each view communicates with the single data model implementation via its expected interface. Each inherited

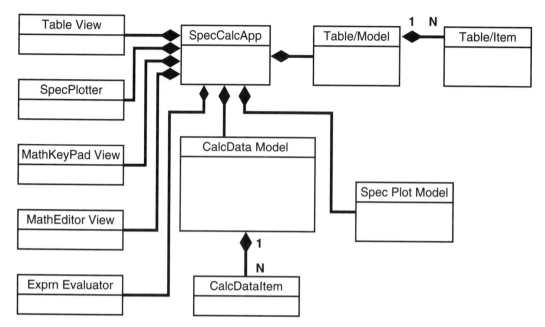

FIGURE 6.4   One Approach to Coordinating Multiple Interfaces and Data Models

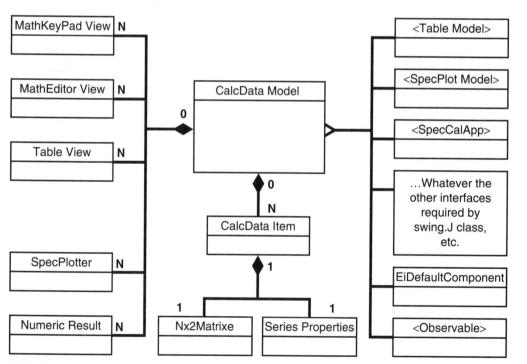

FIGURE 6.5   Integrating Several Data Models and Views Effectively

interface serves as a role for the data contained by the data model. While implementing such a large number of interfaces appears unwieldy, it is an overall better architecture, as it lends itself well to future extension and reduces the overall design complexity.

EXERCISE 6.2 TEAMWORK EXERCISES: For each of the following two scenarios, write a brief analysis of what is motivating the behavior of each character type and what actions can be taken to resolve the situation. Both stereotypes are on a software development team of six people, including an architect and project manager.

"Lone Wolf Developer": Team member has little patience for the overall team goals. Instead he/she insists on being given a well-defined piece to develop in isolation. On previous tasks, he or she has tended to disregard agreed-upon interfaces and has been extremely reluctant to provide detailed designs prior to beginning implementation. Whatever is provided before implementation is always in a state of flux, with most of the documentation being delivered after the implementation is complete.

"Unilateral Consensus": Team member's opinion dominates the group to the point where there are never any dissenting opinions. The team member has technical superiority and a forceful personality. When his/her opinion on an issue is known, other options are no longer considered.

BACKGROUND FOR SOLUTION: "LONE-WOLF DEVELOPER": This person appears to lack a buy-in into the common purpose of the team. His/her actions indicate a shirking of responsibility to the team and no belief in mutual accountability. There is a feeling that success on his or her part is separable from the overall success of the team. Allowing the "lone wolf" to continue destroys the mutual trust between him/her and other team members. Infighting is inevitable when interfaces change without warning, vital documentation is missing, and integration is needlessly delayed by a continually changing codebase.

Regular design and code reviews are essential in ensuring that some communication exists between lone wolves and the rest of the team. By reviewing work products that they have a personal vested interest in, obtaining their attention is assured, and hopefully, constructive "forced" interaction will lead to more regular informal interactions in the future. From the management perspective, the lone-wolf tasks should be scheduled in small increments, ideally no more than three days in length. After each task, they are responsible for documenting their work and integrating with other people who, ideally, work closer to the baseline. Finally, make it clear that proactive communication with team members is the primary determinant of future responsibility. Specifically, an individual should neither spend an inordinate amount of time stuck on a particular problem, nor allow anyone else to spend time on problems whose solution is already known within the team.

"UNILATERAL CONSENSUS":   First, talk to the expert and make it clear how much his or her expertise is valued and considered an asset to the organization. Next, when he or she suggests an idea, ask for the general heuristics which reinforce why the particular approach is superior. Have either the expert or other team members document and consolidate the design heuristics provided. Over time, the heuristics will demystify the decision-making process of the expert and allow team members to reintroduce relevant heuristics in future discussions with the confidence that their suggested approach is at least valid in some circumstances.

Next, change the way meetings are conducted. Create a rule that the opinions of the less-experienced team members are heard first. This results in two desirable outcomes. Less-experienced team members are given a chance to establish ownership of some ideas which will later be validated by the expert and more experienced team members. Or, and admittedly more commonly, the more experienced members are forced to explain the flaws in the suggested approach of less-experienced team members, which helps them learn by starting the discussion in areas they understand rather than the "foreign ground" of the expert. Also, by getting their ideas out first, they are more likely to defend them, which is better than not having an opportunity to suggest them at all.

COMMUNICATIONS TRAINING

The cornerstone of any significantly large venture is communication. In the military, establishing lines of communication between troops is the top priority. Without communication, it is impossible to adequately allocate resources, coordinate efforts, assess progress, or, basically, to conduct war. Similarly, a software team must communicate throughout a software development effort or it simply cannot succeed. A software architect must define what level of communication is required, what form the communication takes, and how to continually assist in improving communication in order to ensure that the development tasks proceed as expected. The architect frequently has to decide which design problems require collaborative brainstorming and which are more suited to a concentrated focus by one or two individuals. Frequently, the specific artifacts of communication among team members which are shared among stakeholders are decided by the architect. Sometimes, notes are a sufficient record of discussions, while at other times formal specifications in UML, IDL, and other forms are required. Finally, every architect should establish feedback mechanisms to ensure that his own technique and approaches are improving and obtaining the desired results.

7.1   COMMUNICATIONS CHALLENGES

Software development is becoming increasingly complicated, requiring the participation of many diverse people with various skill sets. Dealing with the coordination among different groups is an ongoing factor in the military. As such, the military provides a wealth of lessons which are equally applicable to the development of software applications, the most important of which is how multidirectional communication is handled. Since effective communication is required for proper coordination, it can never be considered an optional part of the life of a software professional. Rather, constant verification through proper communication must be a fundamental part of the overall software development process. If it is determined that there is a breakdown, then top priority must be given to re-establishing communications. Facilitation plays a major role in smoothing over various personal conflicts. If necessary, communication may even have to be forced during critical situations.

There is a substantial industry built around aiding developers in the production of software development artifacts. There are tools for coordinating requirements and use cases, tools for developing software design models, and tools for defining software test plans. Each tool has its own strengths and can reduce the time it takes to produce one or more software artifacts. If the goal of software development was the production of such artifacts, they would be worth their kilobytes in gold. However, what sometimes gets lost in a discussion of the merits of the latest tool is how effectively it facilitates communication. After all, while the external deliverable is the software, the internal deliverable is effective communication among team members to ensure everyone is working toward a common goal.

In that context, software artifacts are a necessary, but not sufficient, element of achieving effective communication between software developers. Regardless of the documents being produced, they are of no value unless they are discussed with and understood by the development team. The following two methods will help ensure that development artifacts are not ignored on some distant bookshelf. *First,* all artifacts should be reviewed by a team composed of developers from other teams. This ensures that the other teams are aware of what is being produced throughout the organization and are on the same page in regard to architectural principles, design heuristics, and coding standards. Once the final review is complete, the final document is disseminated to all reviewers. *Second,* all designs produced are submitted to all team leaders who are expected to be familiar with their contents. When issues arise which are answered in the design documents, the architect should bring it to their attention and continually remind team leaders to stay on top of the designs of other groups. While it may be frustrating to know that few of the team leaders are following through and truly staying current with all of the designs, over time it will become apparent that better decisions are made on the team level, in part due to a greater awareness of the efforts of other teams. Finally, when topics arise which affect several teams, schedule a meeting with representatives from all affected teams. Either have the issues solved collaboratively, or have an agreement to utilize a solution developed by the first group that is affected by the issues. For example, if a new requirement arises that all system logs should be exported in an XML format, the first group which needs to produce a log will present a standard XML DTD which will be used by the other teams for storing and viewing logging information.

7.2   RESPONSIBILITY–DRIVEN DEVELOPMENT

The design process requires special discussion in order to promote responsibility-driven design and development. Responsibility-driven design requires that subsystems and components are identified and designed based on their functional responsibilities. Each subsystem or component has a set of responsibilities which is orthogonal to every other subsystem or component in the system. If a particular responsibility which already exists is required by a new subsystem or component, the new component delegates the task to an existing instance of the component or subsystem. This technique maximizes reuse and redundancy at the expense of the typically small performance overhead of delegation. While responsibility-driven development is already popular in many object-oriented software development organizations, it will likely grow even further in popularity with the advent of components and component-oriented development, which already rely upon delegation for composing new components from existing components.

One of the design deliverables in a software development effort is the creation of a software specification for one or more subsystems. In specification writing, it is important to differentiate between the documentation of an interface and the documentation of the implementation. Since the interface may be relied upon by other subsystems, it is expected that its specification will be less likely to change than classes utilized completely within an encapsulated subsystem.

For software development where developers are not able to remain in constant close contact, design documents should be more akin to a specification, a more rigorous description of a software design than those provided by some methodologies. A design specification should clearly differentiate between the interface between subsystems and components versus the parts which make up the internal implementation of one or more subsystems. The purpose of a specification is to reduce, if not completely eliminate, the effect of multiple interpretations of a design. If every design consistently defined every subsystem to a sufficiently low level of detail, documenting each subsystem by describing the semantics of every class, method, parameter, and data structure, then there would be no need to have a specification, as such a design would be sufficient to resolve any ambiguity. However, in practice, designs often vary in their quality, and the introduction of a specification makes explicit the areas where detail is absolutely essential—the interfaces exposed to other subsystems. Generally, it is exceptionally beneficial to describe these interfaces in an interface specification language, such as OMG IDL.

Having a design specification makes it easier for the architect, as there are several heuristics which can be applied to assess whether certain tradeoffs are made appropriately. For example, the introduction of several user-defined data types indicates a tighter coupling between the subsystem and its clients than if more simple or systemwide data types were used. Frequently, an architect will need to communicate ideas to parts of a development team, and a presentation is deemed to be better suited to the time constraints than conveying the same information through individual mentoring. While a presentation is useful for disseminating quick and dirty guidance, it tends to be rather useless if not supplemented with more substantial material over time. Specifically, guidance given in presentation form without being tied to hands-on mentoring can do more harm than good, as developers gain no additional skills and are demoralized at not meeting a higher level of productivity. An architect should always make clear to project stakeholders what presentations are *not* effective at conveying, and she should emphasize the need to support in-depth studying from academic texts. Even more important are industry white papers, which are frequently an excellent means of learning lower-level architectural details of emerging technologies.

7.3   COMMUNICATION RESPONSIBILITIES

One of the duties of a software architect is to serve as the spokesperson of the development team on technical matters. As such, the architect will frequently need to prepare and present briefings to upper management and other stakeholders. Furthermore, briefings are usually faster to create than white papers and are a good preparatory vehicle for outlining the key concepts for future papers. In order to be effective in creating and presenting briefings, the use of a few straightforward techniques can increase the odds of success.

As a technical person, there is always a tendency to convey too much information on a technical topic. Upper-level management frequently is interested only in conclusions—summary information. Also, other technical people can already figure out the details, once the basic idea has been successfully conveyed. First-time technical presenters nearly always cram much more detail and information onto charts than the briefing-chart medium can effectively handle.

In a military campaign, it is essential that information is appropriately updated as the situation changes. This includes the verification that targets were successfully incapacitated, the position and direction of mobile units, and the additional defensive capabilities acquired by the enemy since the last time they were directly observed. Every commander knows that viewed information is immediately obsolete, as several of the campaign elements are constantly in flux. Similarly, on any software project, the status of a development team is also changing. Initial assumptions about time lines, task complexity, and resources will need to take advantage of new information throughout a project's life cycle. While project management will be responsible for the replanning of the current project plan, the architect should wisely be utilizing feedback to alter his technical approach to the project. The issues of when to get feedback, how to get it, and what to do with it once you have it will be addressed in considerable detail.

In some respects, acquiring feedback should be a continual part of the architect's daily responsibilities. It has already been mentioned that in a walkthrough, the architect should be listening for details which reflect how the project is progressing and what obstacles are occupying the most resources. Furthermore, where time permits, cross-team reviews of deliverables should be a part of every development process. Still, there are a few milestones which provide special opportunities to extract useful feedback.

7.4   HANDLING FEEDBACK

There is definitely a positive benefit just in the solicitation of feedback from developers. However, unless there is evidence that provided feedback is utilized to improve process and organizational issues, the development team will quickly become disillusioned and much more reluctant to comment on development activities. Therefore, a plan to make the most of feedback is vitally important to have in place in conjunction with obtaining feedback. Feedback is generally less useful in evaluating the current performance of an organization than in developing a strategy for future improvements in process and team building.

Admittedly, not all feedback should be acted upon. In the highly stressful software industry it is common for a certain amount of venting to take place. For example, if a deadline slipped, there will always be a tendency for a few team members to look to place blame (perhaps rightly so) on particular individuals. In such cases, feedback provides an understanding ear to people who have an appropriate sense of urgency in meeting the agreed-upon milestones by a particular date. However, rather than deal with specific instances—often well after the time when action can be taken to resolve the situation—look toward long-term patterns in people's actions and short-term steps in process improvements.

An important realization in dealing with people on a development team is that you cannot actually change the people you are working with. You can encourage them, flatter them, and negotiate with them; however, ultimately they bear the responsibility for being productive members of a development team. This is true regardless of whether you directly supervise them, share the same level of supervision, or are in a lesser position of authority. However, to be effective you can change yourself, how you deal with people, and how you react to people. First and foremost, a software architect should lead by example and demonstrate the qualities he expects others in the team to share. This includes acknowledging that you respect that people are trying to accomplish the same goals as you are, even if their methods are different. It may take time to listen effectively to gain an understanding of the underlying reasons for a person's behavior. As an architect, it is important to accept responsibility for the efforts of everyone on the team. If the goal is shared by everyone on the team, it is illogical not to accept shared responsibility when various problems arise. Different organizations provide the software architect with varying degrees of authority in working with software developers. When you have greater authority as an architect, you can be even more effective by making the decisions which no one else on the development team is empowered to make.

7.5   EXERCISES

EXERCISE 7.1   To facilitate brainstorming, the "spitwad technique" is a practical, proven method to generate ideas. The facilitator first passes around identical slips of blank paper. The facilitator then reviews the discussion topic and purpose of the brainstorming session. Next, everyone is requested to write down his or her ideas on one or more slips of paper. Each slip of paper should contain a single idea which is relevant to the discussion topic. Every idea should be complete and self-contained, requiring no additional information or explanation. Each idea is wadded up into a ball and tossed into a wastebasket, a box, or, in a pinch, a corner of the room. Ideally, the end result will be a pile of indistinguishable wads of paper. The entire process should take about five minutes.

When everyone has finished, pass around the wads of paper evenly throughout the group. Go around the room and have each person read his or her wads of paper aloud. After hearing all of the ideas, gather suggestions for categories to group the various ideas into. For each category for which there is a general consensus, have someone create a tagboard and tape it to the wall. Next, have the group tape their paper wads to the tagboards under the appropriate category. Every wad should be attached to a category, including duplicates and even ideas which may seem initially to be inappropriate or already part of the existing situation. Finally, the facilitator should proceed to each category and lead a discussion about each of the topics. Participants can provide additional ideas or expand upon existing ideas.

The notes from the discussion should be preserved and distributed to the meeting participants. The information gained from the spitwad brainstorming activity can be utilized in a future meeting devoted to evaluating the ideas and making decisions about appropriate actions to take. The advantage of the spitwad approach is that ideas are submitted anonymously, which allows participants to submit ideas without fear of being judged and being held personally accountable for the merit of their ideas. Therefore, they are more likely to contribute whatever knowledge they have on the discussion topic.

SOFTWARE ARCHITECTURE: INTELLIGENCE OPERATIONS

Intelligence operations are knowledge-gathering procedures. Intelligence operations go beyond basic data collection (assembling uncorrelated information) to the point of collecting fully assimilated practical knowledge—knowledge that affects important architectural decisions.

Gathering knowledge is an essential element of being a software architect. Ordinary knowledge gathering for a project comprises end-user requirements capture and perhaps some commercial product evaluation. We believe that proper architectural practices go well beyond these project-centric traditions, which we consider to be *isolationist* when used exclusively.

Instead, we would augment these practices with some additional procedures which we have found to be effective, including *architecture mining*, *architecture iteration*, and *architectural judgment*. In this chapter we define specific meanings for these phrases as we explain their intelligence-gathering potential.

Architecture mining is a practice that breaches classic intelligence barriers between projects. It can have an intelligence scope as large as an entire industry, or as small as one company's systems. Architecture mining is a conscious effort to eliminate the *ignorance of silence* that characterizes many system developments.

Architecture iteration is a process focused upon a single architecture or specification. It tracks the architecture through its development and life cycle, improving quality through intelligence gathering on each project.

Architectural judgment is a process of decision making, based upon intelligence gathering. Making quality decisions is at the very heart of being an architect. In today's changing world of technology, it is increasingly difficult to make long-lasting judgments without a systematic process.

8.1   ARCHITECTURE MINING

Architecture mining is rapid intelligence gathering for making better decisions. Its benefit is intelligence amplification; it makes the architect appear smarter and more experienced.

Architecture mining should be fast and effective, or it should not be pursued. The industry changes too quickly for any procedure to be effective which takes more than a few days, weeks, or months, depending upon the scope of the decision. Architecture, in its role as a *planning* discipline, should reduce timelines and make software development more effective and efficient. We make this point here because architecture mining has the potential for becoming a career-length activity, instead of a short-turnaround intelligence amplification.

Top Down and Bottom Up

In a top-down design approach, abstract concepts are progressively transformed to concrete designs and implementations. The highest level of abstract design might be the system vision or its initial requirements document. In a bottom-up approach, a new design would be created from fundamental programs or parts. Bottom-up design can be very productive when it involves incremental change or reuse from existing designs.

We contrast top-down and bottom-up with up-front and after-the-fact. An up-front approach would generate plans for designs before implementation commences. In an after-the-fact approach, the project would document designs based upon the as-built configuration.

In general, we consider software architecture to be initiated as an up-front approach. Architecture embodies a system plan that enables estimation and efficient system construction. Ideally, architecture is configured through a bottom-up approach called architecture mining.

Interestingly, object-oriented approaches usually define architecture after-the-fact, as an outcome of the detailed design process, whereas the recommended approach would create architecture as an input to detailed design.

Architecture Farming

Most software design approaches assume that design information is invented as the process proceeds. In a top-down process, design information is generated from requirements, which may be represented as software analysis models. Requirements-driven architecture design is called *architecture farming*. In a spiral process, design information is invented during each iteration. As the spiral process proceeds, architects invent new design information as they learn more about the application problem. It is fair to say that these approaches *reinvent* much of their design information.

Precursor designs exist for most information systems applications and problems. These designs are in the form of legacy systems, commercial products, standards, prototypes, and design patterns. In my experience, it is not difficult to identify a half-dozen or more precursor designs for any given application problem. Valuable information is buried in preexisting designs—information that allowed earlier architects to build useful systems. Extracting this information for use in software architectures is called *architecture mining*.

Architecture Mining Process

Architecture mining is a bottom-up design approach. It exploits historical design and implementation experience to create new software architectures. Because we are relying on successful previous designs, there is substantial risk reduction. The challenge of software architecture mining is to discover, extract, and refine the nuggets of design knowledge. Because there is often a great deal of implementation detail to review, the process is analogous to mining the earth for precious metals.

Mining is a bottom-up design approach, incorporating design knowledge from working implementations. Mining can incorporate design input from top-down design processes, too, so that there can be both top-down traceability and bottom-up realism.

Before mining starts, it is necessary to identify a set of representative technologies that are relevant to the design problem. Technology identification can be done by various means, such as searching literature, interviewing experts, attending technical conferences, and surfing the net. All available resources should be pursued.

The first mining step is to model each representative technology. Technology modeling produces specifications of relevant software interfaces. I recommend using OMG IDL as the interface notation because it is concise and free from implementation detail. OMG IDL is also a good design notation for the target architecture because it is language independent, platform neutral, and distribution transparent. By modeling everything in the same notation, we create a good basis for design comparison and tradeoff.

In the modeling step, it is important to describe the as-built system, not the intended or desired design. Frequently, relevant design information is not documented as software interfaces. For example, some of the sought-after functionality only may be accessible through the user interface. Other key design lessons may be undocumented. It is useful to capture this design information, too.

In the second step, the mined designs are generalized to create a common interface specification. This step entails more art than science, more architectural intuition than meticulous engineering. The goal is to create an initial strawman specification for the target architecture interfaces. It is usually not sufficient to generate a lowest-common-denominator design from the representative technology. The generalized interfaces should resemble a best-of-breed solution that captures the common functionality as well as some unique aspects inspired by particular systems. Unique aspects should be included when they create valuable features in the target architecture or represent areas of known system evolution. A robust assortment of representative technologies will contain indicators of likely areas of target system evolution.

At this point it is appropriate to factor in the top-down design information as one of the inputs. Top-down information is usually at a much higher level of abstraction than bottom-up information. Reconciliation of these differences involves some important architecture tradeoffs.

The final step in the mining process is to refine the design. Refinements can be driven by the architect's judgment, informal walkthroughs, review processes, new requirements, or additional mining studies.

Applicability of Mining

Mining can be a fast, inexpensive process that yields significant benefits in risk reduction and architecture quality. The real product of mining is the edification of the software architect. With a mature understanding of the problem and previous solutions, the software architect is well prepared to make good architectural decisions.

Other mining artifacts include the OMG IDL interface models, but they should not be treated as formal deliverables. These artifacts are simply design notes used in the creative process that produce good architecture.

I believe that mining should be done for most high-quality reusable designs. It is not necessary to do mining for all designs in a system, especially the ones that impact only a small number of developers or subsystems. It is appropriate to consider mining for high-risk or widely used interfaces that impact significant aspects of the system or enterprise.

Given the right documentation and access to expertise, architecture mining can be done very rapidly. In our experience, most mining studies can be completed within a few days for each representative technology. After several mining studies, it is possible to undertake significant designs with confidence.

Mining for Success

How does a software architect gain sufficient knowledge to design and defend a good architecture? Knowledge can come from years of experience of designing similar architectures. Alternatively, the learning process can be greatly accelerated by explicit mining of design knowledge from existing technologies and experts.

In our observation, most software architectures are designed in a vacuum. It is easy to ignore or reject preexisting designs when confronted by a new design problem, but there are serious consequences. "Design-in-a-vacuum" invariably produces immature, custom designs with minimal potential for reuse, interoperability, and adaptability. Because technology transfer between multiple systems rarely occurs in practice, the positive effects of software architecture mining can be quite dramatic.

Horizontal versus Vertical

It is essential to understand the subtle differences between horizontal and vertical design elements. In particular, we refer to aspects of a software interface design at a system level. At this scale of design, we are interested in managing complexity and change effectively. Designs must be flexible, but simple and reusable, if at all possible.

An important goal of architectural design is to have a well-thought-out balance between horizontal and vertical elements. When we say *horizontal* and *vertical,* it often confuses people, because these essential design extremes are unfamiliar concepts to most programmers. When referring to these extremes, we are talking about a continuum of design choices, which vary in flexibility and reusability (on the horizontal extreme) with its ability to solve the point-design solution (on the vertical extreme).

When we say *vertical* design, we mean designs that are unique to one software implementation, unique to one system, or unique to one set of application requirements. Vertical designs are the norm. It is likely that most of the designs that you have ever created or encountered (except for vendor APIs) are decidedly vertical. And people wonder why software reuse is so difficult to achieve in practice?

What makes a design vertical is the presence of specialized details which are hard-coded into the solution. It is well known that attribute names and schemas are application specific and vary over time in an application-dependent way. If these attributes are hard-coded into the system APIs, then we have a vertical API. Other examples include APIs that specify very specialized functions, or contain uniquely constrained sets of parameters.

As programmers, we favor vertical designs because they resolve the current design problem in an obvious way. We have certain attributes and operations to implement, and we code them in a straightforward and direct way. Why should we do it any differently?

As architects, we are concerned with additional design forces which have longer-term impact. From experience, we know that requirements change frequently. We know that certain ways of designing can support change more flexibly than other ways of designing. We could do a rational approach to change management that lists the likely sources of change and their design impacts. One such approach is called the Software Architecture Assessment Method [Bass 98]. These methods address coarse-grain issues of change. But as architects, we can make hundreds of fine-grain decisions that accommodate for change, as we proceed with design. The rationale for these fine-grain decisions could be called our architectural intuition (or the *art* of architecting). However, we also want to balance our quest for flexibility with practicality.

CAN A DESIGN BE TOO FLEXIBLE?

In a nutshell, YES. It's easy to make designs that are too flexible for their own good. Proper architecting is all about common sense and balanced design. When designing system-level interfaces, we certainly don't want to hard-code vertical design details that we expect to change overnight. On the other hand, we certainly don't want to propose a design so flexible that it has flexibility disease. The potential consequences of making a design too flexible include:

▶ *Inefficiency.* Highly flexible designs require extra runtime processing on both sides of an interface. For example, parameter encodings for flexibility may require application-programmed translations from native types to dynamic self-identifying types. In a distributed system, additional marshalling time may be required for dynamic parameters. These inefficiencies can lengthen interface processing latencies by two orders of magnitude or more. Inefficiency will be the most frequent complaint that you encounter when attempting to insert some architecture qualities into a design. In most cases, you should resist this argument. Over-optimization is a source of many unnecessary architectural compromises.

▶ *Lack of Understandability.* Another thing you will notice when the designs are too flexible is that your developers won't understand the flexible features. Some developers will tell you this directly; others will ask questions (that you will have a hard time answering). But the most dangerous response is when developers don't understand, yet go ahead and make assumptions and use the features in ways that you had not intended. We view lack of understandability as a primary limiting force on design flexibility. You should make your designs flexible, but only up to the practical limit of how easy to understand the designs will be for your developers. That includes the likelihood of developers misusing the designs due to lack of understanding (which is also a failure to communicate on your part as the architect).

▶ *Extra Coding.* Flexible designs do require extra software on both sides of the flexible interface. If you look at this extra code, you will notice that it often hard-codes exactly what you had intended to make flexible in your design. For example, passing a set of dynamic attributes could be hard-coded as a fixed set of attributes for each usage of the interface. This situation is normal, since some part of the implementation must do data- handling operations; hard-coding is the most direct way to do it. The benefit of flexibility is that the attribute set is not hard-coded into the architecture, and attribute sets may vary without architectural modifications.

▶ *Extra Documented Conventions.* A key price of flexibility is the need to constrain usage through conventions. Without usage constraints it is often impossible to achieve interoperability between implementations, no matter how carefully specified the interface is. A design may be too flexible when the usage conventions become cumbersome or may even outweigh the original specification. There is an important design balance in trading off implementation details between hard-coded architecture and usage conventions.

A vertical design often has many potentially negative consequences. Vertical elements are tied to application-specific requirements. And we know that requirements are always subject to change or reinterpretation. Vertical designs are unique to one implementation and embody the antithesis of reusability. Vertical designs are often complex, containing many application-specific details. In that sense, it is difficult to manage complexity effectively in a vertical design.

Horizontal Design Elements

Horizontal design represents the common requirements from more than one application. One way to describe horizontal design is that it is the design that remains after the vertical elements are removed or refactored. The elimination of the vertical design elements is an explicit intellectual exercise practiced by software architects. If you take a design and remove or refactor vertical elements into horizontal elements, then the remaining design often addresses the needs of multiple applications; hence it is horizontal by definition.

One formalized approach to vertical design elimination is called *domain engineering*. Domain engineering is the systematic management of reusability. It starts with domain analysis. Typically, domain analysis begins with a set of application requirements [Rogers 97]. The requirements are sorted into groups representing various application functions. Functions that are judged more horizontal (e.g., common to multiple applications) are selected for rewriting. These requirements are rewritten iteratively to remove application-specificity, while still retaining their domain functionality. The rewritten requirements are checked with domain experts to ensure that they retain their value to the domain.

Software design begins after the requirements are domain-analyzed. The horizontal requirements are used to define software interfaces in an application-independent manner. Several software authorities claim that domain analysis helps programmers to design much higher-quality interfaces [Rogers 97] [Coplien 99]—in particular, much more adaptable and reusable, and subjectively better structured.

We believe this observation is due much more to the experiential process than to the artifacts. The process of domain analysis not only yields the deliverable of horizontal requirements, it also gives the software designer new insight and perspective about the design problem. This new knowledge is an invaluable resource for creating high-quality designs.

It is important to note that domain analysis is an *exercise* that helps designers differentiate between horizontal and vertical design elements in a given problem domain. Another such exercise is architecture mining. In both cases, the knowledge gained by the analyst is more important to the design process than the artifacts (e.g., documents) generated by the domain analysis or architecture mining process.

Good horizontal designs meet the requirements of multiple applications. Logically that should be very hard to achieve in practice. However, in a perverse sense, horizontal design is easier to do than vertical design. In a famous result from a mathematics educator, George Polya claims that solving more difficult, generalized problems is often easier than solving specific problems (i.e., solving vertical specializations) [Polya 71]. In other words, solving a more general (harder) problem is often easier in practice. This result is called Polya's Paradox. We believe that this result applies to software design, as well.

One reason why Polya's Paradox works is that specialized problems are often overwhelmed by details. Because a specialized problem refers to one concrete instance, we can extract as much detail as desired from the real-world situation. This excess information itself becomes a problem for the designer. In the more generalized problem, we are freed from addressing the details of any single situation, except as an example from which we can easily discriminate the relevant and irrelevant details.

In the abstract world of the generalized problem, we can define the solution structure in a most advantageous way. This new solution structure is relatively easy to formulate at the abstract level, unburdened by details. When we apply this solution to specific cases, the generalized solution defines the underlying principles for the specialized solution. And we can resolve any similar specific problem with these same principles. In effect, we have defined a reusable solution.

In software, the situation is often not so clearcut. It is possible to have mixtures of horizontal and vertical solutions. Whether we have a good or bad structure depends upon how these elements are intertwined. For example, the vertical qualities of an API are not diminished if it contains intermixed horizontal design elements. In fact, intermixing of vertical and horizontal design elements is the norm, and the design problem for the architect or programmer is to separate these elements from each other. If horizontal design elements are properly separated (for example, in a separate interface), then it is possible to intermix these design elements (e.g., through inheritance) in a controlled way that does not compromise the inherent advantages of separation.

In many instances, the differentiation between what is vertical and what is horizontal is an intuitive, subjective judgment. We believe that the ability to distinguish between these extremes is an important and essential ability of software architects. An important design choice (e.g., between horizontal and vertical) for an architect may be invisible or unimportant to programmers on the project. And that's okay. That is one of the reasons why we believe that software architects are different from programmers. The ability to clearly see these distinctions and know why they are important is an important indicator of the architecture instinct.

What about Traceability?

Internal and external designs are different views of the system. It is relatively easy to prove traceability for vertical designs, because the details correlate closely with external requirements. As we refactor a design into its horizontal form, the traceability becomes less obvious. A horizontal design (of an interface architecture) represents the internal structure of a software system. The internal structure is different and separate from the external requirements. The relationship between the two can be shown only indirectly, at best. When a design comprises horizontal elements, the dichotomy between internal and external views can be extreme.

One approach to show how the internal design supports the external requirements is through scenarios. Each scenario is the performance of an externally significant function, expressed as a thread of execution through multiple layers of the system. In effect, the internal design is exercised in direct response to the execution of an externally meaningful function. Typically, each horizontal design element will be involved in multiple scenarios, indicating that the design is traceable to many external requirements, but not any individual requirement that solely justifies its design.

Designing for Future Applications

Horizontal designs resolve problems across a range of applications. For a horizontal design to be effective, it must meet the potentially conflicting requirements of several independent applications. The horizontal design must satisfy not only current application needs, but also future application needs whose requirements have yet to be specified. But how can we address future, unknown requirements?

The apparent ability to predict future features of systems is a strength of the architecture mining approach. This phenomenon is easiest to understand in terms of commercial software, if we consider that in any given commercial software market there are a number of competing products with differentiated features. For example, the software market includes word processing and geographic information systems (GIS).

There is a common functionality across all products in the market, but there are also key differences that make each competitive. For example, one word processor has great layout abilities, and another has great graphics extensions. As the market evolves, each product will tend to be extended in ways that have proven successful in competing product lines.

This same phenomenon of product differentiation occurs much more dramatically in other situations. For example, in geographic information systems, the product differentiation is so successful that most large companies need multiple vendors' GIS systems to meet their needs.

Because information about commercial products is readily available, it is difficult for competitors to hide anything significant about their products. Competitors monitor each other's products and customers to keep in touch with current conditions and future market directions. With custom in-house software systems, information is less readily available.

In our experience with architecture mining, every legacy system implemented some unique and advanced capability that surprised us in comparison with other known systems. Legacy systems within the same functional area have unique capabilities (that was probably why they were developed in the first place), and all of these capabilities are quite different. It was clear that if the legacy owners were aware of all these capabilities, then they would want a new system that embodied most of them. In effect, study of legacy capabilities showed us the future best-of-breed for custom systems.

In a limited sense, a future software system is a best-of-breed display of successful features in current software systems. Of course, we can factor in some untested features supporting novel requirements which may or may not become successful. One can predict, with some success, how future system features will evolve, given a study of system differences today, and how well these product differences are thriving in today's market.

8.2   ARCHITECTURE ITERATION

Architecture iteration relies upon intelligence gathering during a project. Whether, how, and when to change an architecture are some of the most important decisions for a software architect. An architecture is a plan, and it is said that no plan survives first contact with the enemy. The enemies in this case are change and ignorance. As software architects, we want our decisions to be flexible enough to survive changes. But according to Alistair Cockburn, we don't know what we don't know [Cockburn 98]. Ignorance is the more dangerous enemy. What we don't know can change our architectural assumptions to the breaking point. This intelligence operation is intended to defeat these enemies through the preplanned strategy of *architecture iteration.*

Architects can be very insulated from the realities of software development. The most active time for any architect is at the start of a project. During this time, the architect is free to envision the system without much concern for downstream constraints. Early in the project, an enticing vision is often preferable, both to impress the funding sources (e.g., with apparent progress) and to attract potential staff to the project.

We would urge restraint at this stage for several reasons. First, on average, software projects are over budget by 184% by the time of delivery [Johnson 95], and the systems seldom deliver what was expected. Overestimation of what is feasible is one of the most common failings of up-front estimators, among which architects are key participants. Second, it's more important for projects to prove credibility through demonstrated results, rather than paper plans, known in a derogatory sense as "slideware" or "viewgraph engineering" [Brown 98]. It is important to help projects to identify what is feasible for early demonstration and delivery. Rather than to define "the big vision" for what the system could potentially become in an unconstrained-budget environment, it is important to architect for reasonable implementation costs and long life-cycle maintenance.

Software Process Background

The two traditional types of software processes are waterfall and iterative. *Waterfall process* is a sequence of steps, such as "analyze requirements," "design," "code," and "test," which are of long duration and are scheduled only once during the software project. It is widely accepted that waterfall process does not work for software development in most organizations.

Waterfall fails because of change and the nature of software development. A waterfall process is unable to effectively respond to changes, because changes often require rework in earlier parts of the process. Rework would require violation of process and scheduling constraints. So the project continues ever onward in denial of changes that may cause it to deliver the wrong system. The nature of software development is chaotic. Software projects are products of one or more minds. Communication and miscommunication between people have chaotic effects upon our ability to assess progress and quality. As these things we don't know are discovered, responsiveness, rework, and redirection are often required.

Iterative process reuses the waterfall sequence, but makes each step much shorter and the whole sequence repetitive. The steps are shortened because the scope of the problem addressed in each step is greatly reduced. The sequence is repeated so that the efforts can be redirected in response to changes and discoveries. Iterative process is sometimes called risk-driven development, because in each iteration of analyze-design-code-test there is a feedback assessment (perhaps with user input), and a new plan can be formulated for the next iteration in response to what is learned. Each iteration is an opportunity to rework elements of each process step in accordance with lessons learned.

A key variation of the iterative process model is the *iterative-incremental process*. Incremental processes focus on specific functions of a system, one at a time, not all system functions at once, as may be the case in waterfall and pure iterative processes. For example, an increment may focus on prototyping selected screens. This would be called an external increment, because it is focused on the externally observable behavior of the system. In another example, an increment might focus on building a data access layer, an API for transparent retrieval and update of multiple databases. This would be called an internal increment, because it is focused on internal functionality that is not directly observable to end users.

In an iterative-incremental process, particular functions are selected in sequence for incremental development. Each increment becomes an iteration of the process. The goal of iterative-incremental process is to complete an entire function in an increment, so that it will not require rework downstream in the process. This means that the analysis, design, coding, and testing of that one function must be exhaustive enough to reduce or eliminate the need for later rework.

Iterative-incremental process is a widely accepted approach to software development. Some authorities have called it a "spiral" process, because each iteration increases the scope of developed software, and builds upon the results of previous iterations. Planning a spiral process is one of the most important functions of project management. The balance and sequence of project iterations are critical to project survival, balancing factors such as progress, risk reduction, and upper management support.

External iterations are critical to demonstrating progress (for management support) and usability risk reduction (i.e., making sure we are building the right system). However, external increments usually require throw-away coding, since certain internal functions that have not been implemented must be simulated. In contrast, the objective of internal increments is finished code that can be used throughout development and the system life cycle. In general, the most cost-effective way to build a system starts with internal increments. There are often stronger motivations to perform external increments early in the project.

The Role of Architecture Process

Software architecture helps the project manager in planning increments, because the architect breaks up the system into well-thought-out functions—for example, subsystems and system use cases. The process for software architecture is only one of the tasks in the overall software development process. Much of the software architecture activity takes place early in the project; thus, software architecting comprises early project iterations.

Spiral processes are intended to be quite flexible when applied. How much depth and how often each step is applied can vary from iteration to iteration. Also the length of iterations can and should vary. Software architecture requires this flexibility to be applied sensibly. Ideally, iterations are longer at the beginning of a project. These initial iterations can be called "architecture iterations" because the principal deliverables are architecture artifacts (e.g., higher-level systemwide technical plans).

Generally, the first two iterations are the longest and are applied to architectural planning. A total of three to six months for these iterations is not unreasonable, although as little as two to four weeks is commonplace.

Explicit architecture planning has some distinct benefits in software process. First, the architecture iterations do not require an entire project team. Hordes of programmers are unnecessary during the architecture iterations. In fact, adding programmers too early in the project can lead to much dissension and wasted labor expenditures. Many programmers resent having to participate in lengthy requirements analyses and architecture processes. As might be expected, many programmers would rather be designing and coding hands-on. Also, it is difficult to creatively design in groups larger than 5 people. So, ideal architecture teams are kept small, as are ideal programming teams, with 4 people for 3 months being the most effective size and task duration for development.

A key benefit of architecture is planning the partition of large systems developments into smaller subprojects. As you might expect, our ideal goal would be to form subprojects for about 4 people working for 3 months. Architecture can plan the partitions and define the boundaries between these subprojects. The most detailed partitioning of boundaries is in the form of software interface definitions, i.e., computational architectures. As such, architecture planning makes the whole software process more efficient.

During the architecture phases, commitments can be minimized. For example, it is not necessary to purchase a lot of equipment or software licenses for a small, short-duration architecture team. Any expensive licenses that are required (e.g., for assessing software technologies) could be demonstrator or evaluation versions. The project can also save on labor costs by using a small team during these initial phases.

Architecture planning defers commitment of resources until they are needed. Once the development phase starts, it can be accelerated, because the development effort and many crucial technical decisions are preplanned by the architecture team. A desirable partitioning ratio between architecture planning, development, and deployment is 2:1:1—in other words, half of the project for planning, one quarter for "doing" (i.e., software development and testing), and one quarter for training and deployment. This is a classic result from general project management, which has been applied successfully to software projects. We would consider this as a "goal," not a hard and fast rule. In a sense, once development starts, it continues throughout the software system life cycle, with about 70% of the expenditures occurring after the completion of the formal development project, during operations and maintenance.

Development of a maintainable system is one of architecture's key benefits. In our opinion, architecture planning is essential for achieving higher-level qualities such as maintainability, reliability, extensibility, and others. Many of these qualities are directly or indirectly linked to system complexity. It may be simple common sense, but excess system complexity makes it difficult and expensive in virtually every respect. For example, complex systems are hard to document, develop, test, maintain, debug, and so forth. Architects understand that a system must be as simple as possible, but not too simple (i.e., simplistic). Most systems can be architected in a much simpler way than developers would normally assume.

In any problem there is an inherent complexity, but there is an even greater complexity in solutions (assuming that the solutions work). The necessary complexity in the solution is due to the inherent complexity in the problem. The excess complexity in the solution (beyond the inherent complexity) varies greatly. From experience, most excess complexity derives from a lack of design coordination. Excess complexity can be a natural result of uncoordinated designs, particularly at the system level of software scale. Knowing this, architects can manage and minimize the excess complexity.

ARCHITECTURE BY DELEGATION

The good old days of software promulgated a practice that continues today. Software architecture was and is often designed by delegation. To architect by delegation, a manager identifies candidate subsystems and then delegates the details of interface specification to individual developers. The number of subsystems selected is usually based upon the number of programmers. Six programmers equals six subsystems, four programmers equals four subsystems, and so forth. Having the preexisting structure of the software organization drive the technical solution is a dubious practice, but what happens next is even worse. In order to define subsystem interfaces, programmers engage in pairwise negotiations to define the software interfaces. Since all the interface decisions are decentralized, the process inevitably leads to unique interfaces, also called an "order N by N" solution. The interfaces are unique to each implementation, and unique to each system.

The tragedy of architecture by delegation is that architecture qualities of design are seen as desirable by developers, but virtually always are sacrificed to expedience. Commonality of interfaces is viewed as a desirable objective, but is seldom pursued in practice. Management of complexity is not a significant issue if you have face-to-face technical support from fellow programmers, and the ability to change things whenever agreeable.

Architecture planning enables organizational decisions to be made after their consequences are clearly understood. A classic problem for software projects involves mismatches between the technical requirements of the solution and the preexisting structure of the human organization. Once the human organization is established for a project, with ownership for specific architectural partitions, it is most difficult to change. It is even worse when the architecture is ill-defined, because technical decisions are equivalent to political decisions. It is very undesirable when political compromises become the most important drivers in the design of the system. Doing architecture, up-front, with a small team, allows management to establish the proper organizational structure, one that does not conflict with technical imperatives.

From a management perspective, architecture is a useful planning activity because it defines the solution in sufficient detail to provide a dramatically improved basis for project planning. While estimation methods (e.g., *function points*) are capable of forecasting project costs, these methods cannot define an architecture for the solution. Estimation methods cannot indicate how the system is configured, how to organize the project team, or how to decompose the project. Architecture planning can.

The Macro Process: Architecture Iteration

Architecture iteration is a process for quality improvement in project/system architecture. The process spans the entire system life cycle. In this description of architecture iteration, we will assume that extensive review and feedback are applied at every step in which the project makes an important selection. Once the architects are willing to make a commitment, the information value is lost if it is not reviewed, validated, or confirmed through consensus of peers, developers, or other system stakeholders.

Typically, a software project begins with an informal vision, or an inspiration that may be the result of a creative discussion, or someone's bright idea. This occurs long before the project is a formal project. We could call this Architecture Iteration 0.1 (we will refer to the version and iteration synonymously here). This vision is then documented in some form that sells the concept to the system stakeholders (Iteration 0.2). As a result, time or money becomes available to pursue the vision. In follow-on iterations, projects diverge greatly, depending upon industry, participants, and corporate culture. In this case, we assume that an architecture planning activity occurs next.

After Iteration 0.2, the architecture planning proceeds through requirements analysis and architecture specification, followed by architecture prototyping. During the paper planning phase of architecture specification, any number of design alternatives can be considered. Ten iterations of paper design is not atypical. The architect (or architecture team) is seeking the best solution. And they cannot effectively evaluate solutions without committing them to paper or software for criticism.

Design concepts can (and should) vary widely. For example, designs that are highly vertical should be attempted, as well as designs that are broadly horizontal, and hybrids of the two extremes. At the paper stage of design, commitment to any specific design is inconsequential; therefore, bizarre ideas should be explored in order to discover their potential benefits, if any.

Having gathered the best ideas, from paper design studies, architecture mining, and other intelligence, the architects select the final design. We can call this Iteration 0.9. In the architects' judgment, it represents the best design candidate for realization.

An architecture prototyping activity is appropriate at this point. Its purpose is to validate the key design decisions, in particular the dynamic behavior of the solution. The architecture prototype is a simulation of the system, with all architectural boundaries implemented, but with the internals of the subsystems stubbed out (e.g., throwaway code).

Lessons learned from the architecture prototype are incorporated into the final iteration of the architecture phase, which we can call Iteration 1.0. It produces a paper specification and architecture prototype representing the best design that the architects can produce (with respect to paper studies and simulation), without actually building the system.

The publication of Architecture Iteration 1.0 is an important project milestone, and the most critical milestone for software architects. At this point, the architecture is transferred to the development teams for detailed design and construction (i.e., iterative incremental development). As the conceptual basis for the entire software project, the architecture should be stabilized or frozen, while this detailed work proceeds. The architecture represents the key assumptions of the project. Changes in key assumptions can have dire consequences. The architecture also represents the boundaries of the project, both internal and external. If these boundaries are unstable, much negotiation or worry-mongering may result. The architects work with project management to reduce these negative consequences through architecture stabilization.

The keys to stabilization include (1) doing your homework during the architecture iterations, and (2) *sticking together,* including architects, management, and lead developers. The team is ill-prepared for Iteration 1.0 if its members can't defend their architecture when facing simple and complex questions.

During the development iterations, the architecture team is available to communicate the design. The architects can answer developer questions and interpret designs. The architects should not try to micromanage the internals of each subsystem's design, but simply reinforce the larger-scale boundaries defined by the architecture through well-articulated explanations.

At the same time, the architects are beginning their intelligence collection for Iteration 2.0. As people ask questions and raise concerns, architects should take notes. Any immediate change to the architecture is unwarranted because the experiment is just beginning. It is important to respond with good judgment and not to react in a reflexive manner.

Developer Reaction to Architecture

As the developers near completion of their first prototype, the result of a major development iteration, the architecture team begins active intelligence collection, preparing for the next iteration of the architecture. We can categorize what the architects observe in terms of three developer reactions: (1) implementation as planned, (2) misunderstanding, and (3) defect workaround.

When the system is designed on paper, the architects envision various design benefits. These benefits are unproven until they provide advantages to developers in practice. When the architects inspect the implementation, and it appears to be implemented as planned, that is evidence that the design benefits have been realized. In order for this to happen, the architecture vision and design must be communicated and understood, then implemented, and the design must be technically sound. Evidence of implementation as planned is confirmation of adequate communications and design soundness.

What happens in practice is that some parts of the design are implemented as planned, and other parts in unexpected ways. Each design element has an intended purpose that defines how it should be used by developers. However, architectural intentions do not always match implementation reality. The three developer reactions apply to each and every architectural decision that affects their work. The architect needs to inspect the designs carefully in order to discover the developer reactions. This involves conversations with developers as well as inspection of software and subsidiary design documentation.

We emphasize that it is not the architects' role to be judgmental. During this discovery phase, the architects should be neutral fact finders, using informal discussions and casual reviews to collect their information. This is not the time to enforce architectural decisions; rather it is the time to rediscover the architectural reality, having been through the cycle of design and development.

When the design is not implemented as planned, there are two alternative reasons: there was a misunderstanding of the architecture, or there is a real design defect. The architect must decide which is which. In a misunderstanding, a sound design was implemented in a creative way by the development. The developer could have done what was achieved by using the architecture as planned, but didn't. The developer proceeded to implement the design in a discretionary way that exploited other elements of the design to achieve the same purpose.

As professionals, we make the assumption that everybody in our work environment is trustworthy and has good intentions with respect to architecture and implementation. If possible, we also make the *competent engineer assumption*, that all of the developers are sufficiently educated and competent to understand and implement a properly articulated architecture. We know that the competent engineer assumption does not always apply in many of today's programming shops, so we can work with management to make necessary adjustments to project policies and procedures. Architecture is particularly valuable in this respect, in that it provides technical guidance to the developers that eliminates much guesswork. We can supplement that architectural benefit with training and mentoring.

Using effective management practices, we never jump to the conclusion that developers have bad intentions. When there is a misunderstanding, we always assume that further explanation is needed (perhaps in the form of additional education and training). In this sense, a misunderstanding is a failure of the management and architecture team to communicate the design effectively. Procedures for architectural release and rollout should be modified. For example, if there is a consistently misunderstood part of the design, spending more time communicating that part of the design is warranted in the next iteration.

As our primary architectural communication mechanism, we favor the one-day architecture seminar. This is a lecture-tutorial format which is not a review. This should be emphasized to the audience, because there is an implicit assumption in many development cultures that every meeting is some form of review. In this one-day seminar, the architecture is explained by the architects, section by section and level by level. In our experience, a written document, alone, cannot be an effective means of coordinating implementations without some form of face-to-face explanation. In other words, the stand-up tutorial imparts some missing element of communication that cannot be effectively replaced by architectural documentation.

At first impression, this missing communication factor appears mysterious. What the stand-up tutorial imparts, that no document can, is the architects' commitment to the system design, in every important detail. Through a stand-up tutorial, the architect can make the system vision understood and much more believable. In addition, the architect can quickly explain rationale for design details that no amount of documentation can replace. In a perverse sense, architectural rationale can be nearly unlimited. Design decisions can be based on long experience or on design insights gained through lengthy studies. You can attempt to explain these experiences at length, but the real knowledge can be gained only by experiential learning.

It is possible, as a last resort, that the design has a flaw which must be changed. Flaws and defects can come in many forms and for many reasons. They can be mistakes, oversights, ignorance, and so forth. Many such defects are unpredictable and are discovered and remedied only through experience. As architects, it is our last resort to change the design. Design changes have consequences. A change may fix a certain problem locally, but may cause many other problems and hardships for the project. For example, a significant change to a system-level API used by a dozen applications would involve substantial reprogramming. Sometimes such changes are necessary if there are great technical advantages to the new design.

After Intelligence, Iterate the Design

The architects have learned much during the initial paper design process. They have gained additional insights during architectural prototyping, but the real test of the architecture occurs during development and testing of engineering proto-types and production releases. At every step, the architects strive to improve the quality of the design; they use the lessons learned to make the design better and better. Since quality is the satisfaction of human needs, architects are continually working toward a design that will realize the most stable balance of design features supporting a quality solution addressing the stakeholders' needs.

In terms of our architectural iteration process, at the end of architecture iteration 1.0, we froze the architecture design during development iteration 1.0. Near the end of the development iteration we collected substantial intelligence about how the architecture was implemented. Any changes to the architecture must be inserted during the transition from development iterations 1.0 to 2.0. The key idea of architecture iteration is to keep the architecture stable during development, changing it only at discrete times synchronized with work-stopping transitions in the development process.

The architecture activity is vigorous near the beginning and end of major development iterations, where most developers will work on finishing and stabilizing the current release, before branching off and building the next major release of the code. It is the intention of architects to *catch the train* of the next major release, without derailing the project through ill-timed archi-tecture fluctuations.

Changes are made to the architecture through a decision process called *architecture concentration*. Through our intelligence gathering we know about design comments, criticisms, and actual usage. Each of these inputs to the process comprises an architectural design force. The design forces are balanced by the architect through improved communications or design changes. Many forces are required before a design change is justified. If we are too responsive to forces, design changes will be frequent and violent. This is the opposite of the stable environment that architects are attempting to create. If the architect does not respond to emerging design forces, it creates an equally indefensible situation. So the architects find balance between these extremes by using the architecture iteration process. In other words, there will be changes to the ar-chitecture, at discrete times, according to the project plan. Any inputs received are considered intelligence for the next architectural iteration.

In the architecture concentration process, many forces are resolved by each change. The appropriate analogy is "killing two birds with one stone." The influences of several design forces are combined to cause a single change to the design that addresses the needs. The architect must distinguish between what is needed and what is desired. The provision for "what is needed" must be satisfied, but the provision for "what is desired" should be considered with moderation. Also, it is important to realize that the explanation of the revised architecture can be as important as design changes. In other words, how the features of the architecture are explained is a way of resolving forces, which is often more effective than direct technical changes.

Architecture iteration works like a critical damping factor. If we are too responsive, the architecture changes too rapidly and does not converge for a long time. If we are too stubborn to be responsive, the architecture also takes much longer to converge, perhaps after our dismissal. We want to play our role in the project so that the architecture converges as rapidly as possible, but without much oscillation, which is over-responsiveness to change.

As architects it is our mission to ensure that the system converges on a high-quality design, at least for design decisions having systemwide impact. And if we truly believe in the principle of encapsulation as promoted by OO and component paradigms, that's all we should really care about, because any internal design defects (outside of the architect's control) are isolated within subsystems. Quality convergence is a goal unique to architects, because it is seldom seen as a priority by developers (who are focused on coding issues) or management (who are focused on short-term results). However, we know that architecture quality will contribute significantly to the ease of coding and the delivery of short-term project results, as well as the longer-term issues of usability, extensibility, and maintenance.

The Micro Process: Architecture with Subprojects

The core process of architecture iteration is called *architecture with subprojects*. Because architecture planning partitions the problem into subsystems with stable boundaries, it is possible to design and develop these subsystems as subprojects in relative isolation. By *relative isolation* we mean that the subprojects may be conducted concurrently or in a distributed organization, with relatively minimal need for intersubsystem coordination (assuming that the architecture "does its job").

We can describe architecture with subprojects as a viewpoint on the overall process of system development as follows:

1. *Identify subsystems.* A key result of the architecture planning activity is the designation of a stable of subsystems. Each subsystem has high cohesion (functional connectivity) but minimal coupling to the other sub-

systems. In addition to its technical role, each subsystem has a corre-spondence to the human organization for the project. For example, on small projects each subsystem may denote the scope of responsibilities for a single development. Alternatively, with a high ratio of subsystems to developers, each subsystem may correspond to one of several signifi-cant responsibilities of each developer. On larger projects, a subsystem is usually assigned to a team of developers.

2. *Define subsystem interfaces*. Subsystem interfaces are the concrete defin-ition of boundaries between parts of the architecture. Proper isolation between subsystems (and the groups implementing them) cannot be achieved unless this part of the design is well coordinated across the sys-tem (i.e., managed by architects). It is not always possible to completely define and stabilize interfaces during the architecture planning phase, but these interfaces should at least be considered as a part of the architecture. On large projects and distributed developments, preplanning the subsys-tem interfaces is more necessary than on smaller projects.

3. *Project planning*. The designated subsystems form the basis for develop-ment team organization, project planning, and cost estimation. Project planning is most effective given a reasonable technical plan as a starting point. Project planning can determine how the existing human organiza-tion can be mapped onto the desired architecture, perhaps through redraw-ing boundaries in the human organization for the purposes of the project.

4. *Subprojects in parallel*. With the project plan and the architecture plan well defined, individual subprojects can be spawned to realize parts of the archi-tecture. Ideally, the subproject partititioning is closely matched to the parti-tititioning of the technical architecture. As the parallel subprojects complete their deliverables, they need to synchronize at various points in order to test interoperation across system boundaries. Internally, each subproject conducts an iterative incremental development process. The subproject it-erations do not need to be synchronized, except at major iterations involv-ing systemwide integration. A subproject can have several internal iterations for each major iteration that involves other subsystems.

FROM-SCRATCH DESIGNS VERSUS SMART ARCHITECTING

The practice of architecture involves some engineering, some psychology, some art, and a great deal of intuitive judgment. However, we believe that ar-chitecture is not magic. When designing a new system, it is insufficient to "throw something together" and expect to generate good design. When starting on a new design, the worst approach is to give all the developers a blank sheet of paper (or analogous situation) and ask them to design from their own knowledge of the problem under a tight deadline. Almost as bad is an approach where the architecture team tries the same thing. We call this situation *designing in a vacuum*, because there is no intelligence gathering. In contrast to other fields of endeavor, a software architect has no particular advantage over ordinary developers when designing in a vacuum.

We can overcome the limitations of designing in a vacuum in several ways. One approach that we described at length is architecture mining. Architecture mining gives the architect substantial, detailed information about how to design similar systems effectively. It also conveys a sense of perspective, beyond experience with a sole implementation. Another approach is domain analysis, where a set of requirements is iterated, with user involvement, from a disorganized jumble into distinct horizontal and vertical elements. In both cases, the experience of domain analysis is more valuable than the artifacts generated, because it trains the architect to think about the problem and realize the advantages of increased intelligence and vicarious experience.

Architecting in Chaos

Architecture attempts to bring some additional technical order to the chaotic process of software development. Development can appear chaotic because of apparent changes in the environment of the project. It is the strong desire of software management to give their sponsors what they want—and what they want can change as frequently as the wind direction. In addition, a software project is a learning experience, in which business requirements and real-world constraints are discovered during the project, not during initial requirements elaboration.

The technical environment is also changing; innovations that occur during a project can motivate changes in technical plans. As commercial technologies increasingly address the vertical needs of industry, it becomes easier for external marketeers to impact organizational decisions about software. For example, we have seen extremely well-planned projects completely change direction and technologies, almost overnight, because of vendor influence.

Software design models are inherently intolerant to change. Design models are crafted with respect to certain assumptions, and an emphasis on what's important and what's not. When changes in fundamental assumptions occur, the models are invalidated because their hard-wired assumptions no longer hold true. Most projects find this acceptable. It is a very common failing to deny that invalid models are indeed invalidated. Instead, projects pretend to make progress with broken models, which become progressively more corrupted.

Another source of chaos is in the software process itself. It is devilishly hard to assess software progress, especially by word of mouth. A common joke in the software profession is that the software is always 85% done. Of course it is, and the last 15% can easily add another 90% to the development time and budget. As the truth emerges about software progress there are many surprises, including many pitfalls and unknowns and necessary reworks that impact the project's schedule and direction.

Architects are not the primary responsibility holders when it comes to controlling chaos; that is properly the role of management. However, architects are a de facto part of the management team and can influence management decision making. Architects are responsible for eliminating as much technology-driven chaos as possible, and for mitigating chaotic conditions in other areas touched by architecture, such as enterprise architecture models. Architects should use their influence with management to make suggestions about how to handle important situations that they may have encountered on previous projects. In addition, architects work with management to affect decisions, solutions, and policies that moderate chaos.

Architecture iteration is a primary approach for dealing with chaos, from the software architect's perspective. Some additional strategies that should be used with architecture iteration for dealing with chaos include:

1. *Frequent sampling.* Having frequent and regular meetings can give the project a way to identify and cope with chaotic change. One can address the challenge of change through the frequency of sampling, including regular meetings, perhaps daily. In this approach, the way to keep ahead of change is keep an eye on it. There is an emerging methodology based on this theory called Scrum, in which the project has stand-up team meetings on a daily basis [Rising 00].

2. *Managed environment.* Knowing the potentially devastating consequences of change on a project, management can help a great deal to control the timing and impacts of change. Architecture iteration supports this principle, in which the impacts of architecture change are infrequent, and always crafted to reduce the possibility of future change. Management can control the dissemination of changes in several ways. First and most important is what management says to the development team. If

management parrots and amplifies every known source of change, it becomes the source of chaos. Alternatively, management can limit its comments to those which have necessary impact on the project. An important part of the architect's job is to assess the technical consequences of changes. Management and architects can work together to process change inputs and formulate plans and messages for dissemination to the project staff. Traditionally, management had control of organizational communications; everything was communicated through the chain of command. Today, email has changed that situation a great deal, allowing people to communicate across all organization boundaries and levels at the push of a button. Management should encourage the staff to come to them for decisions regarding change inputs. In addition, management should enforce old-fashioned chain-of-command rules regarding changes requested by other persons and organizations.

3. *Short projects.* You can minimize the effects of change by keeping the project's duration within one year. The shorter the better. The rationale for this guideline particularly addresses changes in the technology environment. Over the course of a year, major technology changes can occur, but complete obsolescence of the existing technology base is unlikely. Over two years, that assumption may not hold. This challenge is especially apparent through the burning-in of year numbers in product names, such as Rational Rose 98 and Microsoft Office 97. There is an inherent 12-month planned obsolescence built into these product images. And the human-interpreted images often are much more influential than the real-world technological consequences of obsolescence.

4. *Low commitment planning and fast execution.* Ideally, an enterprise should have many architectures in planning stages, but few development projects. During the architecture phase, the commitments are very low: a few people for a few months with free-evaluation software. Architecture plans can be changed without much trepidation. Once programming begins, there is usually a larger commitment of resources: many programmers, much equipment, purchased software, and so forth. The commitment to particular decisions increases as code is written. Whereas changes during the architecture phase are easily accommodated, changes during the development phase can be expensive, often resulting in cancelled or unsuccessful projects. Executing the low-commitment approach, development phases are no longer than 6 months, and architecture phases can be as long as 3 to 6 months. The architecture phase defines a project plan and technical design that make it possible to develop the system rapidly.

8.3   ARCHITECTURE JUDGMENT

All architecture benefits depend upon a critical assumption: that *architecture decisions are fundamentally sound and will not be subject to significant change*. If architecture decisions are no better (or even worse) than chance, then it would be appropriate to conduct a software project without architectural planning. In particular, this is why the quality of judgment of the architect is vital. Architecture is all about making important technical decisions for a system or project. By definition, the scope of architecture comprises the important decisions, also known as "architecturally significant" decisions.

How do architects use judgment? Judgment guides our advice to project management and developers. Judgment is used in the evaluation and selection of technologies. Judgment is used in the definition of a "system vision," including the envisioning of architectural frameworks that are detailed to realize the design. Judgment is used in virtually every detail of architecting—for example, designing subsystem interfaces, elaborating enterprise requirements, and allocating engineering objects. We rely on judgment in many cases, because more logical engineering methods are not available or are inapplicable to many intuition-based architecture decisions.

A key role of the architect is to assess the impacts of changes in requirements and technologies. This is a proper role for architecture judgment, because the architect must assess whether these changes impact "the architecture," which also means "affect important system decisions and assumptions." With a systemwide view, the architect is in the best position to make such judgments. The architect should also rely upon specialists to provide answers about specific technologies, as inputs to a decision.

Judgment is the application of the intuitive aspects of architecture. When we say "intuitive," we do not imply impulsivity and ad hoc guesswork. Usually the architect's judgment is backed up by intelligence gathering and experience, as well as systematic decision-making processes. It is infeasible to justify every decision in writing, so we attribute much of what we do to intuitive judgment. Even if we could document all of our decisions, we cannot recreate all of our experiences for the reader, so that he draws the exact same conclusions as our own intuitive judgments. It is essential to have our management and developers trust our judgment in order to be effective architects. We usually do this by enlisting one or more of the lead developers into the architecture decision-making process.

Problem Solving

Architectural judgment is one form of problem solving. If we consider problem solving as a paradigm, we can argue that it fits many human activities. We can map the problem-solving paradigm upon most project activities, including what we do in meetings and day-to-day on the job. In order to be good problem solvers, we believe we should use a problem-solving process for important decisions.

Some alternatives to problem solving include: ad hoc decisions, "whoever yells the loudest," management by caveat, and flipping a coin. Sometimes these are expedient approaches; sometimes it is more important to move on to the next topic, rather than dwell on an inconsequential decision.

To establish a process, we first define the problem-solving paradigm as a reference model. The *general problem-solving paradigm* is to first decide upon the question to be addressed, then identify alternative solutions, elaborate the alternatives, select among them, and implement the solution [VanGundy 88]. At each step we have decisions to make about which process to utilize, and which content alternative to select. Considering each of the generic problem-solving steps, we have the basis for a problem-solving process:

1. *Identify the Question.* The first step is to define the problem. What questions should we answer in order to resolve the situation? The search for the right question can be a miniature problem-solving exercise in itself. In the case of architecture, the questions may be broad and complex, as are the solutions. In a meeting situation, one of the best ways to identify the question is to write down some candidate question (on a flipchart or whiteboard) and let the group edit it through discussion.

2. *Identify Alternative Solutions.* The second step is to discover several potential solutions. In a perfect world it would be nice to identify all possible solutions, but this is seldom feasible (or desirable) in practice. We want to find a reasonable number of candidate solutions that are all worth investigating further. Sometimes if there are many potential solutions, it is useful to redefine the problem or to downselect the alternatives before detailed study.

3. *Elaborate the Alternative Solutions.* Each alternative can be studied further—for example, by detailing the steps involved in implementing that solution. Simply creating a written description of the proposed solutions is a major step toward reducing ambiguity. In this step, we want to share information about the proposed solution, in order to make a more informed decision. In many cases, it is necessary to "make up" information

about a solution—for example, by providing a strawman definition of a plan of implementation.

4. *Select among the Alternatives*. Given the sufficiently elaborated alternatives, the studies are done and it is time to make a decision. Decision making itself can be a drawn-out process, or it can be a simple choice among obvious tradeoffs. By understanding the more complete decision-making processes, we can effectively simplify with known consequences. In particular, decision analysis is a process based upon a matrix (also called "Olympic scoring") [Kepner 81]. The alternatives are listed in columns, and decision criteria are listed in rows. The criteria are in two categories: the essentials and the desirables. The desirables are sorted by priority. Note that we need a problem-solving process to select criteria. The alternatives are scored in rank order: 1, 2, 3, ... Then the scores are tabulated with respect to priority weightings, and the best score wins. The full decision analysis process is considerably more rational and objective than ad hoc decision making. The winner is usually a good choice, and we have a rationale for explaining why in the form of the decision matrix.

5. *Implement the Solution*. Once we have selected a particular solution, we can elaborate the design and implementation plan for that solution and realize the results. Having made a sound decision and eliminated consideration of many unnecessary options makes the implementation step much more focused.

Sometimes the powers that be will disagree with a carefully rationalized decision. One way to explain this mismatch is that the decision criteria have different priorities than the real-world priorities. It is an interesting spreadsheet exercise to revisit the decision analysis and discover the likely priorities.

In any decision-making process, the ability to prioritize is essential. It is not productive to view each choice as an exclusive selection, because that arbitrarily excludes desirable choices. Instead, it is preferable to prioritize among options or among criteria in order to rank-order the alternatives or considerations. One of the most effective ways to prioritize is to use situation analysis, essentially scoring each option by its seriousness, urgency, and growth in importance as high/medium/low, and ranking the results [Kepner 81]. This prioritization process can be used with arbitrary lists of ad hoc concerns. It is not always necessary to rank equal items, and you should not insist on perfection before considering rank ordering. What is important is to determine what is most important, and then focus energies on exploring those alternatives. All this advice can be summarized in the saying "First things first and second things never." Determining what's first (i.e., most important) and what's second is done through a process of prioritization.

Review and Inspection

In some organizational cultures, every meeting is a review. Review is an important process, but it tends to be overused and overestimated. Any time you have more than six people, the meeting is by default a virtual review. With six or more people (and typical meeting processes), it is very difficult to design and proceed creatively. However, it is relatively easy to get sidetracked on discussions.

What's wrong with the review process is that its results are uneven. At its best, it helps to form consensus for good ideas. At its worst, it is a pernicious form of group-think, where everybody concedes to the boss's wishes. Most likely, the review process will focus on issues that are not the most important. And some people with long meeting experience can manipulate the review process by exploiting its weaknesses. One macabre review game is to search for the question that can't be answered (e.g., "What about security?"). It does not have to be the most important question, or even a significant one. Groups are easily led in such a direction, even though it may be irrelevant to the accomplishment of the group's purpose.

We have seen too many review meetings where every idea is pooh-poohed (criticized). This often happens when multiple competing interests are present, such as competing software companies. One interesting process, used by Sun's JDBC team, is to bring one company in at a time, instead of the more typical multicompany meetings. Without the pressure of imminent competition, the companies were more willing to share their technical opinions and help with the creative process.

One firm-and-fast rule that we insist upon in review meetings is that we shouldn't redesign on-the-spot. Technical design decisions should be considered carefully, off-line, and not become the victims of group-think. Untold numbers of bad design decisions are made in review meetings, for spurious reasons. Each review comment is considered to be a design force which must be balanced with other forces in order to make a reasonable choice. Often, many design forces are resolved with single changes, or the solution can be explained in terms of the current design, and how it can be used more effectively.

Also, it is important to clearly define which meetings really are review meetings and which are not. For example, a tutorial is not a review meeting. In some cases, we meet to disseminate completed specifications. We must switch from review mode sometimes in order to stabilize work, distinguishing which decisions are closed and which are open for choice. Otherwise, every decision is up for reconsideration at virtually every meeting.

There is another, more structured, version of review called software inspection [Gilb 93]. We do not claim to describe the process completely here; suffice it to say that this is a process that is very effective. Some experts claim that software inspection "always works."

Instead of an unstructured review, software inspection is a highly structured process. Proper inspection requires a list of quality criteria as well as a basis document (e.g., requirements) with which to compare the designs. Inspection differs primarily from review in that it involves a closer examination. Forty-five minutes per page is not uncommon in an inspection process. The inspections are performed off-line, outside meetings. At inspection meetings, the potential defects are collected as efficiently as possible from the inspection team members. No document can enter the inspection process without meeting certain quality criteria beforehand. These entry criteria are assessed by the inspection leader, a key role in this process.

Inspection can be used at any phase of software development. It is most effective while reviewing written specifications and architectures, although it has been used for code review.

8.4 CONCLUSIONS

In this chapter we covered several intelligence-gathering techniques that can improve our architecture practices and probability of system success. One of the most important lessons learned is to *consider architecture as a deliverable*. In the opinions of some software authorities, architecture is the most important deliverable of the project. We tend to agree; however, we seldom brag about this openly, especially in the presence of developers. The truth is that everybody's contribution to the software project is vitally important, but not all are equally important. Each person can provide a positive or negative contribution to the project's outcome. For example, negative contributions can result from exacerbating chaotic project inputs, rumor mongering, and unwarranted dissension. Architecture is helpful for moderating the chaos of a project but is not the only or most effective means for doing so.

The intelligence-gathering process is interleaved with other architecture processes. For example, we freeze architecture during active code development and gather intelligence near the logical end of each phase. Intelligence is applied to make architectural decisions when and where they can cause the least disruption and most benefit. One of the benefits of intelligence gathering most difficult to achieve is the definition of stable interfaces that maintain system qualities throughout their life cycles. Stable interfaces are required for system-level architecture, distributed computing, and component-based development.

8.5   Exercises

Exercise 8.1   Work with a peer or manager who is very familiar with the organizational systems. Identify the focus of the study, such as: "We want to find a way to exchange accounting information between our systems for monthly and yearly reporting" or "We want our customer service representatives to access information and post transactions across as many lines of business as possible." Then make a list of the systems, standards, prototypes, and products you already know about that are relevant to the problem. Check the Internet, too. Sort this list in terms of the importance of each system for the business and problem resolution. You are done; you have a plan for architecture mining. The next steps would be to track these resources down (leverage the knowledge of managers) and set up some 2- to 3-hour appointments with their one or two architects to walk through their interface specifications and/or schemas, depending on the problem.

Background for Solution: Maybe we chose the wrong name for this process, but architecture mining is a quick and lightweight procedure, compared to what most people expect. You can plan a mining mission in an hour or less (e.g., this exercise) with the right pair of people in the room. Over a 2-week period, you can complete this mission. And your architectural knowledge will be increased immeasurably.

There is no deliverable from architecture mining; it's all about making architects smart. Pick the best-of-breed of the ideas you gather, and you are well on your way to specifying a quality architectural solution to a problem that is vitally important to your business organization. We can't recommend an easier or faster way to get these kinds of results. We know many groups of architects who have spent years trying to find the answers that architecture mining easily delivers within a couple of weeks.

Architecture mining has a second important benefit: it cross pollinates information between projects, creating technology transfers that are otherwise organizationally impossible. The SunSoft people who created Java Database Connectivity (JDBC) used a similar process. They met one-on-one with contributing organizations, eliminating competitive worries that larger multiorganizational meetings would surely trigger.

EXERCISE 8.2 Using your organization's current software process, how would you synchronize the architecture iterations to minimize fluctuations in architecture during development tasks? How would you coordinate architecture changes between iterations? On large projects, will this architecture coordination benefit from synchronization with management communications/meetings, or should architecture coordination be an entirely separate process?

BACKGROUND FOR SOLUTION: The key concept of architecture iteration is to keep the architecture stable when the code is changing, and vice versa. Stabilizing the architecture during coding yields significant benefits. It eliminates much developer confusion. It reduces the wasted time spent on system discovery (estimated to consume up to half of the developer's time). It enables programmers and groups of programmers to work in parallel and in distributed laboratories.

EXERCISE 8.3 List the elements of your organization's design process and the resulting design elements. How would each element and step be characterized with respect to engineering procedure versus architectural judgment? In the execution of judgment, how is the judgment rationalized and/or documented? How could each judgment be re-evaluated at a later time? Who is responsible for defending key judgments when changes occur?

BACKGROUND FOR SOLUTION: Software engineering has suffered from physics envy. Ideally, every process step could be decomposed into rational engineering analysis techniques. Analogies such as automobile manufacturing have been applied to software process, with disappointing results. There is an intuitive level of decision making which is often discounted and buried in software engineering processes. In this age of software architecture enlightenment, we are making these issues explicit and assigning responsibility to architects to manage these intuitive forces. To make the incredible transition from unstructured natural language requirements to a brutally logical binary machine, we must, at a minimum, insert some intermediate steps, in order to minimize risk. This is the role of software architecture, in addition to system planning, which maps the intuitive forces in rationalized steps into the logical abyss of machine code. Architectural judgment is vital to this transition, whether explicit or implicit in the software process.

SOFTWARE ARCHITECTURE: PSYCHOLOGICAL WARFARE

In psychological warfare, we use the term *grounding* to mean a state of quiet confidence. Grounding comes from knowing "how things happen." And usually, you gain knowledge of how things happen through experience, including making mistakes, trial, and error.

9.1   ALTERNATIVE LEARNING

There is another way to learn (rather than making mistakes), and that is through learning from other people. In order to do that effectively, you need two skills that most people lack: how to read between the lines how to take advice. A famous technical editor said, "People don't read," meaning that it's very rare to find someone who's really done his/her homework, reading technical publications and so forth. It is equally true that people don't listen to advice. Including you. Us, too. We all have to try harder to do these basics more effectively. They seem really simple, but most people don't acquire these basic skills in much depth, and therefore waste a great deal of time and energy by not benefiting from the knowledge of others.

The phrase "reading between the lines" is only a figure of speech. You don't literally read anything between lines of text. What you do is analyze what the author is saying at a level of detail somewhat beyond the surface discussion. To do this you need to use your knowledge, experience, and imagination.

Suppose you are reading a story about human experiences. Try to imagine how those people were feeling and acting that motivated what they did. Were they lazy, angry, ignorant, misinformed, or biased? Now read an article by a vendor or consultant. Is the writer competent to speak and act on this subject? Does he have an agenda, perhaps product or standards centric, and is he trying too hard to persuade you? How does what he is saying compare to your own experience and knowledge? Is he right or wrong or somewhere in between? When did he write this, and what was the historical context of these comments?

These are impressions that you should be able to pick up naturally while you read. Reading between the lines gives you the ability to discriminate what you will add to your knowledge, and what you will reject. Every piece has some good and some bad information. To win the psychological war, you need to know the difference, almost instinctively.

9.2   INTERNAL CONTROL

When a friend comes up with bright ideas, it's human nature to try to talk them out of it, because (psychologists say) we are trying to help them avoid being discouraged. We are helping them avoid discouragement by discouraging them verbally. Makes no sense, but most of us engage in this behavior unconsciously. It's natural. In order to change our behavior, we first observe "how things happen."

Similarly, taking advice is not natural. It just seems obvious that any mature adult knows how to take advice. But we don't. Not naturally. Normally, we all think that we know what we are doing. And that we can handle the situation with the force of our own will. In a sense, we mistakenly assume that we can control the world, even when we are in a brand-new situation where we don't have a clue "how things happen."

We use the term *brain in gear* to mean that you achieved a deep state of understanding (about a set of related topics), so that you can articulate your points very persuasively. A trial lawyer works hard to achieve the state of being in gear.

9.3   EXPECTATION MANAGEMENT

Expectation management is one of the most powerful weapons in psychological warfare. In expectation management, we take our instinctual need to discourage other people's ideas, and we use the technique consciously, regarding our own ideas as we present them to other people.

The concept is simple. If you tell someone that your idea will deliver wonderful benefits, and it doesn't, then the person will be dissatisfied. And you lose credibility. However, with expectation management you carefully articulate the potential good and bad outcomes, even emphasizing the negatives. Then with the same idea and same outcome, the person will be pleasantly surprised. You delivered more than they were led to expect! Congratulations.

This technique is essential for group dynamics (e.g., meetings). Always promise less than you can actually deliver. In meetings, tell people clearly what you expect them to do, explain the caveats (i.e., expectation management), and they will often overachieve.

Expectation management is used in a convoluted form in software product marketing. Since marketeers are selling to the customer's needs, an inflated product image is created. This is called the expected product [Moore 96]. People buy the expected product because it appears to meet their needs. What they actually buy is the generic product, which is what the vendor can deliver. In marketing terms, "crossing the chasm" is the transition from a customer base who will buy based upon sexy technology expectations to customers who will buy based upon real-world quality to satisfy needs. If the product is successful, there will be time to enhance it to actually meet expectations. The product can then become an augmented product through extensions and up-selling options. However, this standard model for software marketing almost always leads to disappointment.

Ideally, expectation management is a form of truthful disclosure. By telling people the truth about the potential outcomes, you establish a psychological framework of expectations. In reality, you can contribute to causes but you cannot control the absolute outcomes. If you do a good job, you are contributing to the desired outcomes. And chances are you'll be able to deliver upon expectations, most times. If you don't manage expectations, then you will underperform in people's perceptions, even with the same outcomes. We highly recommend that you apply expectation management; it is a technique that we use every day.

9.4   PSYCHOLOGY OF TRUTH

It is important to understand the meaning of truth, and how to use it, as the basis for your psychological warfare. In an absolute sense, everything that you know is an abstraction of reality. We could say that "everything you know is wrong," which is true in an absolute sense, but not very productive. Thinking more constructively, we can describe our understanding of reality as a set of patterns and models. These patterns and models are an illusion (or, more accurately, a self-inflicted delusion). For example, one can say: "History never repeats itself," which is true in an absolute sense because the world is always changing, always progressing in time. Or so we think.

Software architecture knowledge consists of models. In the hard sciences, it is common knowledge that nature knows nothing about physics. Newton's models for classical mechanics are wrong, when taken out of context. So are Einstein's theories of relativity. However, within their intended contexts, these theories are accurate descriptions of how things happen in the universe. Research in design patterns and AntiPatterns explains why these models work in practice. With the right context and forces, the appropriate model for the solution usually works and produces predictable outcomes.

Despite its weaknesses, classical mechanics is the theoretical model behind numerous human achievements, including rocket science, machinery, buildings, and bridges. In proper context, Einstein's theories accurately describe nuclear energy and near-light-speed digital communications in distributed systems.

9.5   PERCEPTION IS NOT REALITY

It is essential for you to understand some important aspects of mass psychology. Most people believe that "perception is reality" and "seeing is believing." And there may have been some time, before technology, when that was a reasonably effective way to think. But it is not so today. Perception is not reality because technology can falsify perceptions. Technology can create powerful illusions. And especially with computing technology, illusions are becoming easier and easier to manufacture.

For you as an architect, the ability to envision new illusions and impress them upon people's imaginations is vitally important. The architect works in the gray area between intuitive perception and the logical certainty of software. In order to translate intuitive system concepts into software reality, we must have a talent to envision architectural structures. Then we must be able to document these visions and articulate (explain) them in a way that sells the concepts to other people. In other words, we start system envisioning by creating an illusion, and then proceed to architect the system, providing more and more depth to the illusion, until it appears obvious what the system is about, why we should build it, and how it can be realized.

Not all system illusions are worth building even if they are very "sexy." It has been said that "whatever man can see and believe, man can achieve." Software development is an ideal refutation of this kind of wrong-think. A great majority of software projects envision illusions that cannot be effectively realized. In effect, many software projects are subject to the illusion of "imagination run rampant." The architect is responsible for moderating this situation. The architect has the power of imagination, like most people, but the architect is also responsible for managing risks, both technical and people-oriented, that could impact project success.

In an often-used analogy, software efforts are like building different types of cars. First we build a Ford Pinto (or Yugo). The system does something useful, but the engineering and manufacturing are not superb; in fact, they are just the opposite! Often the system does not meet the full expectations (system illusion) of the users. But in the eyes of the developers, if the system actually works, they gain much confidence and are ready to try again with much more ambition. When the team tackles the next system challenge, it builds a Cadillac with all the bells and whistles. With encouragement from the users, the system developers create overly ambitious requirements that cannot be effectively realized. Cadillac projects are likely failures. The project bogs down in trying to create too complex a system; the effort lacks focus. After this failure, the team takes a much more sober approach to the next system. This time they envision and build a Volkswagen Beetle, a modest system, but very practical and well engineered. It meets human needs and works reliably. That's the whole point.

As architects, we want to facilitate our projects to avoid these extremes. Architectural planning creates a solid system structure that goes beyond the engineering limitations of the Pinto/Yugo. We give the developers an excellent chance to avoid this phase of system evolution. We also argue against building the Cadillac system. We want to advise our colleagues to be practical and avoid the pitfalls where so many other projects have failed. Ideally, we want to design and build the VW on the first attempt. Sometimes you can't talk people out of making these classic mistakes, so you may get forced into building the Pinto/Yugo or Cadillac. At this point, it is okay to make your opinions well known, perhaps vehemently (we favor the adult-assertive approach). If they don't understand your concerns, then document them clearly and move on to new challenges. Do not dwell on lost battles or try to undermine the committed direction of a project, whether you are right or wrong, once you have lost the argument. As a computer scientist once said, "It is the fate of competent advisors to have their best advice ignored." As you already know, people don't listen.

9.6   EXPLOITING HUMAN WEAKNESSES

One of mankind's greatest psychological weaknesses is that we jump to conclusions too easily. Competent software architects can turn this weakness into a strength for their software organization and the software industry. By creating compelling reference models of software knowledge, we lead our organizations to the appropriate conclusions.

Software architects command extensive knowledge about software technology, software organizations, and real-world business processes that our systems support. Knowledge is power—in this case, the power to change perceptions. For most people, perception is reality. Reference models are the pattern of the solution for transforming perception into real-world success. Let's explore some examples.

Reference models are commonplace in other fields of human endeavor. They facilitate successful practice in sales, investment, journalism, public relations (PR), economics, psychology, digital hardware design, and consulting. A classic sales reference model is: person, organization, goals, and obstacles (POGO). The analogous reference model for investment analysis is: strengths, weaknesses, opportunities, and threats (SWOT). Journalists and PR professionals use a reference model comprising six questions. These reference models provide an invaluable structure for human discourse that assures quality. Interestingly, many of these models have been incorporated into software standards and practice. For example, the Zachman Framework adopted the journalistic reference model directly. The Reference Model for Open Distributed Processing (RM-ODP) assimilated models from economics and psychology to standardize software architecture viewpoints.

The Hardware Design Level Model (HDLM) has been used in digital engineering practice for more than two decades. HDLM separates design context and forces, so that every EE student learns in college how to design and optimize digital logic circuits with relative ease. Reference models simplify problem solving, so that ordinary professionals can practice their disciplines with world-class results.

Hence the contradiction: Why haven't reference models been used to structure effective software practice? In our opinion, the most effective reference models are unknown by the profession and academia—for example, the Software Design Level Model and RM-ODP. Other powerful reference models have been imposed with unfortunate consequences. For example, Capability Maturity Model (CMM) certification has become the software equivalent of the Spanish Inquisition. Articulating reference models so that they assist in individual decision making is a kinder, gentler way to reform software practice, and ultimately more effective.

Reference Models as Perception

Applying the classic reference model for consulting intervention, there are three basic questions that the readers (software architects) should consider:

1. *What is the problem?* Reference models are basic intellectual tools that are virtually nonexistent in software practice. Effective reference models exist but are relatively unknown by the profession. The corpus of software knowledge is not expressed in terms of reference models. The lack of reference models inhibits our profession from separating design forces and evolving software into an engineering discipline with successful, predictable outcomes.

   Software professionals need reference models in order to understand abstractions. For example, the founders of the software design patterns movement (The Hillside Group) have claimed that four out of five software developers cannot abstract effectively. The Hillside Group's classroom experience is supported by Meyers-Briggs surveys of the general population; only 20% of adults have the appropriate world-perspective to define abstractions. Reference models are a necessity in the confusing, rapidly changing technology environment in which we practice.

2. *What are other people doing to contribute to the problem?* The hard technology problems addressed by reference models are "application problems"—a phrase vendors repeat laughingly, all the way to the bank.

3. *What are you (software architects) doing to contribute to the problem?* This question leads to a Gestalt turnaround: What can we (software architects) do to resolve the problem? We can learn the available, effective reference models for software. We can educate and evangelize the profession toward the use of existing, effective reference models. When we see an important issue unresolved by available models, we can create a new model, optimize it, and contribute it to the corpus of software knowledge. The instantaneous global reach of the Internet make this imminently feasible. We can mentor our peers constantly about reference models, design patterns, and other forms of software problem solving. We (software architects) can take responsibility for our part of the mind-boggling problems and opportunities that the software industry is confronting. Through the articulation of reference models, we can help the software profession become more enjoyable and successful.

Biological Response Model

One of the most universally useful reference models describes biological response (Figure 9.1). This model shows what happens as a biological system is stressed to various degrees. It can be used to describe how people behave, psychologically, when stimulated, and how people can change their minds or behaviors. It is also a good description of how you might respond to external stimulation, so with an understanding of this model, you can choose to follow your biological instincts or choose another path.

The biological response model works according to various stages of excitement. Initially, if the stimulation is small, it is ignored, either deliberately or unconsciously. Consciously our response might be: "It's not important" or "I'm ignoring it." Biologically we are drawn toward small stimuli.

As the intensity of stimulation increases, our attraction changes and we are increasingly repelled. The next level of psychological response is denial, or deliberate ignorance. In denial, we deny the truth or existence of a stimulus event. We turn away from it. We do this automatically; it's human nature, which makes it very difficult to control this part of the response.

As stimulation continues to increase, so does excitation. When a stimulus becomes impossible to deny, we become angry—or joyful—depending upon the situation. It is not possible to maintain a high level of excitation indefinitely. So, in short order, psychological energy is released, such as an angry display or laughter.

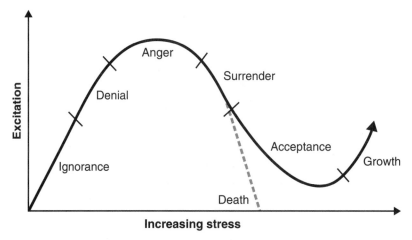

FIGURE 9.1   Biological Response Model

If the stimulation persists beyond a state of excitation, then we experience depression (sadness) or a state of acceptance. Further stimulation above this level of intensity can be fatal.

In psychological warfare we use the biological response model to our advantage, because for most people these are automatic responses of which they are not consciously aware. In fact, some people are so unaware of their own responses that they may not even know when they are angry, until they erupt in an excited frenzy. "Gone ballistic" is the popular phrase for this behavior.

We use this model by adjusting the intensity of our architectural evangelism according to the situation and desired outcome. In some cases, we want to get something accepted without much controversy. This is called "flying under the radar screen." We keep the message at a very low level of intensity and mention the matter infrequently. In some cases, we want people to take notice and to change what they are doing in accordance with our ideas. In this case, we may want to push them right over the top of the model and get them very excited about the concept, with a goal toward changed behavior (acceptance instead of ignorance or resistance).

Group Applications of Response

The biological response model can also be applied to the facilitation of groups, although we are straying from the biological origins of this model when we do so. In theory, each of us individually has a group inside our minds, formed through early childhood experiences. This reference model indicates that we all have interactions between members of our internal group. Real groups are the extension of this concept into interpersonal interactions. So we use these concepts to explain that, if the response model applies to individuals, then it can also be extrapolated to groups.

As the model implies, people often get excited about something before they change their behaviors and accept it. Laughter is one way to push groups over the top and into release and acceptance. Laughter is a great way to diffuse successful situations and win arguments. The experience of laughter involves a high level of excitation and leads to an immediate release of stress (i.e., exactly what we're seeking). Some of the best comedy is self-effacement—in other words, making fun of yourself. Watch standup comedians on television to learn more. Particularly watch for humor based upon self-effacement. Also, the worst kind of humor relates to human body parts. You will see professional comedians use this kind of humor too often for their own good. Avoid this kind of humor at all costs, for reasons such as political correctness.

In groups, we tend to link response models together, so that we create waves of responses. Since death is seldom an option, we continue beyond each state of acceptance into a new curve of excitement. Repeatedly we want to bring individuals and groups to a high level of interest and excitement, make a decision, then move on to the next matter. Meeting facilitation, covered in other chapters, uses the principles of biological response with groups in this way.

We use meeting breakouts to enable people to create something (anything as a first draft), so that they often have ownership and are excited about defending it. It also gives us a starting point for discussion, even if it's bad. We then give them their chance to defend it in public. That's very exciting for the presenter. If the presentation provokes a response from the audience, then he or she can become very excited too. Good things are happening. We have experienced group excitement in very positive and negative senses. Either way is equally beneficial from the facilitator's perspective. In either sense, an excited group is a group that can make decisions and implement choices vigorously. The last thing we want is a group that's falling asleep. In that case, behaviors won't change and little progress is made.

9.7   EXAMPLE: REFERENCE SELLING

One of the ultimate weapons in psychological warfare is the power of illusion. In this warfare we prey on human weaknesses with positive intent. Suppose we had to sell a 10-million-dollar software system (i.e., very expensive). The buying authority for such a product may not even exist entirely within the IT community of the organization; perhaps it resides in the Chairman of the Board of Directors. But even more important than influencing the Chairman will be justifying the sale to the organization, so that the executives have a clear indication of need. It's a lobbying effort on a massive scale, because no one individual needs (or can justify) the whole system, but each may benefit in his or her own way from the purchase.

This kind of salesmanship assignment is a primary activity of software architecture, as it is for software salesmen. But the need to "sell the system" may be just as great for the architect. And the situation, as we have posed it, is within the scope of the kinds of "organizational sales" that software architects participate in and sometimes lead.

The trick for making such a large sale is in the sales pitch. First, you need multiple points of contact in the organization, ideally representing multiple chains of management. We want to talk to each point of contact with the intent of achieving two key things. The highest priority is to convince them that what you are selling is what they want. Then it is important to get them to articulate that need. We will use that information later. Then you want to get additional referrals to other people in the organization. If you succeed with your first contact, you are well on your way. You have a successful sales pitch. However, it often takes three to six months to complete business on this scale.

We use the referrals to lobby additional points of contact in the organization. Remember that leaving a voicemail is not good enough. We need to get them on the phone and/or meet them in person to deliver our pitch. On the second and subsequent contacts, we use the fact that earlier contacts indicated "need" for the product in order to convince our current prospect that it's a growing wave of demand within the organization.

We are telling the customer that it's safe for him/her to support this purchase, because many other people already do. It's a done deal. It's a *fait accompli.* Real salesmen will stretch the truth (via careful articulation) just a bit in order to make their point. In other words, this is a form of namedropping, with a systematic intent. What's important is that we are using the power of illusion to create and consolidate demand for our product.

We are describing a systematic sales process that is used by some of the world's largest software companies, called "reference selling." The software architect should be aware of how this process works, both in order to resist its influence from the outside (if necessary), and in order to use the process to build consensus on the inside of the organization (when needed).

9.8   PSYCHOLOGY OF OWNERSHIP

With individuals and groups, a very important concept is ownership. This is using the "not invented here" syndrome to our advantage in psychological warfare. Ownership can take a long time to develop but is a very important concept for the architect to foster. Ownership can be much more easily eliminated than developed.

Ownership can be quickly eliminated if there is one "know-it-all" person who overrules and makes all decisions on a design or project. For some naysayers, this is the definition of the architect's role. To avoid this perception, the architect cannot be a micromanager. The architect should focus on architecturally significant questions and delegate engineering design questions to the responsible developers. In this way, individual developers acquire and control ownership of their own design space. Interfering with their design decisions, without an overwhelming reason, can be deadly to a project, because it destroys ownership.

Smart people know how to give someone else an idea. This is the key to ownership on the personal level. On most projects there is a "customer," someone who literally owns the project from a financial or responsibility perspective. Many customers are quite insistent that their ideas always take precedence, even if they are not qualified on the technical subject matter. Anyone else's "bright idea" can be either accepted or discarded, based on their whim or fancy. As an architect, you need to be sensitive to this phenomenon. There are some arguments which you can't win, no matter how right you are, because you don't "own" the project. It is not your money being spent, for example.

You must learn to let go of certain cherished ideas, if you can't win over the real project owner. In our work experience, this situation will arise most frequently when there is a direct family relationship between the real project owner and a team member. Many good ideas will get overruled because the family member disagrees—whether or not he or she is really qualified to do so. This is a good example of "life is not fair." And it is something that you will have to live with, unless you leave the project.

Ownership is best fostered in a relationship of trust among the team members and the architect. There must be a division of design responsibilities if there is to be both ownership and quality design. The architect is responsible for architecturally significant decisions. The other team members each have assigned responsibilities. If everyone contributes, and is told how important his or her contributions are, there is the proper environment for establishing a sense of ownership. Ownership requires respect for all team members, no matter how large-scale or narrowly focused their responsibilities are.

In the psychological warfare over ownership, the desired outcome is long-term peace, with mutual respect and trust. A powerful weapon in this battle for peace is showing that you care about team members and their ideas. Some might call it affection or love. People won't listen to you until they know you care about them. Psychologically, what people want most is "to know that they matter," that you think their ideas are important and worth considering, that you think their contributions are essential to the effort. This feeling of mutual respect should be fostered at every opportunity. Showing respect for team members often results in reciprocal feelings for the architect. We use these concepts often in our own daily lives.

Some architects do rule by ego. They do their best to dishonor and discredit other people's ideas through political techniques and/or meeting confrontations. And they can be very successful, professionally. In the wake of such people you will find many discontented persons, crushed by the overwhelming ego. This fosters feelings of resentment which are long-lived, well beyond project completion. We do not like working with people like this, although we have had plenty of experiences with such people. You will have to make your own judgments, if this is your style of interaction. We do know that the person who rules by ego destroys ownership intentionally. And we think that practice is counterproductive.

9.9   PSYCHOLOGICAL AKIDO

Being an architect is a tough job. It can be particularly challenging to your psychological health. It is difficult to stay positive and happy while it sometimes seems that the whole world is upon your shoulders. And bad things happen all the time. It can be quite frustrating at times. Most adults experience frustration often; statistically, a typical adult gets angry about 10 times every day. That's normal psychology.

The common man, inexperienced in psychological warfare, is constantly trying to get himself out of trouble. As experienced warriors, we embrace trouble as much as we embrace success. Good and bad things happen. Most of the events are of small consequence. And many events are out of our control. To be happy in a world of trouble, we must learn to let things go that we cannot control, and to contribute to the success of those events that we can influence.

To acquire the ability to endure bad events and remain happy, we use a philosophy of personal expectation management. We try and try to create success on software projects. We try and try to help our peers and colleagues achieve career and personal success. But in our personal expectation management, we expect nothing—no change in outcome, regarding our involvement. Like medical doctors, we try to do no harm. But there are times when good work leads to bad outcomes, too. It's the luck of the draw. Every day and every decision is a gamble. When nothing happens, great! It's just what we expected. When good things happen, great! It's a pleasant surprise. When bad things happen, there is often a much greater opportunity to be exploited. We should look for it and attempt to bounce forward, instead of being discouraged.

We learn the most from our mistakes, and the least from our successes. Not that we seek to fail. With an attitude of personal expectation management, we don't expect our strategies and patterns to work. So we give it our best effort, acting as if it won't work unless our input is perfect (in a time-bounded sense, of course). For example, suppose we are applying a software design pattern to one of our architectures. If we make a half-hearted effort to apply the pattern, it's very unlikely to generate benefits. Developers will easily ignore it or misuse it so that the benefits evaporate. If we apply the pattern with a reasonable effort, reasonable documentation, and so forth, we are assuming that good things will happen, and with luck the pattern will generate benefits. Developers might understand exactly what we mean, and even add value to our pattern application. We think this is wishful thinking in practice. Finally, suppose that we decide to use the pattern, assume that it's likely to go wrong, and apply it with exceptional care and due diligence, documenting and communicating clearly our intentions to the developers. Even though we expect nothing, we have given the pattern the best chance to perform its function. If nothing good happens, so be it. If it works, that's great, and a very pleasant surprise.

In Psychological Akido, we apply these philosophies in terms of a process of learning. We expect both good and bad things to happen as a result of our architectural work. Our goal is to understand "how things happen." MBAs learn that good things happen when you pull the "action lever." An action lever is anything that you or your project might do to effect change. Unfortunately, we live in world of confusion, of increasing change and information overload. Seeing the action lever is difficult and often requires experience and expertise. That's why companies hire expert consultants; they know where the action lever is. An architect plays this role as well, within the scope of technology and system building.

When good things happen, we have found an action lever, perhaps by accident. The cause may not be immediately obvious. We try to apply the same techniques again in a systematic, experimental way, in order to refine our knowledge of the action lever. When bad things happen, we learn even more. We have found one or more destruct button, which we must try to avoid on future trials. As experience progresses, we learn to avoid the destruct buttons and pull the action levers, becoming more effective.

It is interesting to note that the process of learning to use a computer involves these principles directly. In one dramatic experience, we once took a programming class for a new operating system, in beta test. The software had many defects, as all commercial operating systems do, but these defects were much more prevalent than most of the class had ever encountered (in a near-production release), all of us being experienced software engineers. Because we had not learned the destruct buttons of this new software, everybody experienced frequent crashes, requiring reboot. About 30 reboots were needed on the first day alone, as we attempted to perform simple tasks. The situation reminds us of when we put noncomputer users in front of a demonstration, and they break the software within the first few keystrokes—a well-known phenomenon. In our rebooting laboratory, we learned to "do this and this in a specific order" and "not ever do that," plus remove an erroneous file or two after rebooting. Overnight, many of us thought that it was hopelessly buggy software. By the second day, all students had cut their rebooting needs in half. And we were able to perform more sophisticated programming tasks than we had attempted on the first day. By the end of the week, we were able to perform extremely sophisticated programming tasks, with virtually no rebooting required, except when we chose to reboot intentionally. We had learned the action levers and the destruct buttons. Most surprisingly, we didn't have to think about it; we did it naturally, as we had internalized this knowledge about how we used the system. On reflection, this experience is common to people who use computers. This was just a dramatic example of experienced software engineers repeating the process for new software.

Psychological Akido is much the same, but instead of learning to control a machine, we are learning to survive the psychological warfare that is life. As architects, our life stresses are significant. We use Psychological Akido to help us to cope with life and to learn to perform better and better. Psychological Akido is our quality control process for psychological warfare.

9.10   INTELLECTUAL AKIDO

Psychological Akido is a defensive strategy that works on a personal level. It guards us from the insane situations and environments that we often encounter in our profession. As architects, we should attempt to do more than merely protect ourselves. We should try to help others to grow professionally and personally.

Intellectual Akido is an extension and scaling up of the former practice, to affect many more lives and change the way that people do software. In a sense, the goal of Intellectual Akido is to make the world a better place. Mentoring individuals one by one, we can have some limited impact, perhaps helping a few dozen people over a lifetime. In Psychological Akido, our scope can be much more ambitious, possibly affecting thousands of lives directly.

We apply Psychological Akido as a front-end process, gathering knowledge from good and bad experiences. The next step is to transform our positive experiences into patterns, in the "software patterns" sense. We want to find practices that repeatedly work, so that we can share them with many others. Initially, we prove to ourselves that the patterns work, by applying them in our own work. Then we mentor other professionals to do the same. We learn the ins and outs of the new technique.

When we are satisfied that the quality of this knowledge is worth sharing on a wider scale, we shift knowledge-sharing strategies. We transition from one-to-one sharing (e.g., mentoring) into one-to-many sharing. This transition is an essential idea for affecting the practices of large groups of developers. Suppose you were an enterprise architect or a Chief Information Officer. You would have to execute educational and administrative strategies that change behaviors on a mass scale. One-to-one mentoring simply wouldn't work.

One thing that you must do is to generate documentation. A useful first step is a set of tutorial briefing charts. With these charts you can project your message to groups ranging from a half dozen to several hundred people. The experience of teaching and answering questions will focus your knowledge of the solution and how it is executed. In a sense, you are providing many shortcuts for your student's own Psychological Akido process. You are telling them explicitly where the action levers are, and what to avoid in terms of destruct buttons.

In many cases, some 5% or more will listen carefully, learn the new patterns of knowledge, and apply them to their own work. According to the Nolan Curve, a classic learning theory, if 5% of your skill base can successfully apply much more effective practices, the other 95% will eventually migrate. Within a single organization, a tutorial may be sufficient to effect the required change. Ideally your tutorial includes an even balance of lecture, experience, and feedback (e.g., discussing their experience). From a training perspective, what the students do successfully in class, you can expect them to do on the job. Experience, such as programming laboratories, is vital to their effective knowledge acquisition.

To affect a large group of developers, you need to go further in your knowledge dissemination. A magazine article is a wonderful way to communicate to very large groups. It's wonderful because it's a relatively short-term commitment on your part, and the rewards of professional recognition are superb—almost as good as writing a book. Magazines are continually seeking talent, and if you have something that really works in this chaotic software industry, the knowledge is probably well worth sharing. Posting the same information on the Internet is useful, but not nearly as persuasive as the magazine format.

Everything we have done so far in this process has affected many lives. But the impacts are transient, at best. The tutorial helped us to focus our ideas and develop the verbal articulation of the ideas which is necessary to communicate the message. To create permanent knowledge we must go further. In particular we are talking about books and standards. A standard is a documented technical agreement. It has great moral hegemony. Most standards focus on detailed technical solutions that are intended for vendor implementation. If your ideas are applicable, this is a reasonable mechanism to pursue, given its shortcomings—primarily compromises and long delays. We do not discourage standardization, since we have pursued this approach on a number of occasions.

A book defines intellectual standards. Note that the role in society of journalism and publishing is to confer credibility upon authors, people, and organizations. A book is the ultimate form of journalism. It yields substantial credibility, as well as professional recognition. Hence the phrase that he/she "wrote the book." It is also said that "he who writes, writes history." Exactly. The book author is in a unique position of defining a new ground truth, a new reality—new ways of thinking and perceiving that are a permanent part of human history.

For example, many more people (perhaps 1000X) have read our books on CORBA than will ever read the standard. It is an awesome responsibility. As architects involved in the CORBA standardization process, we use this authority to articulate the technology in a way that is more effective than the standards alone. If you study this situation, you will discover that there is a great gap between what can be readily assimilated (and what is useful in practical applications) and what appears in a typical standards document. A standards-oriented book resolves this gap and makes the technology usable to much greater numbers of developers.

Winning the War

After the book, the job is not nearly finished. As a result of the book, good things happen. In our early book experiences, we were surrounded by naysayers prior to publication, and they all disappeared around the time it was published. They quit their jobs or were transferred into obscurity. Miraculous, to say the least. We were asked to do many more tutorials, worldwide, and to write magazine articles—an almost endless demand for knowledge and wisdom. You can leverage your newfound popularity to enrich your business, or you can go further in the process, which is not nearly complete.

The transition from grunt to expert began on the day you stepped up to the podium and gave your first tutorial. You became the expert (whether you deserved it or not) because you had the courage to put yourself on the front line for the sake of your message. That warfighting spirit can carry you through step after step of Intellectual Akido, until you are affecting many people's lives, and making the world a better place. According to surveys, public speaking is the number one fear for most adults, more so than death. Since you were able to overcome a fear worse than death, you have earned the "right to speak" and a position of respect and authority.

As you travel about the world sharing your message (post book), two important things happen. First, you learn to articulate your message an order of magnitude better than before you wrote the book. You grow and transition from imparting a little bit of knowledge (which everybody knows is dangerous) to communicating lethally effective practices. This newfound confidence does not continue forever, so enjoy it while it lasts. Second, you gain a much deeper sense of how things go wrong by applying your knowledge. What are people's basic misunderstandings? How did they try and fail to succeed?

A second book, describing the AntiPatterns of the misapplication of your ideas, might be an appropriate follow-on. This will help many more people to avoid the common pitfalls. Also, you have gained much more knowledge by following through with this process. Since you have so much more to share, someday you may want to write again—and repeat this final step in the process.

As a series editor, and an advisor to many authors, I always tell them: do not be afraid to share everything that you know about that topic. Be generous with references and citations. The emotional instinct is to hold things back. Save some key bits and pieces for myself, so that I can make money. Not necessary. Not even close. In Intellectual Akido our philosophy is to give it all away. And when you give it all away, you gain so much more. Because there are so many people in this industry who try to hoard their knowledge, the Akido practitioner is a welcome and refreshing alternative. It is also a principle of entertainment, that the actor/actress who gives everything on stage is the most appreciated. The more you give, the more people will enjoy and benefit from your message. And you will grow in knowledge, much faster than anybody can attempt to "catch up" to you.

Winning the Peace

Most of the people capable of "catching up" to you technically will probably scoff at your work and not bother reading it anyway. That's one of the unpleasant shortcomings of this way of life, but probably unavoidable. Professional jealousies will arise. People will be on your case because they feel resentment about your popularity and success. Luckily, there will be few and infrequent encounters. Be sensitive to this.

To follow our way of coping, you must become a kinder, humbler, and nicer person. Do not give these people a reason to criticize you. Never win an argument by implying that, "I wrote the book, so shut up!" Never brag about your accomplishments; let others do that for you. Win by explaining your ideas, which by this time are very well thought out. Let naysayers make up reasons to dislike you, and eventually they will fade away. When you must go up against these people, stay off "front street." Let other people do your talking, while you quietly work in the back room writing the architectures and specifications, doing work that you love.

As your success grows, some of your peers will want to beat you up for any number of reasons. You may have become the symbol of a technology that they don't like. You may be a competitor to their business or their ego. You can attack them head-on, but we wouldn't recommend it. We have tried and failed using this approach.

What's much more effective is an age-old secret of psychological warfare. Be gracious. Turn the other cheek. Most outside observers won't see the situation in terms of issues; they'll interpret a confrontation in terms of personalities. If you are the cool guy (or gal) they'll see the other player as a hothead—someone who is venting anger, not someone who is rationally motivated. We were cheered up, after a recent scuffle, when one of the observers commented that: "At least Tom Mowbray is cool." Remember that "the people have the power," not your hotheaded peers.

An even deeper warfare secret, which always works, is a four-letter word. Love. It's almost unbelievable, but this word has the power to erase all bad feelings, and reverse insurmountable conflicts. We have seen it work for us in recent days, resolving impossible situations that most people assumed would be protracted indefinitely in the fires of war. If you know someone well, it is perfectly reasonable to wish them well and send your love and respect to them and their families. Do it. Don't hold back. Express your feelings honestly and sincerely. You don't need to say much. Once is sufficient. And it is merely a small personal gesture. But it is the key to winning the peace. This is the ultimate weapon of psychological warfare.

9.11   CONCLUSIONS

Psychological warfare requires essential skills for maintaining your own peace of mind and affecting the world about you. As a software architect, you endure tremendous psychological pressures which you must manage, both for yourself and your software organization. Using these techniques, you can progress from small successes to global influence. We emphasize that you should apply these powerful techniques "for the right reasons." Hopefully, your number one motivation for being in this profession is not to make money. To be a true professional you must love your work.

We can unkindly describe the person who's in this business only for the money as a confidence trickster. Another popular terminology for describing these sorts of people is "trough guy," as in a pig trough. We fully understand that there are some roles in the IT business where this way of thinking is appropriate, such as sales engineering. And we have seen several friends follow this path, which leads to quite abrasive ways of interacting. But we take strong exception to this attitude in software architects. It is simply bad behavior and highly inappropriate to attain success as a software architect.

In our philosophy of software architecture, we don't use psychological warfare for purely personal or selfish reasons. These techniques are strictly apolitical. Both good guys and bad guys can use them. And nobody is either all bad or all good. To be the good guys, and do our jobs properly, we must be sophisticated about psychological warfare techniques. We use this knowledge to defend ourselves, defend our projects, and make progress in otherwise intractable situations.

9.12   EXERCISES

EXERCISE 9.1   You will need two 15-minute segments of time to complete this exercise in "reading between the lines."

FIRST SET: Select a historical or fictional book that you might consider to be rather dry reading material. Depending upon your tastes it could be the *Holy Bible* or *Catcher in the Rye*. Find a story about people, and read a paragraph or two carefully. Think about what was it like to be those people. What motivations could they have? What pressures were they under? What do they want and why are they doing what they're doing? Use your imagination to fill in the details of their lives that further explain and enlighten the story. Have someone ask you these questions about the story and hear what you come up with.

SECOND SET: Now select some technical reading material, perhaps a recent magazine. Pick articles written by vendors or consultants, individuals who are likely to have an agenda (selling something) for writing the story. Read a few paragraphs and think about them. Why are they telling you this? What is their agenda? How does their message compare with what you already know about the topic? Did they neglect to mention something germane to the topic?

Do they claim something which you suspect is misleading or blatantly false? Did they include proper citations for verifying their claims, or are they vague about their sources? What is their surface motivation, e.g., telling you about the Java language? And what is their true motivation, e.g., selling you their Java tool by telling you how hard your work will be without some great tool?

BACKGROUND FOR SOLUTION: This is an exercise in subtlety. You are learning to perceive beyond the surface content and get into the author's head. What you know from your perspective is equally as important as the content that you are reading. Most messages that we encounter every day come from biased sources and there is a hidden agenda for sharing this information—for example, advertising and commercials. But more important, much of what you assume is unbiased editorial content (e.g., newspaper stories) is actually based upon press releases from highly biased sources. In fact, some large software companies have hundreds of public relations agents feeding information to the media as quickly as they can assimilate and print it. This is the world of managed perceptions that we live in. Either learn to see through it, or be misled by most of what you read.

EXERCISE 9.2 To learn the concept of internal psychological control, there are a few things that you can practice all the time to consciously modify your natural reactions.

FIRST SET: When someone comes to you with a technical idea, it is natural to try to talk him out of it. We naturally want to discourage people from attempting things that lead to disappointment. In this exercise, try to spend a whole day encouraging people, instead of discouraging them. Before you reflexively blurt out your discouraging message, STOP! Take a breath. Think of a positive message, one that will give them ownership and permission to try it on their own recognizance. This exercise is about changing your own behavior. This discouragement behavior is one of the most obvious natural reactions, so we use it as a classic example which you can work on.

SECOND SET: Unless you are in a high light environment, like San Diego beach, most people don't smile as a regular habit. In this exercise, try smiling when you encounter people—friends, acquaintances, and nonthreatening strangers. Inside your head, the message you want to convey with your smile is, "I want you to know that you matter and I care." This conscious modification of behavior will have a positive impact upon the people around you. You'll be having a good day, and you won't know why.

BACKGROUND FOR SOLUTION: There is a distinct difference between what we would do naturally and emotionally, and what we should do for ourselves, our friends, and our businesses. Psychologically, we may be stressed out, we may be frustrated, we may want to lash out at people emotionally, sometimes for the slightest implied insult. In psychological warfare, we know that it is "always a mistake to take things personally." Before we react emotionally, internal control should kick in, directing us to respond, not react. By responding with internal control, we can maintain important relationships in our lives and our businesses, which might otherwise be destroyed in a few heedless moments.

EXERCISE 9.3 Try the following. Soon. Suppose that you know that you are about to be asked to deliver something, and you are on your way to management to discuss the details. In this exercise, we apply expectation management to our commitment for delivery.

Let's say that you think it's about one day's work, but you're likely to get interrupted and miss a one-day deadline. You believe that if you had two days, you could easily complete the task and deliver. And in three days you could deliver a gold-plated high-quality version.

When you talk to management, I would propose three days, initially, and claim that, "I'll be able to deliver what we basically need by that time." If management balks, and claims they need it in one day, I would tell them the truth, with a bit of underselling. "I really need two days to do an adequate job. I'm very likely to get pulled off into other tasks during those two days, so it will be a struggle." If they absolutely insist on one day, tell them the truth again. State your conditions. "The only way I can deliver is if I get absolutely no interruptions. The only way I can ensure that is if I work at home and unplug the phones."

They should buy on this basis, or find someone else to do the task. So, worst case, you get to spend a luxurious day at home. Take a long hot bath. Do a few hours of uninterrupted work. And take the rest of the day off. Worst case. More likely is that you'll get your two days, they'll expect a minimal job, and you'll deliver a more-than-minimal product, exceeding expectations. You'll be a hero. You kept your word. You delivered on time. And your quality exceeded expectations. Well done! You should give yourself a day off for working so hard!

BACKGROUND FOR SOLUTION: It is quite natural to want to oversell something that you can do in order to quickly generate consensus. However, if you oversell, you have set yourself up for underdelivery. And that's the opposite of expectation management.

EXERCISE 9.4 Applying the principles of Psychological Akido, let's turn around your next negative situation and find the positive lessons learned. Suppose your boss (or customer) is in the habit of getting quite angry because the software is late and buggy, or some other equally normal occurrence. How should you react? Most people would have a reflexive emotional response (without thinking) which varies widely based upon early childhood experience (or so the psychologists claim). Some people might get angry, right along with the boss: "Those darn programmers, they're always late, and their code stinks, damn them to hell!" Other people can't tolerate anger, and they close down. They become very passive, afraid, and quiet. Or they find a reason not to be there and leave.

As an expert martial artist in Psychological Akido, our response is to stay balanced. This is the boss's emotional trauma, not ours. We don't have to be afraid or angry. That's the boss's process erupting, not ours. We want to be there for the boss, and help him work through his feelings. Sensitively. I might say something like, "I'm sorry you feel that way about this situation, how can I help?" Neither angry, nor afraid, but compassionate. Ideally, let the boss sort his own problem. You might ask some leading questions to get him started on identifying alternatives. Perhaps, "What do you think is causing this problem?" and "If you had a magic wand, what would we do to fix this?" Help the boss channel his/her energy into constructive brainstorming of alternatives, and then to selection of positive actions.

BACKGROUND FOR SOLUTION: There are always alternatives. Using this martial art, we channel negative energy into constructive planning and action, because fundamentally we believe that positives and negatives are the same. Both express energy that leads to equally constructive possibilities. From the experience, we learn "how things happen," and a new way forward for dealing with negative situations.

EXERCISE 9.5 Suppose our job was to redirect 100 software projects to use a common process or standard, such as CORBA, within one year. If we were brilliant enough to redirect one project every week, through face-to-face mentoring, it would take two years to complete the task. Nobody is that brilliant or consistently productive. We can't succeed working one-on-one. That's working hard, not smart.

The techniques of Intellectual Akido show a way forward. The core of the strategy is to prepare and present tutorials on CORBA that will evangelize and train the developers to use the technology effectively. In addition, various process and guidelines documents can make it easy to transfer lessons learned to projects, so that they can adopt the desired technology readily. In addition we would add a few other elements, such as an executive policy letter directing all projects to make the transition. We would also add CORBA to the enterprise operational environment (i.e., site licensing and easy acquisition and installation by any project) [Brown 98].

When given an intractable task such as the one described in this exercise is to approach it confidently with a firm grounding in the psychological warfare techniques that will make you ultimately successful.

ARCHITECTURE EXAMPLE: TEST RESULTS REPORTING SYSTEM

A.1   INTRODUCTION

This appendix describes a case study architecture for a test results reporting system (TRRS). The TRRS is a software system initiative that is intended to help software developers resolve incompatibilities between reusable components. The application vision is further explained in [Weiler 99]. We begin with a description of the system concept within the context of UML. Next, the target architecture is defined as an open distributed processing (ODP) system specified in UML. The target architecture provides secure database access for a community of software developers and vendors via the Internet. The architectural prototype is described as a Java language application, specified in UML.

A.2   COMPONENT INTEROPERABILITY CHALLENGE

In the development of large-scale distributed systems, there is a recurring need for teams of developers to share information about systems. Architecture mismatch is the term made popular by the Software Engineering Institute to describe the pervasive incompatibilities between the architectures of software systems [Garlan 95]. This problem is also an artifact of the increasing use of commercial-off-the-shelf (COTS) software in application systems. Multivendor solutions are the norm for both legacy and distributed object environments.

Today, corporate software development organizations must support COTS products from hundreds of suppliers. Managing the compatibility relationships between numerous COTS products is a significant and costly problem in most medium to large corporations. The increasing frequency of software releases from COTS vendors exacerbates this problem for software developers.

The TRRS is an initiative that attempts to resolve these challenges. Today, software developers perform a great deal of in-house testing of COTS products in an attempt to resolve these issues. The TRRS would enable software developers to share testing and development experiences about successful configurations of software products. In addition, technology suppliers could participate in the clearinghouse by integrating their web presence and product information.

A complex, multienterprise system like the TRRS requires significant architectural planning, including the use of design patterns, architectural styles, and modeling tools. We describe here the part of the architecture involving UML case studies and initial Java prototyping. The sections that follow describe the target architecture for the TRRS's Internet presence; then the initial prototype is discussed.

A.3   Target Architecture for the TRRS

The target architecture for the TRRS is described in UML and organized according to the Open Distributed Processing (ODP) standard. As described in other parts of the book, ODP is a standard conceptual framework for object-oriented architectures [ISO 96]. The ODP framework provides a separation of design forces for managing the complexity of large-scale distributed architectures. ODP is quite flexible, and its flexibility is utilized to advantage in this example. For example, not all viewpoints are architecturally significant for this example, so we selectively exclude those viewpoints that are not necessary for the purpose of this system.

A.4   Target Enterprise Viewpoint

The TRRS enterprise viewpoint comprises a number of UML use cases that identify TRRS community participants and their policy relationships. Figure A.1 shows the UML use cases from the application software developer's viewpoint. The three use cases in the UML diagram indicate that software developers will be able to determine product compatibility from the TRRS in a number of ways.

Important enterprise policies concern integrity and liability for product statements in the TRRS databases. Semantic definitions in the UML Object Constraint Language (OCL) can define the policies (i.e., permissions, prohibitions, and obligations) of the enterprise actors in the TRRS process.

A.5   TARGET INFORMATION VIEWPOINT

The TRRS information viewpoint comprises a set of UML class models. The information viewpoint identifies the key concepts that comprise the persistent state of the TRRS system.

Figure A.2 is a UML diagram showing interoperability relationships between COTS products. Conformance Statements (Figure A.3) are vendor

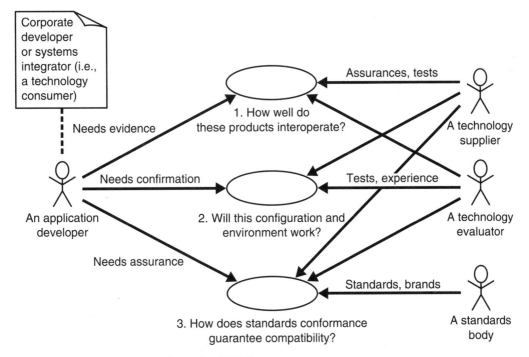

FIGURE A.1   UML Use Cases for TRRS

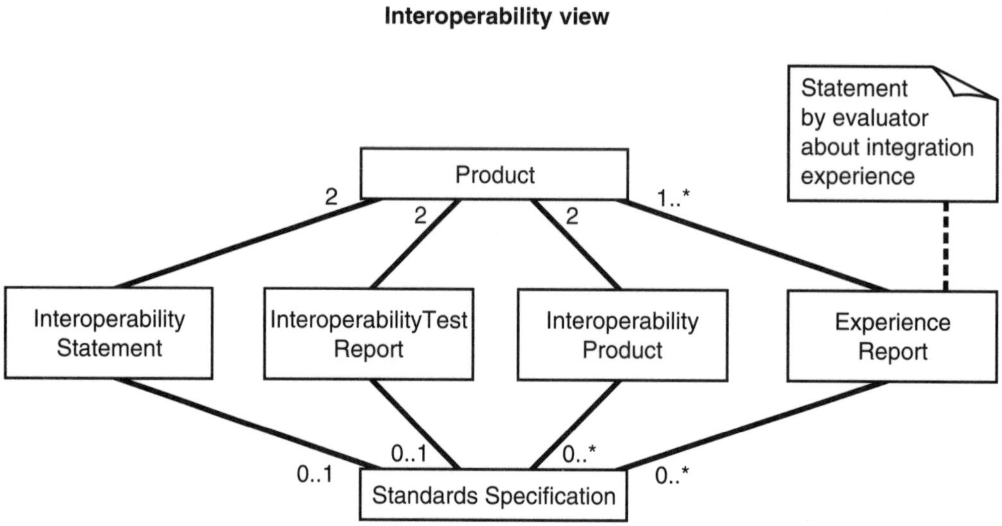

Interoperability view

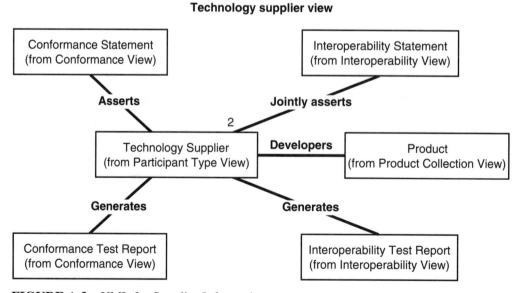

FIGURE A.2   UML for Product Information

Technology supplier view

FIGURE A.3   UML for Supplier Information

assurances of product conformance to standards. Interoperability Statements are a similar concept, except that pairs of vendors assure mutual product compatibility. Interoperability Test Reports contain test results from multiproduct interoperability testing. Interoperability Products are specific COTS solutions for multivendor compatibility. Experience Reports are documented case studies about successful product integration experiences. Together, these are the key document types stored in the TRRS database.

An important tradeoff in UML modeling concerns the number of concepts on each diagram. As shown in Figures A.2 and A.3, simpler UML diagrams are easier to understand because they portray a handful of closely related concepts. Simple UML diagrams can be combined to portray larger sets of concepts on fewer pages. When combined, the technical meaning does not change, but the understandability varies. Too many simple diagrams can be just as hard to understand as too few complex diagrams.

A.6   Target Technology Viewpoint

The TRRS technology viewpoint includes three phases of prototype planning (Figure A.4). These phased prototypes are selected to support incremental system evolution and scalability. The evolution from phase to phase is enabled by the choice of technologies and the provision of multitier interoperability boundaries in the implementation.

Phase 1 is a rapid prototype configured as a standalone Java application with a flat-file database. Phase 2 supports multiple clients on an intranet using RMI or IIOP technologies for distributed infrastructure [Malveau 97]. Phase 3 supports database scalability by replacing the flat file with a JDBC interface to a back-end database.

The technical architectures for Phase 4 and beyond resemble Phase 3. Beyond Phase 3, the addition of TRRS software functionality for database entry, database integrity, and Internet-capable security means significant development challenges. Other development challenges include the provision of tools for architecture planning and management that utilize the TRRS data. For example, notification to software developers about relevant TRRS product entries (using push-technology) introduces a dynamic aspect to software architecture.

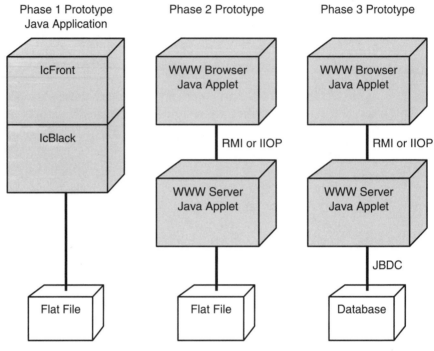

Phase 1 Prototype
Java Application

Phase 2 Prototype

Phase 3 Prototype

IcFront

IcBlack

WWW Browser
Java Applet

WWW Browser
Java Applet

RMI or IIOP

RMI or IIOP

WWW Server
Java Applet

WWW Server
Java Applet

JBDC

Flat File

Flat File

Database

FIGURE A.4   UML for Prototype Deployment

A.7   PROTOTYPE IMPLEMENTATION

In order to plan this prototype, we needed to define an affordable scope
of capabilities to demonstrate the TRRS concept within tight budget and schedule deadlines. The UML modeling of the TRRS assisted greatly in identifying
the core functionality for this first prototype increment.

A low-fidelity (LoFi) mockup of the Phase 1 user interface was prepared
and validated with potential users of the TRRS. LoFi is a useful paper-and-pencil
exercise that enables rapid evolution and validation of user interface concepts.

As a first programming step, the developer used Java AWT Library objects to construct the user interface. Using cut-and-paste programming techniques from working Java code, the overall control structure of the application
was configured. Additional programming customized the code for the TRRS
application, working on both front-end and back-end capabilities iteratively.

The sample database syntax was defined using a predictive-keyword
parsing strategy. Multiple record formats were defined to represent the attrib-

utes of the key object types from the UML model. Product data was collected to populate the sample database using on-line information from vendors' Internet sites. Data collection was limited to a target market comprising selected database products and compatible CORBA products [Malveau 97]. The data collection process yielded interesting examples of vendor architecture mismatches and product data specification.

The resulting prototype is shown in Figure A.5. The main TRRS window displays the product options (upper left). Software developers select a configuration of products using the ADD and REMOVE buttons to create the configuration list (upper right). The RETRIEVE RESULTS button accesses the database from the back end. The bottom panels display the retrieved clearinghouse documents, including standards conformance statements, product

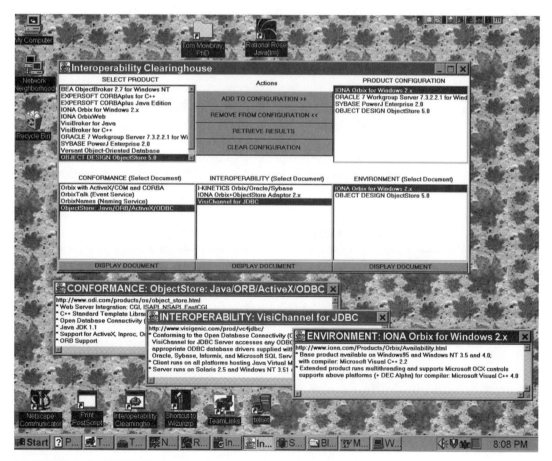

FIGURE A.5   TRRS Prototype

```
Public NamedObject[] retrieveProducts()
public NamedObject[] retrieveConform(NamedObject[] configList)
public NamedObject[] retrieveInterop(NamedObject[] configList)
public NamedObject[] retrieveEnviron(NamedObject[] configList)
public String retrieveDocument(NamedObject theDoc)
```

FIGURE A.6   Computational Viewpoint Signatures in the Java Language

interworking evidence, and product installation requirements. The software developer then reviews the desired information using the DISPLAY DOCUMENT buttons. Figure A.5 is an example of the final screen appearance after document retrieval and display.

A.8   PROTOTYPE COMPUTATIONAL VIEWPOINT

To support future evolution of the TRRS prototype into a deployed distributed system, a partitioning strategy was employed between the front-end and back-end application code. The coupling between these computational modules was limited to five operation signatures (Figure A.6). These Java operations were chosen to directly support a thin-client implementation for the user interface. The majority of the application logic is allocated to the back-end. This strategy enables future distributed implementations of the TRRS prototype, as well as the integration of alternative front-ends and tools by vendor-participants.

A.9   TRRS TERMINOLOGY

In our opinion, sorting out terminology is an important task for the architect, just because it seldom gets done on its own by other project members. The architect requires consistent terminology to articulate the architecture specification. In addition, the architect often creates new terminology in order to give the developers a handle on key concepts. The following is a preliminary TRRS glossary:

Experience Report—A report by an independent organization (not the product vendor) about a set of products.

Feature (or Product Feature)—A significant product capability that is selected from an enumerated list in the TRRS Categories. *Examples:* Security, Directory, Database Access

Operating Environment—An enabling hardware/software platform configuration upon which products can execute.

Organization—A participant in the TRRS, which may be a standards group, a product vendor, a testing organization (providing product-related services), or an IT user.

Product—A unit of commercially available software (i.e., readily available).

Product Related Service—A technical service that relates directly to product capabilities or utilization. *Example*: Training and testing.

Standard Profile—A "technology" that is published as an open systems specification (publicly available specification adopted by a standards group). A standard profile may be a derivative from a publicly available specification.

Technology—A reference to the specification of a "feature." Either the technology is a standard profile, or there is a default technology category: PROPRIETARY. *Examples:* For Security Feature: CORBA Security, GSS API, Secure TCP/IP Sockets. For Directory Feature: CORBA Naming, CORBA Trader, LDAP, X.500.

A.10   USE CASE DEFINITIONS

In this section we describe the essential system-level use cases, identifying key interactions with the TRRS system.

The essential interactions with the TRRS system involve the following actors and transactions:

1. *UC001 Product Information Retrieval Session*
   Key Actor: Information Technology User (IT User).
   Key Transaction: Retrieving product information and experience reports from the TRRS system.
2. *UC002 Product Information Entry Session*
   Key Actor: Vendor.
   Key Transaction: Entering product information into the TRRS system.
3. *UC003 Experience Report Entry Session*
   Key Actors: Solution Providers and Testers.
   Key Transaction: Entering experience reports into the TRRS system.

This first set of use cases can be diagrammed as shown in Figure A.7.

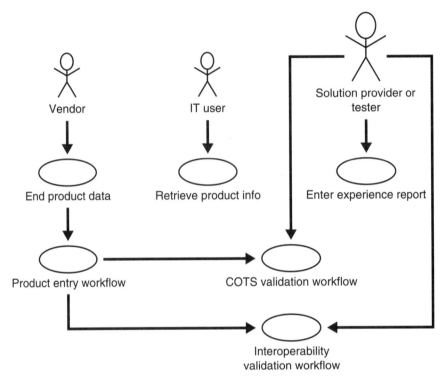

FIGURE A.7   Core Use Cases for TRRS System

Use Case 001 Product Information Retrieval Session

High-level sequence of actions:

1. User directs browser at TRRS web site.
2. User logs in with IT user privileges.
3. System identifies user "domain" and presents reference model graphic.
4. User navigates to selected architectural level and product category using domain reference model.
5. User requests display of a specific product category.
6. System displays a list of alternative products.
7. User selects a specific product.
8. System displays product attributes.
9. Extension: User can display attributes of other products.
10. User exits TRRS site.

Use Case 002 Product Data Entry Session

High-level sequence of actions:

1. Vendor staff directs browser at TRRS web site.
2. Staff logs in with vendor privileges.
3. Staff requests creation of new product data entry.
4. System displays product data entry form.
5. Staff selects product level and product category.
6. Staff enters product attributes. Uses Product Entry Workflow (UC004).
7. Staff submits form.
8. System validates entries.
9. Extension: System can request updates to form before accepting it.
10. System confirms receipt of valid form, displaying entries.
11. Staff confirms form submission.
12. Extension: Staff can return to data entry form to modify entries and re-submit (Steps 7–11).
13. Staff exits TRRS site.

Use Case 003 Experience Report Entry Session

High-level sequence of actions:

1. Staff of system solution providers or testers directs browser at TRRS web site.
2. Staff logs in with tester or solution provider privileges.
3. Staff requests creation of new experience entry.
4. System displays experience report data entry form.
5. Staff selects product(s) from TRRS database.
6. Staff fills in experience report data entry form.
7. Staff submits form.
8. System validates form entries.
9. Extension: System can request updates to form before accepting it.
10. System confirms receipt of valid form, displaying entries.
11. Staff confirms form submission.
12. Extension: Staff returns to data entry form to modify entries and resubmit (Steps 7–11).
13. Staff exits TRRS site.

A.11   CORE WORKFLOWS

These are core business processes of the TRRS organization. They provide supporting information for the primary use cases.

UC004 Product Entry Workflow

Key Actors: Product Vendor

Context: Workflow initiating with the creation of a new product entry in the TRRS system.

1. Vendor collects product data sheets and standards references to prepare for submission to TRRS.
2. Vendor selects product features from TRRS categories to create a class features list.
3. Vendor selects standards for asserting product conformance by completing conformance forms.
4. Vendor identifies product's interoperability capabilities, completing interoperability forms.
5. Vendor establishes linkages to own product information and external documentation.
6. The product entry is committed to the TRRS system product directory.
7. The product conformance and interoperability templates are entered into a workflow queue to solicit the following kinds of TRRS entries (see use cases UC005 and UC006):
   a. Standards Testing
   b. Independent Testing
   c. User Experience Reports

UC004 Extension: Vendor nominates an additional feature category.

UC005 COTS Validation Workflow

Key Actors: Testing Labs, Solution Providers, IT Users, Product Organizations Context: Workflow initiated when new conformance statements are asserted.

1. Conformance statements are sent to independent evaluators, including Testing Labs, Solution Providers, and IT Users, soliciting test and experience inputs.
2. a. Independent laboratory test generates test results, entered in TRRS system as experience report (see UC003).

b. Solution providers using the product in systems development submit integration testing experience reports (UC003).

c. IT Users submit usability results as experience reports (UC003).

3. Continue with UC007.

UC006 Interoperability Validation Workflow

Key Actors: Independent Evaluators: IT Users, Testing Labs, Solution Providers, two or more Product Vendors.

Context: Workflow initiated when new interoperability statements are asserted.

1. Interoperability statements are sent to independent evaluators.
2. Evaluators perform interoperability tests, product integrations, and usability experiments.
3. Evaluators submit results to the TRRS as experience reports.
4. Continue with UC007.

Extension (from Step 3 above): Interoperability Solution

1. Solution provider or third-party vendor may create an interoperability solution between two or more products.
2. The interoperability solution can be registered with the TRRS as a product with these asserted interoperability statements.
3. Solution providers can report their level of effort to create the interoperability solution.

UC007 Experience Report Update

1. Vendor assesses the experience report submissions.
2. Vendor concurs with each report. (See Extensions A and B.)
3. Report is stored and published in TRRS system.

Extension A: Vendor does not concur (as in Step 2 above).

1. Vendor does not concur with experience report
2. TRRS returns report to author with comment.
3. Author modifies report and resubmits. (Resume from Step 2 above.)

Extension B: Deadline Passes
Context: Vendor does not concur

1. Sixty days pass since vendor has received report without concurring.
2. Report is stored and published in TRRS system.

A.12   INFORMATION MODEL

This information model is provided for requirements purposes, as identifying the business classes and their attributes in the Interoperability Clearinghouse business environment. Note that it does not represent an engineered data model.

The primary business objects in the TRRS system are shown in Figure A.8. The following is a basic description of these objects. TRRS member *organizations* include standards groups, independent software vendors (ISV), testing laboratories, and IT users. *Product related services* are value-added capabilities provided by TRRS member organizations, such as testing, systems integration, and value-added reselling. A *standard profile* identifies a particular standard (or a user profile of a standard). An *operating environment* is a configuration of horizontal products and/or infrastructure products that enable the utilization of other higher-level products. An *experience report* is documentation of the use of a product. A *product* is a commercial software artifact.

The entities shown in Figure A.9 identify the anticipated information requirements for the TRRS system. The sections that follow outline preliminary definitions of the associated information for these TRRS entities. Note that this

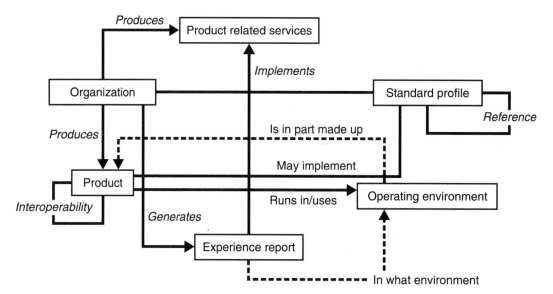

FIGURE A.8   Key Information Objects and Associations

does not constitute a normalized or engineered data model. Asterisks indicate fields which are anticipated to be indexed for the purposes of searching, e.g., primary and foreign keys.

Product Information

Product Name and Version*—The trade name of the product and the version number. The version number should be detailed and distinct for each product release.

Release Date—The date of initial general availability of the product.

Organization Name*—The vendor of the product.

Organization URL*—The web site URL of the vendor of the product.

Product Class—The class of product selected from TRRS Categories.

Organization
OrganizationName
OrganizationType
Industry
ContactInfo
StandardsAffiliation
ServiceOfferings
ProductOfferings
Experience Reports
ValidationAwardsInfo

Product Related Services
ServiceName
ServiceClass
OrganizationName
Description
Associated Product Suites
ContactInfo
Pricing
Contract Vehicles
Accreditations
Experience Reports
Certifications

Standard Profile
StandardName
StandardsOrganization
ProductClass
StandardNumber
StandardsVersion
ReleaseData
Functionlist
UML Specification
Bibliography
URL or XML Tag
Reference Implementation
Testing Tool
Approved Testing Org
Confirming Products

Product
ProductName
ProductVersion
ReleaseData
OrganizationNameMfg
Organization URL
ProductClass
FunctionList
ProductData Sheet
InterfaceSpecification
OperatingEnvironment
Interoperability Validation
Standards Conformance Tests
Usability Testing Awards
User Implementation Validation

Experience Report
ReportName
ReportType
OrganizationName
ProductNames
Environment
CompleteResult URL
Results and Status

Operating Environment
Operating Platform
EnvironmentClass
ProductName
Device Drivers
DatabaseRuntime
ProtocolStack
Industry Adoption of Platform

FIGURE A.9 Preliminary Information Requirements

Function List—A description of the product features from a business perspective.

Product Data Sheet—A detailed description of the product from a technical perspective.

Interface Specification—The external interface specification of the product.

Operating Environment*—The operating environment which this product supports.

Interoperates with What Product—Vendor-asserted interoperability relationships with specific product(s).

Conforms to Standards—Vendor-asserted standards conformance.

Product Dependencies—Additional products required for this product to operate.

Is a Part of a Suite—Name of the product suite of which this product is a member.

Unit Price—Manufacturer retail price for this release.

UML/ADL Functional Specification—Product specification in terms of Unified Modeling Language and formal specifications.

TRRS Status and URL Links

Interoperability Validation—Links to TRRS documents that are evidence of interoperability between this product and other products.

Standards Conformance Testing—Links to TRRS documents that are evidence of conformance between this product and standards.

Usability Testing Awards—Links to TRRS documents that are evidence of product usability, or awards for usability.

User Implementation Validation—Links to TRRS documents that are evidence of experience of utilization of this product, e.g., Experience Reports.

Standard Profile Information

Standard Name—The title phrase that identifies this standard.

Standards Organization—The organization(s) which issue this standard.

Class—The product class to which this standard applies.

Standard Number and Current Version—The formal standards number and version numbers of this standards release.

Release Date—The date of initial public availability of this standard.

Standard Function List—A description of the features that are standardized, explained from a business perspective. Corresponds to the terminology and keywords used for the Product: Feature List.

UML Specification—The Unified Modeling Language specification of this standard.

Bibliography—A document bibliography corresponding to this standard (e.g., including ANSI National Standards Number).

URL or XML Tag—A web site URL or XML description to provide a referral for more information about this standard.

Standard Price—Cost of obtaining the standards specification.

Reference Implementation or Testing Tool—Description of an implementation of the standard which is inexpensively available as a reference to implementers. Alternatively a description of a testing tool which can be used to assess conformance of implementations to the standard, including instructions or contacts on how to obtain the reference implementation or testing tool.

Approved Testing/Branding Organization*—Cross reference to a testing organization or branding organization, where a testing organization provides conformance testing as a "product related service," and/or a branding organization grants trademarks with associated conformance guarantees.

Conforming Products—Links to products with some level of conformance to the standard.

Organization Information

Organization Name—Legal or business name of the organization.

Organization Type—Kind of organization as characterized by a TRRS Category.

Industry—Industrial domain for this organization, e.g., manufacturing, telecommunications, etc.

Contact Information—How to contact this organization, including: principal point of contact, address, phone, fax, and email.

Standards Affiliation—Membership in a standards organization or organizations.

Service Offerings*—The kinds of services performed, including "Product Related Services," e.g., conformance testing.

Product Offerings*—The products offered, cross referenced to "Product" entities.

Experience Reports*—Cross referenced to published experience reports, registered with the TRRS.

Validation/Awards Information—Description (and cross reference) to the standards conformance validations or awards received.

Product Related Services Information

Service Name—Name of the service performed.

Service Class—Kind of service.

Organization Name*—Name of the organization performing the service.

Description—Description of the service performed.

Associated Product Suites—Cross referenced to the product suites upon which this service is performed.

Contact Information—Instructions and information for how to request the service.

Pricing—Cost of the service.

Contract Vehicles—In-place mechanisms for acquiring the service, e.g., basic ordering agreements, etc.

TRRS Status and URL Links

Accreditations—Credentials associated with the service.

User Experience Reports—Cross referenced to experience reports pertaining to this service.

Certifications—Certification credentials relevant to this service.

Experience Report Information

Report Name—Name describing this experience.

Report Type—Kind of report, from TRRS Categories.

Organization Name*—Cross referenced to the organization that submitted the report.

Product Name—Name of the product(s) addressed by this experience report.

Environment—Operating-environment context for this experience.

URL Link—Link to the experience report content.

Results and Status—Summary of the experience report outcome.

Operating Environment Information

Operating Platform—Description of the (hardware/software) platform embodied by this operating environment.

Class—Type of operating environment, e.g., client, server, net-server, embedded.

Product Name—Name of the product designating this operating environment.

Device Drivers—Installed device drivers (hardware/software) required in
this operating environment.

Database Runtime—Database products supported in this operating environment.

Procotol Stack—Networking protocols supported in this operating environment.

Industry Adoption of Platform—Endorsements for this operating environment and its components.

A.13   CONCLUSIONS

This test results reporting system is a case study that demonstrates the applicability of ODP and UML notation to architecture and prototyping. The diagram
literacy that UML makes possible benefits efforts like the TRRS by making
technical documentation universally understandable. UML supports the application of powerful tools for advanced software development practices, including: design patterns, OO frameworks, architecture styles, and components.
Combining these UML technologies and practices with Internet applications
makes ambitious concepts like the TRRS feasible. Note that the architecture
does not comprise an engineered design, but does specify details such as information requirements in a form that is much closer to implementation than ordinary prose requirements.

DESIGN TEMPLATES
AND EXAMPLES

B.1   CONCEPTUAL DESIGN

Conceptual design focuses on high-level issues. It defines the scope and limits of the design. It looks at issues from different perspectives. It ensures that use cases are handled naturally and smoothly. It is completed prior to high-level design, detailed design, or implementation.

Conceptual design documentation provides an overview of a component or service (utility). It includes the following sections:

► Goal
► Responsibilities
► Architectural level
► Classes and objects, class semantics, and class relationships
► Description of features, interactions, data types, and constraints
► How the design addresses relevant use cases and requirements

Section 1   Goal

The goal is a single, simple, and complete statement that captures the purpose of a component or service (utility).

Good Example

The trash bag [component] provides people a disposable container for refuse.

Poor Example

The trash bag [component] is used both indoors and outdoors to put refuse in so it can later be picked up by a garbage truck or taken to a garbage dump.

Section 2   Conceptual Overview

The conceptual overview is a one- or two-paragraph statement supporting the goal and describing what the reader can expect from the remainder of the document.

Example (from Profile Service Conceptual Design)

In addition to information that is intrinsic to a business object (BO), it is useful to find other related information about the BO that is not part of what defines that object, but is useful nevertheless. The discovery interface available on these BOs allows one to add and retrieve such related data by means of the Metadata, Property, Ontology and Relationship services. However, the absence of a uniform template that tells one what data can be expected from these services limits their usefulness. It is this template that is provided by the profiling service in the form of one or more profiles for each type of business object.

Section 3   Responsibilities

Responsibilities describe what a component does or what it keeps track of. They are listed in order of priority, with more important or larger responsibilities listed first. Each responsibility must first be captured by a single, simple sentence (not compound with lots of "ands"). A description including important supporting details should follow. The description may introduce subconcepts, but not new or super concepts.

Good Example

The Boy Walking Dog [component]

- ► exercises the dog. He does this twice a day.
- ► prevents the dog from running away. He does this by keeping the dog on a leash.
- ► ensures doggie creates waste.
- ► cleans up doggie waste.

Poor Example

The Boy Walking Dog [component]

▶ uses a scooper. This is part of cleaning up after the dog.
▶ walks the dog and learns to whistle. He also picks up a gallon of milk at the store he passes along the way.

Section 4   Architectural Level[1]

The architectural level is one of the following:

▶ Application. The application level encompasses application and session components, application and session utilities, and user interface classes and utilities.
▶ Domain. The domain level includes vertical domain-specific components and services.
▶ Foundation. The foundation level encompasses common services, such as workflow, naming or metadata, and core components and data types, such as EiObject and FormattedDataRep.

For application components, also note whether the component is generic to all domains or specific to either a single or a limited number of domains.

Section 5   Classes and Objects, Class Semantics and Class Relationships

This section should contain one or more diagrams (probably not more than three or four) identifying classes and objects, class semantics and class relationships. Diagrams should be responsibility oriented, not data oriented. They should show the relationships and interactions between classes, and class semantics. They should show how classes or class groupings fulfill responsibilities listed in Section 3.

Each diagram should be accompanied by a sequence of interactions that are taken to fulfill each responsibility the diagram fulfills.

Diagrams are drawn using Visio or PowerPoint and inserted into a conceptual design document electronically. Diagrams do not have to follow UML standards. They should be drawn relatively quickly, and should have just enough detail to illustrate concepts. In other words, these diagrams should be kept simple.

[1] Architectural level is also used to organize documents in the file system.

Example (See Figure B.1)

1. The boy attaches the leash to the dog and holds it throughout the walk.
2. The leash restrains the dog throughout the walk.
3. The dog exercises.
4. At least one time during the walk, the dog creates waste. This may occur randomly throughout the walk; however, the walk isn't complete until there is at least one occurrence.
5. Following each occurrence of the dog creating waste, the boy operates the scooper.
6. The scooper picks up and stores the waste.

Section 6 Description of Features, Data Types, and Constraints

Features are fine-grained mechanisms for fulfilling responsibilities. There should be many more features than responsibilities, and the features should directly support responsibilities. Data types are supported formats for populating classes. Constraints are limitations imposed on classes, relationships, and interaction.

The detailed description:

► Refers to class diagrams where appropriate
► Does not address implementation details
► Relates each point back to specific classes, objects, or responsibilities
► Does not introduce new concepts

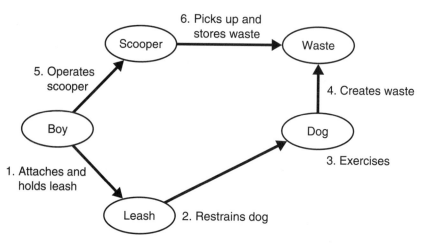

FIGURE B.1 Boy Walking Dog Component Classes

Examples

► The boy component has a watch so it knows when to walk the dog
► The boy component can bend, allowing it to position the scooper effectively
► The leash is made of leather to ensure that the dog can be restrained under any conditions (for example, if the dog starts to run or jerk)
► The dog can exercise at speeds from 0 to 30 mph
► The scooper holds 100 cm³ of waste
► The scooper may be of type Johnson & Johnson Model B or DuPont Model 52-P412

Section 7   How the Design Addresses Relevant Use Cases and Requirements

This section references relevant use cases and requirements and their source documents. No new design concepts are introduced. References to class diagrams and responsibilities are made where needed to clarify how the component fits in with the use case or requirements.

Example

The Boy Walking Dog component satisfies the following requirements from Use Case TCP1: Takes Care of Pet in the Family Household System Scope definition documents.

► TCP1.2.1 The dog must be exercised twice daily
► TCP1.2.2 The dog must create waste when it exercises
► TCP1.2.3 The dog must be cleaned up after

B.2   RELATIONSHIP SERVICE CONCEPTUAL DESIGN

Section 1   Goal

Enable the explicit representation of entities and relationships.

Section 2   Conceptual Overview

The Relationship Service allows entities and relationships to be explicitly represented. Entities are objects. Roles represent objects in a Relationship.

The Relationship Service contains a list of relationship factory objects, each of which contains relationships of a particular type. Relationships are between object instances and are dynamically created from Roles. Roles are defined as part of the description of a relationship and also contain a reference to an object instance and a name for the role instance within a particular relationship. Relationships are typically the result of dynamic system processes versus class attributes, which are part of the object's definition. Relationship types are defined by the processes occurring within a domain model. Typical relationships include owned-by, responsible-for, part-of, and member-of.

The Relationship Service introduces the concept of RelationshipFactory, which is the universe of relationship instances that share the same relationship type. A RelationshipFactory is analogous to a table, where each row constitutes a relationship instance, and every column can be regarded as a Role. Figure B.2. exemplifies this analogy.

▶ *Type*
Related entities and the relationships themselves are typed. In the example, the Patient-Doctor relation is a relationship among two persons. The Patient and Doctor roles constrain their associated object types to the object type Person.

▶ *The roles of entities in relationships*
A RelationshipFactory is defined by a set of roles that entities have. In the example, a person plays the role of Patient, and another one plays the role of Doctor. A single entity (i.e., Ms. Robinson) can have different roles in distinct relationships.

▶ *Degree*
Degree refers to the number of required roles in a relationship. In the example, the Patient-Doctor relation is a degree-two relationship.

▶ *Cardinality*
For each role in a relation, the cardinality specifies the maximum and minimum number of relationships that may involve that role. In the

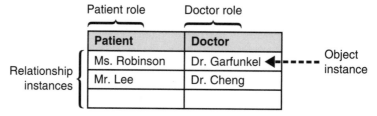

FIGURE B.2 The Patient-Doctor RelationshipFactory Analogy. Relationships can be characterized along a number of dimensions

example, the Patient role may have a minimum cardinality of one and a maximum cardinality not specified (a doctor may take care of one or many patients). The Doctor role may have a minimum and maximum cardinality of one (if a patient can have only one primary doctor assigned).

► *Uniqueness*
Uniqueness describes a constraint among roles in a relation that determines whether the same object name may exist in multiple roles for a single relationship. In the example, the object Dr. Garfunkel is unique with respect to a single relationship because a patient of Dr. Garfunkel cannot assume the role of a doctor and treat Dr. Garfunkel as a patient.

Section 3   Responsibilities

The Relationship Service is responsible for:

► Representing entities and relationships
► Managing the life cycle of RelationshipFactories
► Managing the life cycle of Relationships
► Providing a way to traverse to the related entities

Section 4   Architectural Level

► Foundation

Section 5   Classes and Objects, Class Semantics, and Class Relationships

The following classes support the use of the Relationship Service:

► RelationshipFactoryFactory
► RelationshipFactory
► Relationship

Relation: Contains all the Relationship instances of the relationship type that it defines. Manages the life cycle of a Relationship. Holds the constraints that a set of objects has to meet in order to participate in the relationship type.
Relation Factory: Manages the life cycle of a RelationshipFactory.
Relationship: References the related objects.
Role: Holds the constraints that an object has to meet in order to assume the role.
Role Factory: Manages the life cycle of a Role.

The following structure supports the use of the Relationship Service:

Named Object: Contains the name of the role that the object wants to assume and a reference to the object.

The scenario shown in Figure B.3 depicts the Relation Creation Process, to illustrate the interactions among the different classes in the system.

1. The **Create Relation BPO** passes the role name and cardinality constraints to the **Role Factory** (i.e., Role name = "Doctor," minimum and maximum cardinality = 1).
2. The **Role Factory** creates the **Role** object (i.e., The role Doctor).
3. The **Create Relation BPO** sets the type constraints on the **Role** object (i.e., Adds the object type Person to the role Doctor).

The **Create Relation BPO** repeats steps 1–3 for every role in the relation.

4. The **Create Relation BPO** passes the relation name and the role objects to the **Relation Factory** (i.e., Relation name = "Patient-Doctor," Patient and Doctor roles).
5. The **Relation Factory** creates the **Relation** object (i.e., The Patient-Doctor relation).
6. The **Create Relation BPO** sets the relation properties on the **Relation** object (i.e., Specifies that the role Patient is antisymmetric with the role Doctor).

The scenario shown in Figure B.4 depicts the Relationship Establishment Process that creates a relationship instance between two objects.

1. The **Establish Relationship BPO** asks the **Relation Factory** to find a specified relation (i.e., Find relation "Patient-Doctor").
2. The **Relation Factory** retrieves the **Relation** object (i.e., The Patient-Doctor relation).
3. The **Establish Relationship BPO** passes a set of **Named Objects** to the **Relation** object (i.e., {Role name = "Doctor" and a reference to the Person instance Dr. Cheng} and {Role name = "Patient" and a reference to the Person instance Mr. Lee}).
4. The **Relation** object verifies that the passed objects meet the roles (type and cardinality) and relation (degree and properties) constraints (i.e., Dr. Cheng has to be of the object type Person).
5. The **Relation** object creates the **Relationship** object that relates the passed objects.

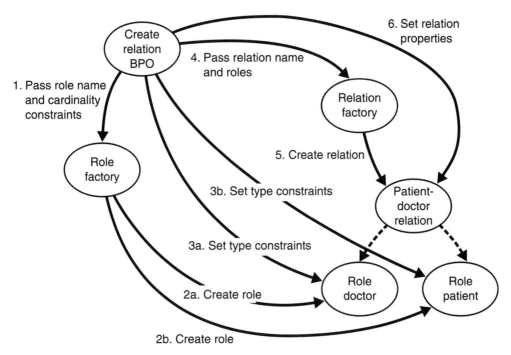

FIGURE B.3   Relation Creation Process

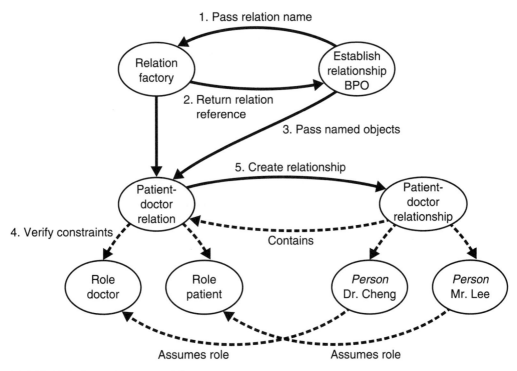

FIGURE B.4   Relation Establishment Process

Section 6   Description of Features, Data Types, and Constraints

Features

▶ Ability to represent entities as objects.
▶ Ability to represent different types of Relationships.
▶ Ability to represent entities participating in a Relationship as Roles.
▶ Ability to characterize Role constraints within a Relationship.
▶ Create/Delete RelationshipFactories.
▶ Create/Delete Relationships.
▶ Traverse to related objects through Relationship objects and Role constructs.

Data Types

The Roles for a Relationship are defined as a structure to decrease the overall number of objects which need to be created per relationship. Also, the definition of Role, including their constraints, and the definition of the Relationship are also modeled as structures. This is to support the expected usage pattern of retrieving descriptive information to display a set of related characteristics, as most of the values make little sense in isolation, i.e., Maximum Cardinality.

```
struct RoleDef {
        string roleName;
        InterfaceDefSeq allowedTypes;
        long minCardinality;
        long maxCardinality;
        boolean uniqueObjectName;
};
typedef sequence <RoleDef> RoleDefSeq;

struct RelationshipDef {
        string relationshipName;
        string relationshipDesc;
        RoleDefSeq roleDefs;
};
typedef sequence <RelationshipDef> RelationshipDefSeq;

struct Role {
        string roleName;
        string objectName;
        CORBA::Object relatedObject;
};
typedef sequence <Role> RoleSeq;
```

Constraints

An object must be a CORBA::Object in order to participate in a Relationship.

Section 7   How the Design Addresses Relevant Use Cases and Requirements

The design supports the following requirements stated in the Virtual Hub Requirements document.

Information Management Requirements

4.4	Photographs will be assigned a role based on the categories listed in Section 4.2 of TEC95
4.9	The user may establish relationships between ground truth data
4.10	The user may establish relationships between ground truth data and products or documentation

Situational Awareness Requirements

12	The user may associate a geographical feature
12.1	With a Business Object
12.3	With Ontology Concepts

Dynamic Linked Documents Requirements

25	Linked Documents
25.3	Embedded objects need to be 'linkable' to other objects.

B.3   HIGH-LEVEL DESIGN

High-level design precisely allocates component or service (utility) behaviors and responsibilities. It also details relationships with other components. High-level design is completed prior to detailed design and implementation.

The high-level design documentation deliverable is a prose document with the following sections:

► Screen Mockups
► UML Diagrams

► Discovery Interface Use
► Component Reuse
► Representative Use Cases

Section 1   Screen Mockups

Screen mockups are created for interesting graphical user interfaces. This includes all interfaces essential to fulfilling component or service responsibilities. Each screen mockup is accompanied by a decription of input and feedback, and how the view changes as work progresses.

Section 2   UML Diagrams

Text description of where to find the component, and how to open and close it.

Section 3   Discovery Interface Use

Section 4   Component Reuse

Section 5   Representative Use Cases

B.4   RELATIONSHIP SERVICE HIGH-LEVEL DESIGN

Section 1   Screen MockUps

The Relationship service will use the Relationship Composer and Relationship Browser to visualize its contents. The service itself will not have a visual component.

Section 2   Design Considerations

Several issues affected the design. This design overcomes several of the flaws in the other industry relationship service while avoiding much of the complexity of the previous relationship service design. The primary capability which existed in the previous version of the relationship which is not included in the new design is the rich set of constraints (i.e., symmetric, antisymmetric, reflexive, transitive, etc.). There are no plans to include such constraints in the future, as the value they provide is not worth the increase in complexity and decrease in understandability of the design.

These were the major issues involved in the design:

▶ There was a desire to limit the number of CORBA objects created to one per relationship instance. The other relationship services are frequently criticized for requiring the instantiation of several CORBA objects per relationship instance, which is expensive and results in poor resource utilization.

▶ A desired feature of the Eidea Labs relationship service was the capability to create new relationship types dynamically. Few other relationship services currently provide this capability.

▶ Another feature which was desired was a more straightforward use of the service when interacting with the Eidea Labs Discovery interface.

▶ CORBA provides very limited support for object equality. This design does not explicitly address this issue nor does it require objects participating in a relationship to implement an interface which uniquely identifies an object instance. Flexibility in describing unusual relationship types was also desired, such as relationships between arbitrary configurations of groups of objects.

▶ The design needed to adhere to the Eidea Labs architectural principles, including minimal interfaces, concise abstractions, and reasonable scalability to support large-scale enterprise systems.

Section 3   Component Reuse

This component will use Objectstore to manage its persistence and Visibroker to manage its distribution. No other reuse of software is expected.

Section 4   Discovery Interface Use

The Relationship Service defines a class RelationshipBag which is stored inside domain objects and accessed through the discovery interface. The Relationship service modifies this class to add relationships to the Relationship bag so they can be accessed by clients to the business object in order to discover the specific relationships an object instance participates in.

Section 5   OMG IDL

This completely replaces the Relationship Service IDL which was used in the Relationship Service implementations.

Complete IDL

```
#include <eiTypes>

module ei {
   module RelationshipService {
      struct Role {
            string roleName;
            string objectName;
            CORBA::Object relatedObject;
      };
      typedef sequence <Role> RoleSeq;

      struct RoleDef {
            string roleName;
            InterfaceDefSeq allowedTypes;
            long minCardinality;
            long maxCardinality;
      };
      typedef sequence <RoleDef> RoleDefSeq;

      struct RelationshipDef {
            string relationshipName;
            string relationshipDesc;
            RoleDefSeq roleDefs;
            boolean uniqueObjectName;
      };
      typedef sequence <RelationshipDef> RelationshipDefSeq;


      RelationshipFactoryFactory {
            exception CannotCreateRelationshipFactory {};

            RelationshipFactory create(in RelationshipDef
                definition);
            void remove(in RelationshipFactory factory);
      };  // end interface RelationshipFactoryFactory


            exception CardinalityViolation {};
            exception UniquenessViolation {};
            exception ObjectTypeViolation {};
            exception InvalidRole {};
            exception NameMismatch {};

      interface RelationshipFactory {
            readonly attribute RelationshipDef description;

            Relationship create(in RoleSeq roles) raises (Car-
dinalityViolation,
                  UniquenessViolation, ObjectTypeViolation,
                      InvalidRole);
            void remove(in Relationship relationship);
      };  // end interface RelationshipFactory
```

```
interface Relationship {


    readonly attribute RoleSeq roles;
    readonly attribute RelationshipDef description;

    RoleSeq findRoles(in string objectName) raises
        (NameMismatch);
    void addRoles(in RoleSeq roles) raises (Cardinali-
        tyViolation,
            UniquenessViolation, ObjectTypeViolation,
                InvalidRole);
    void removeRoles(in RoleSeq roles) raises (Cardi-
        nalityViolation,
            InvalidRole);
}; // end interface Relationship

interface RelationshipBag {
    exception NameMismatch { };

    RelationshipSeq find(in string relationshipName);
    RoleSeq findRoles(in string relationshipName);
    StringSeq getRelationshipTypes();

// The following two operations are used by the Relation-
    ship Service to
// add Relationship reference to object if the Relation-
    shipBag is available
// through the discovery interface

    void addRelationship(in Relationship newRelation-
        ship,
            in string objectName) raises (NameMis-
                match);
    void removeRelationship(in Relationship relation-
ship);
    };   // end interface RelationshipBag
}; // end module RelationshipService
};   // end module ei
```

Section 6   Population

This effort will define the following three relationship types:

Associated-With

This Relationship is used to model general associations between two objects of any type. It provides a straightforward one-to-one mapping, can accept objects of any type, and constrains the two objects to have a different name assigned to their role. The relationship consists of two roles: Subject and Associated.

Composed-Of

This Relationship is used to associate Spectra objects with other objects, with the semantics of one object being composed of a set of materials with the corresponding spectral signatures. It allows up to ten spectra to be associated with an object. There are two roles, a Subject role, which can be of any object type, and a Material role, which must be a Spectra object. All of the objects in the relationship must be assigned different names.

Produced-By

This Relationship is used to associate an object, typically a Feature object, with the WorkItem or Business Process that created it. The relationship has two roles, the Result role, which can be of any object type, and a Process role, which must be an object of type WorkItem or BPO. The process role has a cardinality of exactly one, as does the Result role. The Result and Process roles must be assigned different names.

Section 7   Representative Use Cases For Event Traces

The following use case will demonstrate the base capability of the Eidea Labs Relationship Service.

VHP3c Associates Geographical Feature

The purpose of this use case is to associate a geographical feature with ancillary information to provide a more complete description of the feature.

Section 8   Client Profile

The following Java utility class will provide a more convenient, finer-grained access to the information contained in the Relationship service:

```
class RelationshipWrapper {
    RelationshipWrapper(RelationshipSeq relationships);
    RelationshipWrapper(ei::component eiObject);
    string Name();
    string[] RoleNames();
    string[][] RoleValues(string[] roleNameList);
    long count();
    long minCardinality(string roleName);
    long maxCardinality(string roleName);
    boolean uniqueName(string roleName);
    string[] allowedTypes(string roleName);
    string[] getObjectName(string roleName);
```

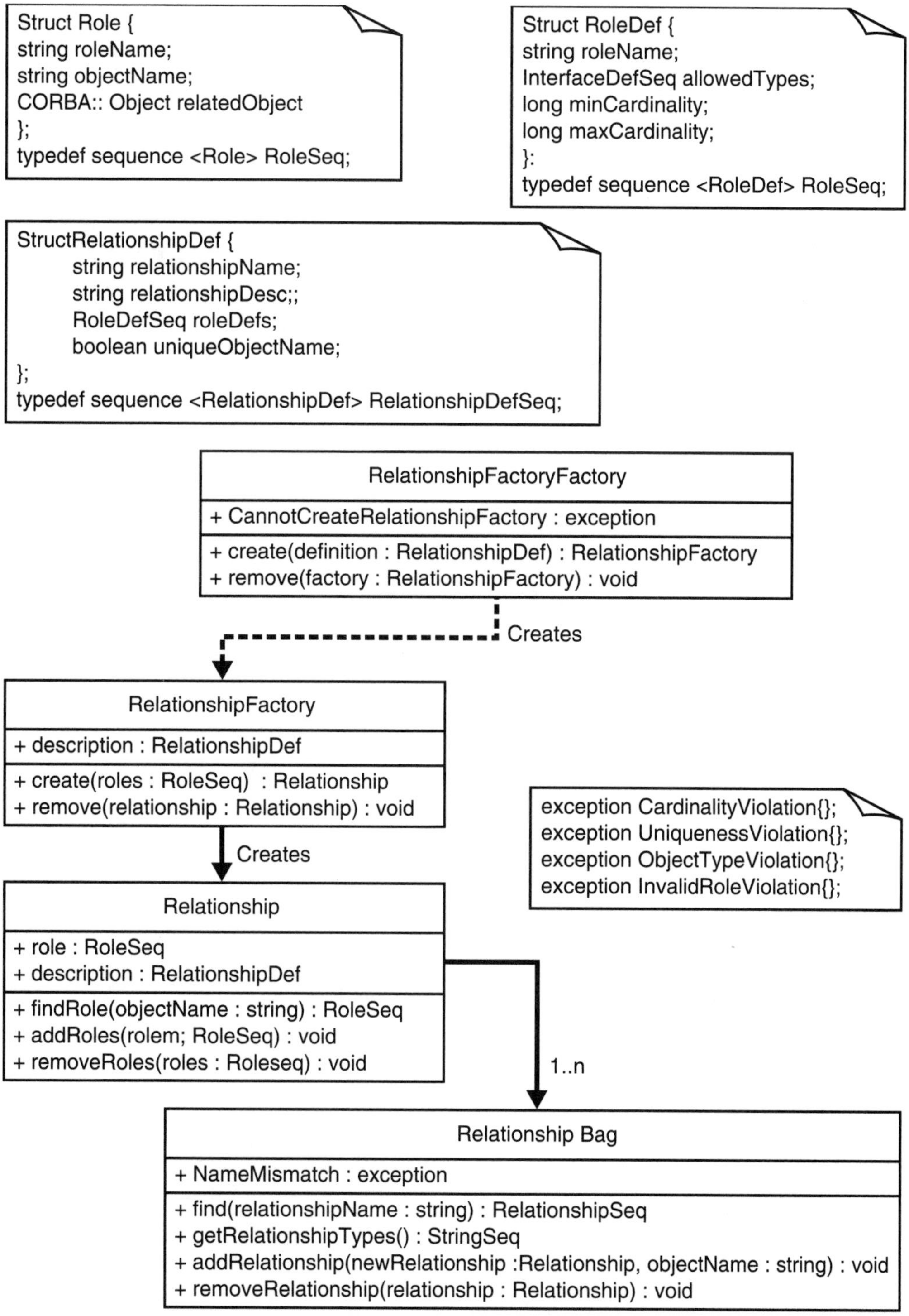

```
Struct Role {
string roleName;
string objectName;
CORBA:: Object relatedObject
};
typedef sequence <Role> RoleSeq;
```

```
Struct RoleDef {
string roleName;
InterfaceDefSeq allowedTypes;
long minCardinality;
long maxCardinality;
}:
typedef sequence <RoleDef> RoleSeq;
```

```
StructRelationshipDef {
      string relationshipName;
      string relationshipDesc;;
      RoleDefSeq roleDefs;
      boolean uniqueObjectName;
};
typedef sequence <RelationshipDef> RelationshipDefSeq;
```

RelationshipFactoryFactory
+ CannotCreateRelationshipFactory : exception
+ create(definition : RelationshipDef) : RelationshipFactory + remove(factory : RelationshipFactory) : void

Creates

RelationshipFactory
+ description : RelationshipDef
+ create(roles : RoleSeq) : Relationship + remove(relationship : Relationship) : void

Creates

```
exception CardinalityViolation{};
exception UniquenessViolation{};
exception ObjectTypeViolation{};
exception InvalidRoleViolation{};
```

Relationship
+ role : RoleSeq + description : RelationshipDef
+ findRole(objectName : string) : RoleSeq + addRoles(rolem; RoleSeq) : void + removeRoles(roles : Roleseq) : void

1..n

Relationship Bag
+ NameMismatch : exception
+ find(relationshipName : string) : RelationshipSeq + getRelationshipTypes() : StringSeq + addRelationship(newRelationship :Relationship, objectName : string) : void + removeRelationship(relationship : Relationship) : void

FIGURE B.5   Relationship Service

```
        boolean objectPlaysRole(string objectName, string role-
           Name);
        boolean objectIsParticipant(string objectName);
};
```

Section 9   UML Class Diagrams

The UML class model for the architecture is shown in Figure B.5, on the previous page. The relationship factory creates relationship objects. These objects are typically contained in a relationship bag. The factory itself has a factory-factory that supports independent distributed creation operations throughout the system.

APPENDIX C

GLOSSARY OF SOFTWARE ARCHITECTURE TERMINOLOGY

This glossary is a derivative compilation of terms, including terminology from the Reference Model for Open Distributed Processing (RM-ODP) [ISO 96]. If the term is viewpoint specific, the viewpoint is indicated in brackets (for example "[ENTERPRISE]").

Abstraction: The process of suppressing irrelevant detail to establish a simplified model, or the result of that process.

Access Transparency: A distribution transparency which masks differences in data representation and invocation mechanisms to enable interworking of objects.

Action: Something that happens. Every action of interest for modeling purposes is associated with at least one object.

Activity: A single-headed directed acyclic graph of actions, where the occurrence of each action in the graph is made possible by the occurrence of all immediately preceding actions (i.e., by all adjacent actions which are closer to the head).

Architecture of a System: A set of rules that defines the structure of a system and inter-relationships between its parts.

Behavior of an Object: A collection of actions with a set of constraints on when they may occur. The specification language in use determines the constraints which may be expressed. Constraints may include, for example, serializability, nondeterminism, concurrency, or real-time constraints. A behavior may include internal actions. The actions that actually take place are restricted by the environment in which the object is placed.

Binder [Engineering]: An engineering object in a channel that instantiates and maintains a distributed binding between interacting engineering objects.

Capsule [Engineering]: A configuration of engineering objects forming a single unit for the purpose of encapsulation of processing and storage. Virtual machines and processes are examples of a capsule.

Channel [Engineering]: A configuration of stubs, binders, protocol objects, and interceptors providing a binding (connection) between a set of interfaces to engineering objects, through which interactions can occur. Bindings that require channels are referred to as distributed bindings in the engineering language. Bindings that do not require channels (i.e., between objects in the same cluster) are referred to as local bindings.

Checkpoint [Engineering]: An object template derived from the state and structure of an engineering object that can be used to instantiate another engineering object, consistent with the state of the original object at the time of checkpointing.

Class: The set of all entities satisfying a type.

Cluster [Engineering]: A configuration of engineering objects forming a single unit of deactivation, checkpointing, reactivation, recovery, and migration. A segment of virtual memory containing objects is an example of a cluster.

Community [Enterprise]: A configuration of (enterprise) objects formed to meet an objective. The objective is expressed as a contract which specifies how the objective can be met.

Compliance: The satisfaction of architectural constraints by a set of specifications.

Composition of Objects: A combination of two or more objects yielding a new object, at a different level of abstraction. The characteristics of the new object are determined by the objects being combined and by the way they are combined. The behavior of the composite object is the corresponding composition of the behavior of the component objects. The composition of a collection of objects yields an equivalent object representing the composition. The behavior of this object is often referred to simply as the behavior of the collection of objects.

Computational Viewpoint: The *computational viewpoint* partitions the system into objects which interact at interfaces. It enables distribution through functional decomposition of the system.

Configuration of Objects: A collection of objects able to interact at interfaces. A configuration determines the set of objects involved in each interaction. The concept of interface and the related concept of interaction are defined terms. From these definitions, the concept of configuration can be seen to encompass not just a collection of objects, but also the way in which those objects are able to interact.

Conformance: The satisfaction of specification constraints by a system or product implementation.

Conformance Point: In a specification, a conformance point corresponds to an architectural reference point. A conformance point is where behavior may be observed for the purposes of conformance testing.

Contract: An agreement governing part of the collective behavior of a set of objects. A contract specifies obligations, permissions, and prohibitions for the objects involved. The specifications of a contract may include:

- a specification of the different roles that objects involved in the contract may assume;
- the interfaces associated with the roles;
- Quality of Service (QoS) attributes;
- Quality of Protection (QoP) attributes;
- indications of duration or periods of validity;
- indications of behavior which invalidates the contract (preconditions, post-conditions, invariants);
- live-ness and safety conditions.

Contractual Context: The knowledge that a particular contract is in place and that a particular behavior of a set of objects is required. An object may be in a number of contractual contexts simultaneously; the behavior of that object is constrained by the intersection of the contractual agreements.

Decomposition of an Object: The specification of a given object as a composition. As an example of the above definitions, an object, A, may be decomposed into a composition of objects, X and Y and Z, and, conversely, objects X and Y and Z may be composed into the single object, A.

Distribution Transparency: An abstraction of the complexity of distribution processing from particular system users (such as application software developers). The standard distribution transparencies include: access, failure, location, migration, relocation, replication, persistence, and transaction. See the corresponding definitions.

Domain: A set of objects, each of which is related by a characterizing relationship to a controlling object. Every domain has a controlling object associated with it. Examples of domains are Security domains and Management domains.

Dynamic Schema [Information]: A *dynamic schema* is a specification of allowable state changes.

Engineering Viewpoint: The *engineering viewpoint* focuses on object allocation, mechanisms, and functions (i.e., services) required to support distributed interaction between objects in the system.

Enterprise Viewpoint: The *enterprise viewpoint* focuses on the purpose, scope, and policies (obligations, permissions, and prohibitions) of the system.

Entity: Any concrete or abstract thing of interest. While in general the word *entity* can be used to refer to anything, in the context of modeling it is reserved to refer to things in the universe of discourse being modeled.

Environment of an Object: The part of the model which is not part of that object. The set of actions associated with an object is partitioned into *internal actions* and *interactions*. An internal action always takes place without the participation of the environment of the object. An interaction takes place with the participation of the environment of the object.

Epoch: A period of time for which an object displays a particular behavior.

Error: Part of an object state which is liable to lead to failures; a manifestation of a fault in an object. Corrective action may prevent an error from causing a failure.

Failure: The violation of a contract. The behavior specified in the contract is, by definition, the correct behavior. A failure is thus a deviation from compliance with the correct behavior.

Failure Transparency: A distribution transparency which masks, from an object, the failure and possible recovery of other objects (or itself), to enable fault tolerance.

Fault: A situation that may cause errors to occur in an object. Faults can be accidental, intentional, physical, man-made, internal, external, permanent, or temporary.

Federation [Enterprise]: A community of domains.

Function: Distributed processing functions are fundamental, widely applicable services that enable the construction of distributed processing systems. There are four standard categories of functions [ISO 96]:

- ▶ Management functions: object management, cluster management, capsule management, node management
- ▶ Coordination functions: event notification, checkpointing and recovery, deactivation and reactivation, group, replication, migration, engineering interface reference tracking, transaction
- ▶ Repository functions: storage, information organization, relocation, type repository, trading
- ▶ Security functions: access control, security audit, authentication, integrity, confidentiality, nonrepudiation, key management

Implementation [Technology]: A process of instantiation whose validity can be subject to test.

Information Viewpoint: The *information viewpoint* focuses on the semantics of information and information processing.

Instantiation of an Object Template: An object produced from a given object template and other necessary information. This object exhibits the features specified in the object template.

Interaction Point: A location where there exists a set of interfaces. A location is a position in both space and time.

Interceptor [Engineering]: An engineering object in a channel located at a boundary between domains. An interceptor performs checks to enforce or monitor policies on permitted interactions between engineering objects in different domains. Interceptors perform transformations to mask differences in interpretation of data by engineering objects in different domains. An inter-subnetwork relay is an example of an interceptor, as are gateways and bridges.

Interface: An abstraction of part of the behavior of an object. An interface comprises a set of interactions and a set of constraints.

Invariant: A predicate that a specification requires to be true for the entire lifetime of a set of objects.

Invariant Schema [Information]: A set of predicates on one or more information objects which must always be true.

Location Transparency: A distribution transparency which masks the use of information about location in space when identifying and binding to interfaces.

Manager: An engineering object which manages a collection (unit) of engineering objects. A cluster (capsule) manager is responsible for managing a single (capsule) cluster of engineering objects.

Migration Transparency: A distribution transparency which masks, from an object, the ability of a system to change the location of that object. Migration is often used to achieve load balancing and reduce latency.

Mobility Schema: A specification of constraints on the mobility of an object.

Name: A term which refers to an entity in a given naming context. A name identifier is an unambiguous name in a given naming context.

Naming Context: A relation between a set of names and a set of entities.

Node [Engineering]: A configuration of engineering objects forming a single unit for the purpose of location in space. The node provides a set of processing, storage, and communications functions. Access to these functions is provided by a nucleus object. A computer and its software (operating system and applications) is an example of a node. A node can be a parallel computer under the control of a single operating system.

Nucleus [Engineering]: An engineering object which coordinates processing, storage, and communications functions for other engineering objects within its node.

Object: A model of an entity. An object is characterized by its behavior and, dually, by its state. An object is distinct from any other object. An object is encapsulated, i.e., any change in its state can only occur as a result of an internal action or as a result of an interaction with its environment. An object interacts with its environment at its interaction points.

Obligation: A prescription that particular behavior is required. An obligation is fulfilled by the occurrence of the prescribed behavior.

Operation [Computational]: An interaction between client and server objects. The syntax of an operation is usually defined by an operation signature (or function prototype).

Permission: A prescription that a particular behavior is allowed to occur. A permission is equivalent to there being no obligation for the behavior not to occur.

Persistence: The property that an object continues to exist across changes of contractual context of an epoch.

Persistence Schema: A specification of constraints on the use of processing, storage, and communication functions.

Persistence Transparency: A distribution transparency which masks, from an object, the deactivation and reactivation of other objects (or itself). Deactivation and reactivation are often used to maintain the persistence of an object when the system is unable to provide it with processing, storage, and communication functions continuously.

Policy: A set of rules related to a particular purpose. A rule can be expressed as an obligation, a permission, or a prohibition. Not every policy is a constraint. Some policies represent an empowerment.

Postcondition: A predicate that a specification requires to be true immediately after the occurrence of an action.

Precondition: A predicate that a specification requires to be true for an action to occur.

Prohibition: A prescription that a particular behavior must not occur. A prohibition is equivalent to there being an obligation for the behavior not to occur.

Proposition: An observable fact or state of affairs involving one or more entities, of which it is possible to assert or deny that it holds for those entities.

Protocol Object [Engineering]: An engineering object in a channel that communicates with other protocol objects in the same channel. Protocol objects achieve interaction between engineering objects which are in different clusters, capsules, and nodes.

Quality of Protection (QoP): A set of security requirements on the collective behavior of one or more objects.

Quality of Service (QoS): A set of quality requirements on the collective behavior of one or more objects.

Reference Point: In an architecture, an interaction point designated for selection as a conformance point. The conformance point appears in a specification which is compliant with that architecture.

Refinement: The process of transforming a specification into a more detailed specification. Specifications and their refinements typically do not coexist in the same system description.

Relocation Transparency: A distribution transparency which masks relocation of an interface from other interfaces bound to it.

Replication Schema: A specification of constraints on the replication, availability, and performance of an object.

Replication Transparency: A distribution transparency which masks the use of a group of mutually behaviorally compatible objects to support an interface. Replication is often used to enhance performance and availability.

Role: Identifier for a behavior, which may appear as a parameter in a template for a composite object, and which is associated with one of the component objects of the composite object.

Schema [Information]: A specification of state, state changes, or constraints. The kinds of schema include: invariant schema, static schema, dynamic schema, mobility schema, persistence schema, and replication schema. See corresponding definitions.

Security—Access Control Function: Prevents unauthorized interactions with an object.

Security Audit Function: Provides monitoring and collection of information about security-related actions, and subsequent analysis of the information to review security policies, controls, and procedures.

Security—Authentication Function: Provides assurance of the claimed identity of an object.

Security—Confidentiality Function: Prevents the unauthorized disclosure of information.

Security—Integrity Function: Detects and/or prevents the unauthorized creation, alteration, or deletion of data.

Security—Key Management Function: Provides facilities for the management of cryptographic keys, including: key generation, registration, certification, deregistration, storage, archiving, and deletion.

Security—Nonrepudiation Function: Prevents the denial by one object involved in an interaction of having participated in all or part of the interaction.

State of an Object: At a given instant in time, the condition of an object that determines the set of all sequences of actions in which the object can take part.

Static Schema [Information]: A specification of the state of one or more information objects at some point in time.

Stub [Engineering]: An engineering object in a channel that interprets the interactions conveyed by the channel and performs any necessary transformations or monitoring based on this interpretation. Stubs are the engineering object in the channel which interface directly with the client and server objects.

Subtype: An entity is a subtype of a given type if and only if its properties satisfy the predicate of the given type and other subtype-specific predicates.

System: Something of interest as a whole or as comprised of parts. Therefore a system may be referred to as an entity. A component of a system may itself be a system, in which case it may be called a subsystem. For modeling purposes, the concept of a system is understood in its general, system-theoretic sense. The term system can refer to an information processing system but can also be applied more generally.

Technology Viewpoint: The *technology viewpoint* focuses on the choice of technology in the system.

Template: The specification of the common features of a collection of entities in sufficient detail that an entity can be instantiated using it. For example, an object template is the specification of the common features of a collection of objects in sufficient detail that an object can be instantiated using it. A object template is an abstraction of a collection of objects. A template may specify parameters to be bound at instantiation time. A standards specification containing interface bindings is a technology object template.

Transaction Transparency: A distribution transparency which masks coordination activities among a configuration of objects to achieve consistency.

Transparency: The property of hiding from a particular user the potential behavior of some parts of the system.

Type: A predicate characterizing a collection of entities. An entity is of the type (or satisfies the type) if the predicate holds for that entity. Types needed are (at least) objects, interfaces, and actions. An entity may have several types and may acquire and lose types (for example: person, employee, homeowner).

Viewpoint Language: Definitions of terminology, concepts, and rules for the specification of a system from a particular viewpoint. The standard viewpoint languages include: Enterprise Language, Information Language, Computational Language, Engineering Language, and Technology Language. See [ISO 96] Part 3 for details.

Viewpoint of a System: A form of abstraction achieved using a selected set of architectural concepts and structuring rules, in order to focus on particular concerns within a system and its environment. Viewpoints often represent the perspective of a particular stakeholder or technical expert involved in the system. The viewpoint model addresses their issues and concerns. There are five standard viewpoints of a system: Enterprise, Information, Computational, Engineering, and Technology. See corresponding definitions.

Acronyms

ACID	Atomic, Consistent, Isolated, Durable	DARPA	Defense Advanced Research Projects Agency
AKA	also known as	DIN	German National Standards Organization
ANSI	American National Standards Institute	ECMA	European Computer Manufacturers Association
API	Application Program Interface	E-R	Entity-Relationship Modeling
CASE	Computer Aided Software Engineering	FGDC	Federal Geographic Data Committee
CD-ROM	Compact Disk Read Only Memory	FIPS	Federal Information Processing Standard
CIO	Chief Information Officer	FTP	File Transfer Protocol
CMU	Carnegie Mellon University	GOTS	Government off-the-shelf
COM	Microsoft Component Object Model	GPL	Gamma Pattern Language
CORBA	Common Object Request Broker Architecture	HVM	Horizontal-Vertical-Metadata
		IBM	International Business Machines
COSE	Common Open Software Environment	IC	Interoperability Clearinghouse
		ICD	Interface Control Document
COTS	Commercial off-the-shelf	IDL	ISO/CORBA Interface Definition Language
CTO	Chief Technology Officer		

IEEE	Institute of Electrical and Electronics Engineers		OQL	ODMG Object Query Language
ISO	International Standard Organization		OSE	Open System Environment
			OSF	Open Software Foundation
ISV	Independent Software Vendor		OTG	Objective Technology Group
IT	Information Technology		PLoP	Pattern Languages of Programs Conference
MVC	Model-View-Controller		RFC	Request for Comment
O&M	Operations and Maintenance		RFI	Request for Information
ODMG	Object Database Management Group		RFP	Request for Proposal
ODP	Open Distributed Processing		SEI	Software Engineering Institute
OLE	Microsoft Object Linking and Embedding		SPC	Software Productivity Consortium
OLTP	Online Transaction Processing		SQL	Structured Query Language
OMA	Object Management Architecture		SYSMAN	X/Open System Management
OMG	Object Management Group		TCP/IP	Transmission Control Protocol/Internet Protocol
ONC	Open Network Computing		TRRS	Test Results Reporting Database
OO	Object-Oriented		TWIT	Third-World Information Systems Troubles
OOA	Object-Oriented Analysis			
OOA&D	Object-Oriented Analysis and Design		UML	Unified Modeling Language
			URL	Universal Resource Locator
OOD	Object-Oriented Design		WAIS	Wide Area Information Search
OODBMS	Object-Oriented Database Management System		WWW	World Wide Web
			XML	eXtensible Markup Language
OOTS	Object-Oriented Technology Symposium			

APPENDIX E

BIBLIOGRAPHY

The following sources are cited in the text using the name-date notation, for example, [Katz 93].

[Adams 96a] Adams, Scott, *The Dilbert Principle: A Cubicle's Eye View of Bosses, Meetings, Management Fads and Other Workplace Afflictions,* Harperbusiness, 1996.

[Adams 96b] Adams, Scott, *Dogbert's Top Secret Management Handbook,* Harperbusiness, 1996.

[Adams 97] Adams, Scott, *Dilbert Future: Thriving on Stupidity in the 21st Century,* Harperbusiness, 1997.

[Akroyd 96] Akroyd, M., "Anti Patterns Session Notes," *Object World West,* San Francisco, 1996.

[Alexander 77] Alexander, Christopher, *A Pattern Language,* Oxford University Press, 1977.

[Alexander 79] Alexander, Christopher, *The Timeless Way of Building,* Oxford University Press, 1979.

[Augarde 91] Augarde, Tony, *The Oxford Dictionary of Modern Quotations,* Oxford University Press, 1991.

[Bass 98] Bass, Len; Clements, Paul; and Kazman, Rick, *Software Architecture in Practice,* Addison Wesley, 1998.

[Bates 96] Bates, M. E., *The Online Deskbook,* Pemberton Press, 1996.

[Beck 96] Beck, K., "Guest Editor's Introduction to Special Issue on Design Patterns," *OBJECT Magazine,* SIGS Publications, January 1996.

[Bezier 97] Bezier, B., "Introduction to Software Testing," *International Conference on Computer Aided Testing*, McLean, Virginia, 1997.

[Block 81] Block, P., *Flawless Consulting: A Guide to Getting Your Expertise Used*, Pfeiffer & Company, San Diego, 1981.

[Blueprint 97] Blueprint Technologies, "Software Silhouettes," McLean, Virginia, 1997.

[Booch 96] Booch, Grady, *Object Solutions*, Addison-Wesley-Longman, 1996.

[Booch 98] Booch, Grady; Jacobson, Ivar; and Rumbaugh, James, *The Unified Modeling Language User Guide*, Addison Wesley, 1998.

[Brodie 95] Brodie, Michael, and Stonebraker, Michael, *Migrating Legacy Systems: Gateways, Interfaces, and the Incremental Approach*, Morgan Kaufmann Publishers, 1995.

[Brooks 79] Brooks, Frederick P., *The Mythical Man-Month*, Addison-Wesley, 1979.

[Brown 95] Brown, K., "DesignByCommittee," on the Portland Patterns Repository Web Site, http://c2.com/ppr/index.html.

[Brown 98] Brown, W.; McCormick, H.; Malveau, R.; and Mowbray, T., *AntiPatterns: Refactoring Software, Architectures, and Projects in Crisis*, John Wiley & Sons, 1998.

[Buschmann 96] Buschmann, Frank; Meunier, Regine; Rohnert, Hans; Sommerlad, Peter; and Stal, Michael, *Pattern-Oriented Software Architecture: A System of Patterns*, John Wiley & Sons, 1996.

[C4ISR 96] C4I Integration Support Activity, "C4ISR Architecture Framework," Version 1.0, Integrated Architectures Panel, U.S. Government Document CISA-0000-104-96, Washington, DC, June 1996.

[Cargill 89] Cargill, Carl F., *Information Technology Standardization: Theory, Process, and Organizations*, Digital Press, 1989.

[Cockburn 98] Cockburn, Alistair, *Surviving Object-Oriented Projects: A Manager's Guide*, Addison-Wesley, 1998.

[Connell 87] Connell, J. *Rapid Structured Prototyping*, Addison-Wesley, 1987.

[Cook 94] Cook, S., and Daniels, J., *Designing Object Systems*, Prentice Hall, 1994.

[Coplien 94] Coplien, James O. *Object World* briefing on Design Patterns, Hillside, 1994.

[Coplien 99] Coplien, James O., *Multi-Paradigm Design for C++*, Addison-Wesley, 1999.

[Davis 93] Davis, Alan M., *Objects, Functions, and States*, Prentice Hall, 1993.

[Dolberg 92] Dolberg, S. H., "Integrating Applications in the Real World," *Open Information Systems: Guide to UNIX and Other Open Systems*, Patricia Seybold Group, Boston, July 1992.

[D'Souza 98] D'Souza, Desmond, *Objects, Components, and Frameworks with UML: The Catalysis Approach,* Addison Wesley, 1998.

[Duell 97] Duell, M. "Resign Patterns: Ailments of Unsuitable Project-Disoriented Software," *The Software Practitioner,* Vol. 7, No. 3 (May–June 1997), p. 14.

[Foote 97] Foote, Brian, and Yoder, Joseph, "Big Ball of Mud," *Proceedings of Pattern Languages of Programming* (PLoP '97), 1997.

[Fowler 97] Fowler, Martin, *Analysis Patterns: Reusable Object Models,* Addison-Wesley, 1997.

[Gamma 94] Gamma, E.; Helm, R.; Johnson, R.; and Vlissides, J., *Design Patterns,* Addison-Wesley, 1994.

[Garlan 95] Garlan, David; Allen, R.; and Ockerbloom, J., "Architecture Mismatch: Why Reuse Is So Hard," *IEEE Software,* Vol. 12, No. 6 (Nov. 1995), pp. 17–26.

[Gilb 93] Gilb, Tom; Graham, Dorothy; and Finzi, Susannah, *Software Inspection,* Addison Wesley, 1993.

[Goldberg 95] Goldberg, A., and Rubin, K. S., *Succeeding with Objects: Decision Frameworks for Project Management,* Addison-Wesley, 1995.

[Griss 97] Griss, M., "Software Reuse: Architecture, Process, and Organization for Business Success," *Object World,* San Francisco, 1997.

[Halliwell 93] Halliwell, C., "Camp Development and the Art of Building a Market through Standards," *IEEE Micro,* Vol. 13, No. 6, (Dec. 1993), pp. 10–18.

[Harmon 96] Harmon, Paul, and Morrissey, William, *The Object Technology Casebook: Lessons from Award-Winning Business Applications,* John Wiley & Sons, 1996.

[Herrington 91] Herrington, D., and Herrington, S., *Meeting Power,* The Herrington Group, Inc., Houston, TX, 1991.

[Hilliard 96] Hilliard, R.; Emery, D.; and Rice, T., "Experiences Applying a Practical Architectural Method," in *Reliable Software Technologies: Ada Europe '96,* A. Strohmeier, ed., Springer-Verlag, *Lecture Notes in Computer Science,* Vol.1088, 1996.

[Horowitz 93] Horowitz, B. M., *Strategic Buying for the Future,* Libbey Publishing, Washington, DC, 1993.

[Hutt 94] Hutt, A., ed., *Object Oriented Analysis and Design,* John Wiley & Sons, 1994.

[ISO 96] International Standards Organization, *Reference Model for Open Distributed Processing,* International Standard 10746-1, ITU Recommendation X.901, 1996.

[Jacobson 91] Jacobson, I., and Lindstrom, F., "Reengineering of Old Systems to an Object-Oriented Architecture," *OOPSLA Conference Proceedings,* 1991.

[Jacobson 92] Jacobson, I., *Object Oriented Software Engineering,* Addison-Wesley, ACM, 1992.

[Jacobson 97] Jacobson, I.; Griss, M.; and Jonsson, P., *Software Reuse: Architecture Process and Organization for Business Success,* Addison-Wesley, 1997.

[Jacobson 99] Jacobson, Ivar; Booch, Grady; and Rumbaugh, James, *The Unified Software Development Process,* Addison Wesley, 1999.

[Johnson 93] Johnson, R., "Tutorial on Object-Oriented Frameworks," OOPSLA93 Tutorial Notes, Association for Computing Machinery, 1993.

[Johnson 95] Johnson, J., "Creating Chaos," *American Programmer,* July 1995.

[Katz 93] Katz, M.; Cornwell, D.; and Mowbray,T. J., "System Integration with Minimal Object Wrappers," *Proceedings of TOOLS 93,* August 1993.

[Kepner 81] Kepner, C. H., and Tregoe, B. B., *The New Rational Manager,* Kepner-Tregoe, Inc., Princeton, NJ,1981.

[Kitchenham 96] Kitchenham, B., *Software Metrics,* Blackwell Publishers, 1996.

[Kreindler 95] Kreindler, R. Jordan, and Vlissides, John, Object-Oriented Patterns and Frameworks, Stanford University, August 1995.

[Kruchten 95] Kruchten, P. B., "The 4+1 View Model of Architecture," *IEEE Software,* November 1995, pp. 42–50.

[Malveau 97] Malveau, R. C., and Mowbray, T. J., *CORBA Design Patterns,* John Wiley & Sons, 1997.

[Moore 96] Moore, Geoffrey, *Crossing the Chasm,* Harper Business, 1996.

[Mowbray 95] Mowbray, Thomas, and Zahavi, Ron, *The Essential CORBA,* John Wiley & Sons, 1995.

[Mowbray 97a] Mowbray, T.J., "The Seven Deadly Sins of Object-Oriented Architecture," *OBJECT Magazine,* March 1997, pp. 22–24.

[Mowbray 97b] Mowbray, T.J., "What Is Architecture?" *OBJECT Magazine,* Architectures Column, September 1997.

[Moynihan 89] Moynihan, T.; McCluskey, G.; and Verbruggen, R., "Riskman1: A Prototype Tool for Risk Analysis for Computer Software," *Third International Conference on Computer Aided Software Engineering,* London, 1989.

[Opdyke 92] Opdyke, W. F., *Refactoring Object-Oriented Frameworks,* Ph.D. Thesis, University of Illinois, Urbana, 1992.

[Orfali 96] Orfali, Robert; Harkey, Dan; and Edwards, Jeri, *The Client-Server Survival Guide,* John Wiley & Sons, 1996. (Also see the third edition, published in 1999.)

[Ousterhout 98] Ousterhout, John A. "Scripting: Higher Level Programming for the 21st Century," *IEEE Computer Magazine,* March 1998. http://www.scriptics.com/people/john.ousterhout/scripting.html

[PLoP 94] *Proceedings of the First Conference on Pattern Languages of Programs,* August 1994.

[PLoP 95] *Proceedings of the Second Conference on Pattern Languages of Programs,* August 1995.

[Polya 71] Polya, George, *How to Solve It,* Princeton University Press, 1971.

[Pree 95] Pree, Wolfgang, *Design Patterns for Object-Oriented Software Development,* Addison-Wesley, 1995.

[RDA 96] RDA Consultants, "Experiences Using CASE Tools on ROOP Projects," Tinomium, MD, 1996.

[Rechtin 97] Rechtin, Eberhardt, and Maier, Mark, *The Art of Systems Architecting,* CRC Press, 1997. (Also see the second edition, published in 2000.)

[Riel 96] Riel, A. J., *Object-Oriented Design Heuristics,* Addison-Wesley, 1996.

[Rising 00] Rising, Linda, and Janoff, Norman S., "The Scrum Software Development Process for Small Teams, *IEEE Software,* vol. 17, no. 4, July/August 2000.

[Roetzheim 91] Roetzheim, W. H., *Developing Software to Government Standards,* Prentice Hall, 1991.

[Rogers 97] Rogers, Gregory F., *Framework-Based Software Development in C++,* Prentice Hall, 1997.

[Schmidt 95a] Schmidt, Douglas, "Using Design Patterns to Develop Reusable Object-Oriented Communication Software," *Communications of the ACM,* October 1995, pp. 65–74.

[Schmidt 95b] Schmidt, Douglas C., and Coplien, James O., *Pattern Languages of Program Design,* Addison-Wesley, 1995.

[Shaw 93] Shaw, M., "Software Architecture for Shared Information Systems," Carnegie Mellon University, Software Engineering Institute, Technical Report No. CMU/SEI-93-TR-3, ESC-TR-93-180, March 1993.

[Shaw 96] Shaw, Mary, and Garlan, David, Software Architecture: Perspectives on an Emerging Discipline, Prentice Hall, 1996.

[Spewak 92] Spewak, S.H., and Hill, S.C., *Enterprise Architecture Planning,* John Wiley & Sons, 1992.

[Strikeleather 96] Strikeleather, J., "The Importance of Architecture," *OBJECT,* Vol. 6, No.2 (April 1996).

[Taylor 92] Taylor, D. A., Object-Oriented Information Systems, John Wiley & Sons, 1992.

[VanGundy 88] VanGundy, Arthur B., *Techniques of Structured Problem Solving,* Van Nostrand Reinhold, 1988.

[Vlissides 96] Vlissides, John M.; Coplien, James O.; and Kerth, Norman L., *Pattern Languages of Program Design,* Addison-Wesley, 1996.

[Walden 95] Walden, Kim, and Nerson, Jean-Marc, Seamless Object-Oriented Software Architecture, Prentice Hall, 1995.

[Webster 95] Webster, Bruce F., Pitfalls of Object-Oriented Development, M & T Books, 1995.

[Weiler 99] Weiler, John A., "From Architecture to Reality, Making the Promise of Plug and Play Work: The Interoperability Clearinghouse," The OBJECTive Technology Group, http://www.theotg.com/archives/whitepapers/.

[Wirfs-Brock 90] Wirfs-Brock, Rebecca; Wilkerson, Brian; and Weiner, Lauren, Designing Object-Oriented Software, Prentice Hall, 1990.

[Yourdon 93] Yourdon, Edward, "Software Reusability," The Decline and Fall of the American Programmer, Prentice Hall, 1993.

[Zachman 97] Zachman, John A.; Inmon, William H.; and Geiger, Jonathan G., Data Stores, Data Warehousing, and the Zachman Framework: Managing Enterprise Knowledge, McGraw Hill, 1997.

INDEX